EARLY PRESBYTERIANISM
in CANADA

EARLY PRESBYTERIANISM
in CANADA

essays by
JOHN S. MOIR

edited by
PAUL LAVERDURE

GRAVELBOOKS

© Laverdure & Associates, 2003.

All rights reserved. No part of this publication may be reproduced or transmitted in any form or by any means, or stored in a database or retrieval system, without the prior written permission of Laverdure & Associates.

COPY EDITOR: Richard Cooper.
COVER AND BOOK DESIGN AND PRODUCTION: Duncan Campbell.
COVER PHOTO: Greenock Presbyterian Church, St. Andrew's, New Brunswick.

Printed & bound in Canada.

National Library of Canada Cataloguing in Publication Data

Moir, John S., 1926-
Early Presbyterianism in Canada: essays / by John S. Moir; edited by Paul Laverdure.

Includes bibliographical references.
ISBN 0-9688813-3-5
1. Presbyterian Church—Canada—History. I. Laverdure, Paul. II. Title.
BX9001.M45 2003 285'.271 C2003-910065-0

Laverdure & Associates gratefully acknowledges the Priscilla and Stanford Reid Foundation for its sponsorship of this book.

GRAVELBOOKS
A Division of
Laverdure & Associates
Historians & Publishers
Box 246
Gravelbourg, SK
S0H 1X0

For

T. Melville Bailey

and

John A. Johnston

friends and historians

Table of Contents

Editor's Preface—xi

Introduction—xiii
The Writing of Canadian Presbyterian History

1. NEC TAMEN CONSUMEBATUR—1
Canada and the Huguenot Connection, 1577-1627

2. 'WHO PAYS THE PIPER . . .'—13
Canadian Presbyterianism and Church-State Relations

3. ROBERT McDOWALL—28
Pioneer Dutch Reformed Church Missionary in Upper Canada

4. THROUGH MISSIONARY EYES—41
The Glasgow Colonial Society Papers as a Source of Social History

5. TO FERTILIZE THE WILDERNESS—56
Problems and Progress of the Synod of Nova Scotia in Its First Quarter-Century

6. THE STOOL OF REPENTANCE—72
The Disciplinary Role of Presbyterian Courts of Session in Victorian Canada

7. LOYALTY AND RESPECTABILITY—85
The Campaign for Co-Establishment of the Church of Scotland in Canada

8. THE QUAY OF GREENOCK—107
Jurisdiction and Nationality in the Canadian Presbyterian Disruption of 1844

9. ON THE KING'S BUSINESS—124
Canadian Presbyterians and the Laymen's Missionary Movement

10. A SENSE OF PROPORTION—141
The Presbyterian Contribution to Biblical Studies in Canada

11. A NATIONAL VISION—156
The Contribution of Atlantic Presbyterianism to Canada

12. LOYALTIES IN CONFLICT—174
Scottish and American Influences on Canadian Presbyterianism

Endnotes—190

A Select Bibliography of Canadian Presbyterianism—207

Editor's Preface

In the quarter century since John Moir wrote the official *Enduring Witness. A History of the Presbyterian Church in Canada,* the quantity and quality of published research in the field of Canadian Presbyterian history have expanded immensely, thanks partly to Moir's work and to the founding of the Canadian Society of Presbyterian History in 1975. The following essays were written over a period of more than a quarter century to supplement his official history; they were sometimes presented to this Society and were available only to its members. Others were published in periodicals now found only in the largest research libraries. These and some unpublished essays were collected so that they may be read by those interested in the study of Canadian Presbyterian history.

The book in your hands is the second of two collected volumes containing the best of Moir's shorter works. The first volume, *Religion in Canada: Historical Essays by John S. Moir,* sets the general context and outlines the issues further explored in the present volume dedicated entirely to the Reformed tradition and, specifically, Presbyterianism in Canada before the formation of the United Church of Canada in 1925. It is hoped that another volume of Presbyterian History after 1925, perhaps culled from the printed papers of the Canadian Society of Presbyterian History, will one day complete this trilogy.

Original typographical errors have been corrected, duplication has been removed, and minor changes have been made in sentence structure and paragraphing. All endnotes have been converted to a single style. A select bibliography is included at the end of these essays for individuals who would further deepen their knowledge of Presbyterianism in Canada. Each essay is preceded by a short account of the reason for which the particular essay was prepared.

I thank John Moir for entrusting me with his many essays and for providing an entirely new essay, "The Writing of Canadian Presbyterian History," to introduce this volume. John's son Ian Moir and his wife Marta did yeoman service in retrieving the texts from ancient computer files. The Priscilla and Stanford Reid Foundation are to be heartily thanked for their support of this publication, one which would have been close to W.S. Reid's heart.

Paul Laverdure
Gravelbourg, Saskatchewan, 2003

INTRODUCTION:
The Writing of Canadian Presbyterian History

THE HISTORIOGRAPHY OF CANADIAN PRESBYTERianism falls into three overlapping periods. The pioneer times from the Conquest to the 1860s and the nationalist period from Confederation to the 1960s were both dominated by clerical authors. The third stage, beginning after World War II, is marked by sharply increased studies of high quality and a variety of themes, mostly the work of academics trained in history or the social sciences. The latter writers, for the most part, are lay persons rather than clergy. Where earlier authors were educated theologians, usually without the benefit of the broader perspective of a historian, these lay successors are generally handicapped by their limited understanding of theological issues.

In the century before Confederation few Presbyterian histories appeared and most of these were hagiographic biographies of clergy, praising their devotion and pastoral influence, sometimes supplemented with selected sermons. Regional chronicles were accompanied by histories of missions to Presbyterian group settlements and one on the unique mission of John Geddie to the cannibals of the New Hebrides (Vanuatu). Of all the discouragements to history writing in that period, the absence of a Presbyterian denominational publishing press was at least as critical as the paucity of documentary sources. By contrast the Methodist printing house, established in 1829, not only published a weekly newspaper but issued numerous Methodist clergy biographies and church document collections, especially after it acquired a rapid steam press in 1850.

The steam press certainly provided the technological means for the production of books in quantity, including religious history, but the event that inspired historical interest and incentive among Canadians generally was Confederation in 1867. On the religious front the spirit of nascent nationalism inspired denominational unions, the first being that of nearly all Canadian Presbyterians in 1875. Four years later the new Presbyterian Church's General Assembly appointed a committee with a broad mandate "to collect . . . books and documents as may be of historical value in connection with any of the Presbyterian Churches of the Dominion." This committee reported in 1880, but then disappeared for over three decades for reasons unknown. Perhaps the reason was the failure to create any central record repository. Or, perhaps it was the congregational independence that developed in virtually every Canadian denomination as a local response to the isolation of the vastness of the country weakening centralized church government.

Inspired by nationalism and the Presbyterian union of 1875, the Rev. William Gregg, professor of Church History at Knox College in Toronto, undertook the writing of a history of Canadian Presbyterianism. Painstakingly he collected primary source materials from far and wide (although he cites these sources indirectly in the text rather than footnotes). Gregg's ambitious project soon convinced him that at least two volumes, if not three, would be needed for a comprehensive history of Canadian Presbyterianism. His 646-page *History of the Presbyterian Church in Canada* (1885) ended at 1834 and covered only the Maritimes and Lower and Upper Canada. Gregg's plans to continue his massive history never reached fruition, but in 1892 he did produce a *Short History of the*

Presbyterian Church in Canada (248 pages) which briefly recounted the denomination's history in all of Canada.

Gregg was not the only historian to concern himself with Canadian history in this period between Confederation and World War I. The stories of foreign missions became more popular as women's missionary activities in the Church provided an exotic international setting. This vital role of church women was joined on the eve of World War I by the highly organized and financially effective Anglo-Saxon-dominated Laymen's Missionary Movement. Some more biographies and regional mission histories did appear, but these were primarily for popular consumption to raise more funds. Many of these volumes were published by James Campbell and Son of Toronto, a staunch Presbyterian family that performed as an unofficial denominational press.

In 1916 the General Assembly established a Historical Committee, but its purpose may have been to stress the virtues and continuity of Presbyterian history as a counterweight against the interdenominational union proposed by the Congregationalists, Methodists and a majority of Presbyterians. As part of the pro-union campaign John Thomas McNeill, Professor of Church History at Knox College, produced *The Presbyterian Church in Canada 1875-1925* (1925, 276 pages) to justify the church union of that year as the God-willed route to evangelize, civilize and christianize a country challenged by cultural and religious pluralism, urbanization, and industrialization. McNeill's avowed purpose was to condemn the denominationalism of the minority of Presbyterians blocking "a brighter day" and "truer music" for coming generations.

Approximately one-third of Canadian Presbyterians rejected the union of 1925, and two volumes defending their position appeared—E. Lloyd Morrow's *Church Union in Canada: its history, motives, doctrines, and government* (1923), and Ephraim Scott's *"Church Union" and the Presbyterian Church in Canada* (1928). The continuing Presbyterian Church in Canada was now anxious to justify its existence and its past and in 1929 the General Assembly decreed that all synods and presbyteries must have historical committees. By the terms of the 1925 Union the Presbyterian archival materials that had been accumulated at Knox College were stored in Ontario's provincial archives until a settlement was finalized in 1950. At that date the United Church acquired the Presbyterian Church Archives, but Knox College retained the theology collection housed in Knox College's Caven Library.

In that quarter century the Presbyterian Committee on History began to gather up Presbyterian archival materials from outside sources in an effort to save some of its denominational history. Unfortunately, the reorganization of the Church after Union (amidst lengthy lawsuits about property, the cataclysmic impact of the Depression in 1929, the disastrous drought of the thirties in Western Canada and the onset of World War II in 1939) left little time or energy to pursue the collecting or writing of Presbyterian church history. At least the Church showed evidence of being conscious of and protective of their heritage both theologically and materially, but the only scholarly history to appear was W. Stanford Reid's *The Church of Scotland in Lower Canada, Its Struggle for Establishment* (1936).

Soon after World War II a number of factors, many interrelated, came into play and produced the current period of Canadian Presbyterian historiography. A new generation gradually took the initiative in the Committee on History, particularly in the person of the Rev. Dr. John A. Johnston. At the same time a new generation of professors of church history, represented by Allan Farris of Knox College and also by Stanford Reid of McGill and Guelph universities, was more aware and receptive to concurrent changes in secular historiography. The celebrations for Canada's centenary in 1967 seem to have awakened the Church to the fast-approaching centennial of the Church itself. A national archival repository was opened in Knox College in 1973.

To mark the centenary of Canada's Confederation the Committee on History produced three books, each somewhat over one hundred pages in length. *The Face of the Church* (1967) contained sermons by a number of ministers; *Enkindled by the Word* (1966) was a series of historical essays, and *A Short History of the Presbyterian Church in Canada* (1965) was intended to fill the gap left eight decades earlier by Gregg until a full-length, updated history of the Church could be written.

Putting Canadian religious history into a broader academic perspective, Donald Creighton promoted the importance of Canadian religious history by supervising several such theses in the Graduate School of the University of Toronto. Beginning in the late 1960s I was also conducting a graduate seminar, "Canadian Religious Traditions," at the University of Toronto. The class attracted a number of Knox College students, who researched, presented, and usually published excellent papers on some aspect of Canadian Presbyterianism. Several of these Presbyterian students have since held teaching positions in the Church colleges.

In 1969 the Committee on History invited me to write a comprehensive account of Presbyterianism in Canada as one of the Church's centennial projects. *Enduring Witness,* published in 1974, may have been the initiative for other historians to delve into Presbyterian history, and was certainly the excuse for founding the Canadian Society of Presbyterian History the following year. That Society's annual volume of *Papers* supplemented the occasional articles that had appeared in the *Canadian Journal of Theology,* and in the

Committee on History's semi-annual leaflet publication, *Presbyterian History*. Simultaneous with the publishing of *Enduring Witness*, the Committee on History began the series *Called to Witness* (volume I: 1975), subtitled "Profiles of Canadian Presbyterians," as a supplement to *Enduring Witness*. This project has now stretched to four volumes while two more, entitled *Gifts & Graces*, profile more Canadian Presbyterian women.

In the post-war decades the interest of both lay historians and social scientists has turned to various aspects of Canadian religious history, and the multi-discipline study of religion became established as departments in many Canadian universities. This widespread development added both to the volume and breadth of publications about Canadian Presbyterian history, and historians of religion acquired a coterie of fellow scholars who brought new dimensions and new methodologies to this particular field. Reflecting this widening interest, a large number of scholarly volumes on specific Christian denominations and topics other than missions and church-state relations began to be published.

Responding to popular changes of religious views and practices, historians began to examine the implications and applications of Presbyterianism. Answering McNeill's 1925 condemnation of denominationalism, Keith Clifford offered a justification for the continuing Presbyterian Church in Canada in his 1985 volume, *The Resistance to Church Union in Canada 1904-1939*. This was followed by Brian Fraser's *The Social Uplifters* (1988), on the Social Gospel in Canadian Presbyterianism until 1915, and by regional studies such as Charles Scobie and George Rawlyk's collection, *The Contribution of Presbyterianism to the Maritime Provinces of Canada* (1997). Other research included histories of doctrinal teaching and the Church's theological colleges, and of Canadian Presbyterianism before the 1875 Union, such as

Richard Vaudry's history of the Free Church (1989), Stewart Gill's biography of William Proudfoot, leader of the United Secession Mission (1991), and Eldon Hay's *The Chignecto Covenanters* (1996).

In the last decade and a half two distinct trends have appeared in the writing of Canadian Presbyterian History. First, the Presbyterian element was frequently included with other Canadian denominations in specialized studies such as Michael Gauvreau's *The Evangelical Century* (1991). The second development is a strong revival in the writing of regional Presbyterian history, of which the most recent example is Peter Bush's excellent *Western Challenge* (2000), an examination of the Church's mission in western and northern Canada before the union of 1925. As the second millennium begins, the writing of Canadian Presbyterian history is a burgeoning field attracting historians and other scholars who are finding publishers and an increasing market for their work. The task of a student of Canadian Presbyterian history has been made simpler by the moving of the Church's archives and a related records management unit to a new climate-controlled facility with more space, state of the art equipment, and the advantage of being located in the Church's head office at Wynford Drive in Toronto.

1. Nec Tamen Consumebatur
Canada and the Huguenot Connection, 1577-1627

To mark the tercentenary of Louis XIV's revocation of the Edict of Nantes and the subsequent exodus of more than fifty thousand Huguenots from France, the Huguenot Society of Canada organized a conference at Trinity College, University of Toronto, in 1985. This was an opportunity to examine the reformed tradition in Canadian history in the time of Samuel Champlain. This paper, which explores the role of the Huguenots in the commerce and settlement of New France before Huguenots were banned from the French possession in 1627, was published by the Huguenot Society, along with the other papers from the symposium, in Canada's Huguenot Heritage *(Toronto 1987) and is reprinted here by permission.*

Canadian awareness of the Huguenot connection in the early history of this country scarcely exists. The primary cause of this near-silence is simply the shortage of clear historical evidence. Few records have survived from that period and those that did were written by unsympathetic Roman Catholic observers. Another factor in this dearth of Huguenot history is probably the historians' habit of emphasizing "majoritarian" history—that is, of concentrating attention on larger elements or forces in history whose records are more readily available, and so overlooking smaller elements such as minority groups or movements.

Nevertheless, it is a fact of Canadian history that during the first quarter of the seventeenth century, when trade, colonization and missions drew the attention of Old France to North America, Huguenots were dominant in the development of New France.

The year 1577 does not in itself specifically mark the entry of the Huguenots into France's enterprises in the New World—it is the date of the Peace of Bergerac or Poitiers which brought an armistice to the wars of religion in France and was the occasion and the reason for renewed French interest in trade and colonization in northern America. D.B. Quinn, compiler of the monumental five-volume documentary on exploration and settlement in America comments that, "In the earlier phase, 1577-1603, the personalities encountered are too vaguely defined, their motives too mixed to show us a clear way ahead."[1] The re-activation of French ambitions in 1577 is the starting point for a generation of colonial undertakings leading directly to extensive Huguenot involvement in the history of early New France.

This renewed impulse to colonial development came primarily from Troilus de Mesgouez de la Roche, a Roman Catholic who convinced King Henry III that France would benefit from colonization in northern America and who was consequently named "Governor and our Lieutenant-General and Viceroy of the said *Terres neuves* and countries which he shall conquer and take from these barbarians."[2] De la Roche was involved in the religious wars until 1584 when his Company of St. Malo brought back five shiploads of furs from Canada. Thereafter two further expeditions were aborted and de la Roche spent seven years in jail as a political prisoner. The year of that isolated trip, 1584, Jacques Noël, companion of his uncle Jacques Cartier on the famous 1535 voyage, revisited the St. Lawrence, probably with de la Roche's expedition.[3] Two years later, in 1586, Noël received from Henry III a reactivated version of Cartier's 1540 commission, with the interesting proviso that only Roman Catholics could work in the officially approved fur trade.[4] By implication it would appear that Huguenots had already been active in the fur trade.

Noël's monopoly was immediately challenged in the courts by St. Malo merchants who wanted to continue to share in the profits of the fur trade, but not in the costs of colonization. Before the wheels of justice even got into motion, Henry III revoked the monopoly in July 1589, just three weeks before his assassination. Noël now abandoned all interest in the valley of the St. Lawrence, but Henry IV continued the policy begun by Henry III, emphasizing trade more than colonization. Trade was profitable—experience was to show that colonization was not. Despite the requirement of royal charters for the founding of settlements and despite such royal encouragements as a free supply of settlers from the prisons of His Most Christian Majesty, company after company found the expense of maintaining settlers in the New World consumed much of the profit from the fur trade. Successive settlements were abandoned or reduced to summer-only trading posts. So the rivalry of trade *versus* settlement persisted more than a century until 1663 when Louis XIV cut this Gordian knot by making New France a province of Old France and by throwing the full resources of his kingdom behind the development of the North American colony. By that date the population of New France numbered only some 2000 souls, but the English colonies on the Atlantic seaboard already contained an estimated fifty times as many settlers.

Historically the Huguenot connection with the early history of New France begins with Henry IV's proclamation of the Edict of Nantes in 1598, an event that ushered in a quarter-century of reconstruction and expansion for France.

Although Henry was assassinated in 1610, this second decade of his twenty-one-year reign appears as a period of religious tolerance when many of Henry's Huguenot supporters and former companions-in-arms shared in Henry's plans for a renewed France. The first chapter of the Huguenot connection in New France opens in 1599 when Henry transferred de la Roche's monopoly to the Huguenot Pierre Chauvin. Chauvin de Tonnetuit (to distinguish him from the contemporary ship captain Pierre de Chauvin de Pierre) was a resident of Dieppe and later Honfleur where he was captain of the Huguenot town guard. Because of his outstanding war service and his influential position at Henry's court, Chauvin was encouraged by the Roman Catholic François Gravé du Pont, a trader and explorer in the St. Lawrence before 1599, to seek royal approval for a trading venture there. When Chauvin was given a ten-year monopoly, however, de la Roche protested, claiming that neither Chauvin nor his Huguenot associate, Pierre du Gua de Monts, had ever been in New France.[5]

King Henry relented his decision to the extent that he recommissioned Chauvin only as a lieutenant of de la Roche, but this was sufficient authority for Chauvin to send his four ships and settlers to found a short-lived colony at Tadoussac. With Chauvin sailed Du Pont, his partner and lieutenant, and also de Monts who came as a passenger. Only five of the sixteen settlers survived the first winter and although the post was used for trade for another two years, no more colonists were sent, which Samuel Champlain later attributed, without any justification, to the fact that Chauvin was a Huguenot.[6] In 1602 Chauvin's monopoly was about to be opened up to rival traders from St. Malo and Rouen, but when Chauvin died early in 1603 the monopoly passed to Admiral Aymar de Chaste, governor of Dieppe and one of the royal commissioners investigating Chauvin's failure to colonize. De Chaste in turn sent a survey expedition to the St. Lawrence—one ship was captained by du Pont with Samuel Champlain as a passenger—but de Chaste died that summer and so the coveted monopoly was again available from the king. This time Henry granted it to de Monts, with the requirement that trade must be accompanied by the settlement of sixty colonists per year and the Indians must be won to Christianity.

De Monts, the central figure in the Huguenot history of New France, was born about 1558 near the town of le Gua, south of La Rochelle, where his family had held land for centuries. Only recently has de Monts' important role in the story of early Canada been appreciated, probably because Champlain, his contemporary and associate from Brouage, the seaport just twenty kilometres from de Monts' properties, has traditionally been hailed as the 'Father of New France.' In his article on de Monts for the *Dictionary of Canadian Biography,* George MacBeath emphasizes de Monts' central place in building New France.

> Despite the tremendous contribution made by this far-seeing and broad-minded individual to the development of Canada, he has seldom been accorded his rightful place in accounts of its history. Here is the man who made possible so much of what Champlain accomplished. He it was who, inspired with the noble impulse of making a new France in America, founded the first permanent colony here. With his interest in trade simply as a necessary source of funds for colonization and discovery, he sacrificed personal gain for the greater goal, one in which Champlain was his staunch ally.... It was de Monts who proved that people from Europe could live here permanently and that agriculture could be carried on successfully.... Had

his monopoly been enforced and maintained by the French government, the undertaking of de Monts in Acadia and Canada might well have succeeded in full measure instead of falling short of the goals he had set.[7]

De Monts had already visited the inhospitable shores of the lower St. Lawrence. Now, with the monopoly in his own hands, de Monts directed his efforts towards the Atlantic coast in search of a more promising site for his trading and colonizing venture. On his first expedition, in 1604 (when the brief settlement at St. Croix Island in Passamaquoddy Bay was built), de Monts was accompanied by his partner Jean de Biencourt de Poutrincourt and by Samuel Champlain, both Roman Catholics, but also by a priest and a Huguenot minister. During the transAtlantic voyage the two men of God engaged in theological disputes that led to blows. Once ashore, the priest Nicolas Augry managed to get lost in the woods. The minister was suspected of having murdered him, but two weeks later the priest was found and their quarrel was apparently resumed where they had left off.[8] Both men remained in the settlement that first winter and must have died almost simultaneously of scurvy. Sagard, the Récollet missionary, later reported that, "the sailors who buried them put them both in a single grave, to see if they would be at peace when dead, since living, they had never been able to agree."[9] Unfortunately, this very human and humorous story-ending is not supported by first-hand information.

De Monts' colonies, first on the St. Croix River and then from 1605 to 1607 at Port Royal on the Nova Scotian shore of the Bay of Fundy, seem to have reflected the religious tolerance introduced by the Edict of Nantes. Probably a sizable proportion of the settlers were Huguenots and, except for the unlucky minister, lived in peace with the Roman Catholic colonists. After 1607, when financial difficulties caused by the high cost of supporting a non-productive colony provided the occasion or the excuse for cancelling de Monts' monopoly, the Huguenot story comes seemingly to an end. After de Monts' withdrawal from Acadia in 1607, his lobbying won him a new monopoly of the more lucrative trade in the St. Lawrence. With Champlain as his principal helper, de Monts succeeded in establishing a permanent trading post at Quebec in 1608. When the Acadian colony was revived by Pontchartrain in 1611 with Roman Catholic settlers only, the efforts of the pious and wealthy Madame de Guercheville to send out two Jesuit missionaries were stalled for a season by the refusal of Huguenot ship-owners at Dieppe to transport the Jesuits across the sea.[10]

Trade, not colonization, was the main aim of de Monts' venture at Quebec, but from this small outpost grew France's permanent interest in northern America and Canada's oldest city. Religious controversies do not seem to have disturbed the early years of settlement at Quebec, but the assassination of Henry IV in 1610 was bound to have a destabilizing effect on the political and religious situation in both Old and New France. Henry's imperious and Roman Catholic widow, Marie de Medici, became regent for the nine-year-old Louis XIII, but political rivalries prevented any sudden revolution in national policies. The process of change began with the removal from power of Henry IV's Huguenot first minister, the Duc de Sully. Sully had openly opposed overseas ventures which might add to the financial plight of the monarchy, but the large reserves he had hoarded for Henry were soon dispersed by the Dowager Queen and her favourites. Even when Queen Marie was exiled from court after the declaration of young Louis' majority in 1614, her influence on policy diminished very little.

Amidst the swirl of court rivalries and intrigues the rising star in France's political firmament was Armand-Jean du

Plessis, Cardinal-Duc de Richelieu, who proved his usefulness in 1619 by bringing peace between the queen mother and the clique that dominated the impressionable young king. Although Marie and Richelieu soon quarrelled, Richelieu's influence over Louis and his virtually absolute control of royal policy was complete after his return to the Council of State in 1624, just one year before the last Huguenot revolt began. This final war of religion ended in total defeat for the Huguenots in 1628, giving Richelieu the opportunity to impose unity under a Catholic monarch by cancelling those military, legal and political powers confirmed to the Huguenots by the Edict of Nantes. As for New France, the Huguenot revolt provided a chance to prevent, in New France at least, those religio-political divisions that Richelieu and like-minded persons blamed for France's weakness and disunity.

The impact of Henry IV's death on events in New France appeared only slowly, but two separate and seemingly unrelated developments were moving the colony's trade and religious relations towards a confrontation. By 1612 de Monts' company was in such financial trouble that in an effort to get a strong friend at the royal court several nobles were successively given the title of viceroy and a generous share of the trade profits. Unfortunately for the company, one viceroy died three weeks after his appointment and another, the Huguenot Prince Henry Bourbon de Condé, spent over three years in the Bastille. De Monts was still a major shareholder but his authority was gradually being challenged as more traders entered the syndicate. More serious than the frustrating search for political friends was this internal struggle for control of the trade growing between a group from La Rochelle (that controlled one-third of the business) and the merchants from Rouen and St. Malo.[11]

There is no evidence that religion was involved in this rivalry, but religious controversy did constitute the second force for change. In 1615 four Récollet friars had been recruited as missionaries to the Indians by Champlain. According to Champlain the Huguenot merchants agreed to transport and maintain the Récollets because the king wished it.[12] When returning to France, however, after a year in the field, Fathers Joseph Le Caron and Denis Jamet convened a meeting at Quebec attended by Champlain who described the state of the trade in Quebec as "a house divided."[13] The proposed solution was the exclusion from New France of the Huguenots who, according to Le Caron, had "the best share in the trade" and whose "contempt" for the Roman Catholic faith endangered the spiritual future of the colony. A resolution to this effect was presented to the king but no action followed.[14] Roman Catholics who advocated colonization would not risk their capital in New France, and Huguenots who would take that risk showed little interest in colonization.

Meanwhile, the administrative picture in New France becomes progressively more confusing. For reasons unstated, de Monts withdrew from the trade in 1617, and Champlain was prevented by the company from returning to the colony in 1619. The following year the monopoly was given to a new syndicate operated by some members of the de Caën family of Dieppe. Although the nominal head of this company was the Duc de Montmorency, the leading figure was the Huguenot Guillaume de Caën, chosen, so Champlain says, in the expectation that he would convert to Roman Catholicism.[15] The new monopolists were required to support six Récollet missionaries, a heavy enough financial burden in itself, but the Rouen-St. Malo company was so firmly entrenched in New France it proved impossible to exclude it from the trade.

Obviously, the situation in the colony was not improved by this rechartering, so the Récollets returned to their plan of 1616 to exclude the Huguenot connection. Father Georges Le Baillif arrived in 1620 and participated in another assembly of notables the following summer. Not surprisingly Le Baillif was chosen to lay the assembly's complaints at the foot of the throne.[16] These complaints included charges that Huguenots had supplied firearms to the Indians. Back in France Le Baillif was received twice at court, where he had influential friends. Louis XIII and his Privy Council examined Le Baillif's documents and, as a result, de Caën was forbidden to send any ship to New France.[17] Le Baillif's documents proved to be forged letters, supposedly from Champlain and other colonists, but this did not deter the missionary from publishing a vicious pamphlet attack on de Caën.[18] Le Baillif's religious superior also asked the king to prevent Huguenots from trading or living in New France. All these efforts produced little result for the moment, since de Caën was now given an exclusive charter in return for compensating the merchants from Rouen and St. Malo. Calm seemed to return to New France, perhaps because Le Baillif did not!

The Huguenots continued to be a visible—and vocal—presence in the colony. Some had actually settled at Quebec and nearly two-thirds of the crew members in de Caën's ships were Protestants.[19] In 1622 de Caën was accused of holding prayer meetings in his cabin while the Roman Catholics had to gather on the bow for religious observances.[20] Later, when Huguenot sailors were ordered not to sing psalms in the St. Lawrence, they complained of being "deprived of their liberty," but they did agree to confine themselves to praying.[21] No sooner was their Roman Catholic commander out of sight than the singing began again, and so loudly that the Indians on shore could hear them. "There is no use in talking to them," remarked Champlain, "it is their great zeal for their faith that impels them."[22] Perhaps some of the sailors' zeal was intended only to annoy Roman Catholics.

At the same moment, some boats came downriver to Quebec where Roman Catholic crew members grumbled that

Huguenot companions had been holding unauthorized prayer meetings, which Champlain said must cease at once.[23] Not long after, an Algonquin chief complained that since the coming of the missionaries many of his tribe had died. Champlain indignantly blamed the Huguenots for putting such "impious words" into the heads of the Indians.[24] This litany of grievances against the Huguenots continued, and the documentary accounts suggest some repetition of evidence because of confused dates. In 1626 it was charged that Roman Catholic sailors had been forced to attend forbidden "sacrilegious" Calvinist services. De Caën condemned this story as a "spiteful fiction."[25] By this date the religious conflict in New France had been intensified by the arrival of three Jesuit missionaries whom de Caën refused to shelter at either the habitation or the fort of Quebec.[26]

The Jesuits, however, had two strong advocates at the king's court—Cardinal de Richelieu and the pious young Duc de Ventadour, the most recently appointed viceroy of New France whose Jesuit confessor Philibert Noyrot returned from a summer visit to the colony and appealed to the cardinal and duke for an end to the Huguenot monopoly.[27] In response, in 1627 Richelieu organized a new company, the One Hundred Associates, all Roman Catholics, and revoked the Edict of Nantes as it applied to New France. Henceforth none but French Roman Catholics could legally trade or settle in the colony. The royal signature for these documents was given by Louis XIIII in the siege lines encircling the doomed Huguenot stronghold of La Rochelle. The Huguenot connection with New France was officially at an end—fifty-seven years later, what Richelieu had done for New France the Sun King Louis XIV achieved for Old France by his revocation of the Edict of Nantes.

In retrospect, the Huguenot contribution to Canada's early history seems quantitatively small and of short duration. On closer examination, however, the historical evidence is certainly open to re-interpretation. Our accounts of these Huguenot activities have all come from hostile sources, and there are indications that after 1629 Champlain rewrote his version of events deliberately to denigrate the Huguenots, to emphasize the Roman Catholic contribution to the creation of New France, and particularly to depreciate the work of de Gua de Monts so that Champlain himself might be hailed— as he has in fact been—as the "father" of New France. The boundary between history and propaganda is indeed only vaguely defined, and in the history of early Canada it now appears that de Monts and his Huguenot associates have been the victims of that process of historical revision with which we have become only too well acquainted. And yet, their memory has not been destroyed. *Nec tamen consumebatur.*

2. 'WHO PAYS THE PIPER...'
Canadian Presbyterianism and Church-State Relations

Two symposia on the theme of "The Presbyterian Contribution to Canadian Life and Culture" were held, the first at The Presbyterian College, Montreal in October 1988, the second at Knox College, Toronto in May 1989. Although a considerably shorter version of the following article delivered at the symposia was published in a Carleton Library Series volume, The Burning Bush and a Few Acres of Snow, *in 1994, the original speech is published here for the first time.*

THE PROBLEMATIC RELATIONSHIP OF CHURCH AND state has been at the heart of every secession and every reunion in the history of Scottish Presbyterianism, and in Canada that same issue, like so many other features of Presbyterian identity, has been shaped primarily by those Scottish precedents and traditions. Most of the arguments used in Canada and in Scotland owe more to John Knox than to John Calvin, but the ultimate appeal to authority leads back to the Bible. Scripture contributes several oft-cited proof texts, but these are both inconclusive and even conflicting. The exhortation "Render unto Caesar" (Matthew 22:21) provides no assistance in determining what belongs to Caesar and what to God. Probably more influential in shaping Presbyterian attitudes have been Jesus' statement to Pilate, "You have no power over me unless it had been given you from above" (John 18:11), and the interjection by the disciples at the Last Supper, "Look, Lord, here are two swords" (Luke 22:38), a gratuitous comment freely misinterpreted and misused in every century since.

The latter two texts have been regularly taken to mean that sacred and secular authority are both of divine origin, and are parallel but distinct and unequal spheres. In his classic study, *The Holy Roman Empire,* James Bryce notes that the Holy Roman Church and the Holy Roman Empire were like two sides of a single coin, "the co-operation of both being needed in all that concerns the welfare of Christendom at large."[1] This accord between papal and imperial powers, between the sacred and secular swords, rested on a theory ("as sublime as it is impracticable") that required a co-operation "attained only at a few points in their history."[2] The symbolism of the two swords was embodied in the coronation ritual of post-Carolingian emperors, but already by the middle of the ninth century Pope Nicholas I was trying to tilt the balance of power in favour of the church. Quoting St. Paul that the secular ruler is God's servant for the general good,—"if you do wrong, be afraid, for he does not bear the sword in vain" (Romans 13:4)—Nicholas claimed that the emperor's right to rule came from the pope because the power to use the secular sword was intended "for the exaltation of his mother, this holy apostolic church."[3]

This concept of the two spheres of jurisdiction passed into Calvin's theology. Calvin stressed the king's responsibility as God's anointed, but he also allowed for the removal of a bad king by the lesser magistrates. John Knox agreed that civil government was divinely instituted and that the authority of rulers was limited by divine law, but he also recognized that the feudal kingdom of Scotland was not the republican city-state of Geneva. He asserted that ordinary citizens shared the power and duty to remove and execute a tyrant—"the sword is in their own hand"—and so both people and king shared the sword committed to them by God.[4] The operating base for this popular resistance grew from Knox's concept of covenanting, and for this his model was the Scottish custom of bonding.

The development of the Church of Scotland as a national, endowed, and protected institution reduced any reality of popularly based power, yet the Knoxian tradition of resistance lingered on in Scotland and in those lands overseas where Scots settled. The Union of 1707 promised to protect the Church's rights in Scotland and establish its equality with the Church of England in their respective kingdoms, but it failed to define their status outside Britain, an oversight fraught with future difficulties for British North America. Within Scotland itself, two other developments also influenced the religious development of the country and of the colonies. Just five years after the Union the united Parliament re-established the power of lay patrons, whether individual landowners or the state itself, to appoint parish ministers, thus negating the congregation's right to call. The second development was the gradual polarization of the Church of Scotland into two competing parties, the strict Calvinist "Evangelicals" and the deistic and latitudinarian "Moderates."

These last two developments played a part in the secession of 1733 when Ebenezer Erskine and his followers separated from the established church over the patronage issue. For the Church of Scotland, particularly the Moderates, it was acceptable that the patrons who paid the piper should call the tune by appointing their chosen candidates to pulpits. The next secession, in 1761, saw three Church of Scotland ministers carry opposition to state interference with the church to its logical conclusion by demanding complete separation of church and state and the adoption of voluntarism. Under the voluntary system the piper would receive only the free-will offerings of the audience—a practice which might leave the party without any music!

The third tradition of church-state relations came immediately from the Disruption of 1843. Once again the seceders—this time more than two hundred members of the General Assembly—left the established and endowed church because of the state's support for the patronage system. The new Free Church did not, however, believe in voluntarism. Reiterating Chapter 24 of the Westminster Confession, the new church proclaimed that the state must not interfere in the church's separate and sacred sphere of authority. Nevertheless, because Christ is head over the nations and over civil rulers, the Free Church still insisted that the state is under divine obligation to support His church materially. Now the piper must still be paid, but whoever pays the piper will not be allowed to call the tune. For the Free Church the two swords still existed but, whereas state intrusion into the church's jurisdiction was anathema, the church could claim to be not only the conscience of the state but by logical extension the final arbiter in all matters involving church-state relations.

The similarity of this anti-Erastian position to the contemporary political arguments of the Oxford Movement and Roman Catholic ultramontanism is striking and results from the events and philosophy of the French Revolution.[5] Reacting to the emergence of modernism and secularism, and specifically to Napoleon's treatment of the papacy, ultramontanes asserted that, because the church is divine, infallible and soul-saving where the state is human, fallible, and materialistic, the church is superior to the state and is the God-appointed conscience of the state. Anti-Erastianism was the bed-rock of the Romantics' opposition to statism, whether voiced in Edinburgh, Oxford, Rome or Paris, yet anti-Erastianism *per se* is not necessarily voluntarist.

The three traditions—endowed church establishment, separation of church and state and, finally, the church independent of but superior to the state—were carried from Scotland to British North America, but here circumstances and personalities created interesting mutations. The ideal of a national establishment, based on the Reformation principle of *cuius regio, eius religio* (the ruler's religion becomes the nation's religion), assumes the existence of religious uniformity—an assumption not applicable here because of *de facto* religious pluralism. Although the Church of England was legally established in the Maritimes, there was little cause for jealousy or cupidity among other denominations because no endowment was provided. Similarly, when the Church of Scotland did claim social and religious superiority over the Secessionists in the 1820s, no demand for co-establishment with the Church of England was ever put forward.

In Upper and Lower Canada, however, the relations of church and state became a Presbyterian *cause célèbre*, complicated by conditions and traditions inherited by the government from the French regime. The Quebec Act of 1774 was designed to integrate a French-speaking and Roman Catholic population into an anglophone and Protestant empire, in part by giving legal recognition to the religion of the "new subjects." The so-called Constitutional Act of 1791 recognized the right of Loyalists to representative government and English law, but it also established the Protestant religion and endowed the clergy with lands equal to one-seventh of Crown land grants. "Protestant Clergy" was not defined, but subsequent clauses referring to rectories and rectors "of the Church of England" are accepted by historians as sufficient evidence that the Church of England was now established in the two Canadas, as in the Maritime colonies. The difference in the two regions, however, was the creation of the Clergy Reserves—3,750 square miles of prime agricultural land—a delayed fuse for church-state relations in the St. Lawrence-Great Lakes basin.

Among Presbyterians in the two Canadas the church-state issue arose soon after the arrival of the Loyalists. The controversy, however, did not begin with the Clergy Reserves. In 1786, when Presbyterians petitioned against the Church of England's monopoly on marriages, their claim for equal treatment of the Church of Scotland was based on the loyalty of Scots. No group in Britain deserved more appreciation from the House of Hanover, for their steady support of the Protestant succession during the Glorious Revolution that had prevented "tyranny by High Churchmen."[6] Lieutenant-Governor Simcoe blamed John Bethune, the Presbyterian Loyalist chaplain, for this petition, which he denounced as "the Product of a wicked Head and a most disloyal Heart." Nevertheless, the petition produced a revised marriage act that added clergy of "the church of Scotland, or Lutherans, or Calvinists" to those licensed to solemnize matrimony.[7]

Two generations passed before church-state relations again attracted Presbyterian attention. This time the issue was government aid to St. Andrew's at Niagara-on-the-Lake after its church was burned by the Americans in the War of 1812. The petition of the Niagara congregation made no claim to co-establishment. It merely suggested that the Clergy Reserves might supply the £100 the Presbyterians wanted.[8] No money was forthcoming, but four years later resolutions of the legislatures of both Canadas called for co-establishment of the Church of Scotland as a legal right, with endowment from the Clergy Reserves or some other public source.

Despite the creation, at government prompting, of a Canadian synod of the Church of Scotland in 1831, John Strachan's successful defence of the Church of England's control over the Clergy Reserves and the campaign by Methodists and other voluntarists to end denominational privileges and religious favouritism in the Canadas by the separation of church and state prevented the achievement of co-establishment.[9] The closest the Church of Scotland ever came to establishment and endowment in the Canadas was its inclusion as an inferior partner in the 1841 compromise division of the Clergy Reserves funds—a division that also made the Church of Rome a beneficiary of the support promised a half-century early to the "Protestant clergy"! That 1841 solution to the issue of state endowment for religion lasted only fifteen years before the Clergy Reserves were secularized by an Act that proclaimed its purpose to be the removal of "all semblance of connexion between Church and State,"[10] the only such reference in the legislative history of Canada.

Before this victory of voluntarism was achieved, however, Canadian Presbyterianism had already faced its own moment of truth regarding church-state relations. In the wake of the Napoleonic wars a flood of Scottish immigrants fled depressed conditions at home to settle in the colonies, and particularly in the area north of Lake Erie which received an estimated 10,000 persons per year.[11] As important as their numbers was the religious persuasion of these immigrants: they were predominantly supporters of the Evangelical party in the Church of Scotland. The issues of "patronage" and "intrusion" did not exist in British North America, yet the Disruption in Scotland called for a sympathetic response particularly among these more recent immigrants. If Disruption was good enough for old Scotland, it should be good enough for the colonies. To an Evangelical, continued connection with the Church of Scotland made one guilty of sin by association.

Orchestrated by that peripatetic advocate of the Free Church cause, the Rev. Robert Burns, the Disruption spread to British North America in 1844 bringing with it that third version of the church-state relationship—pay the piper but do not call the tune. Burns had fought valiantly and written voluminously against voluntarism in Scotland in the late 1820s,[12] and not surprisingly he found clerical allies in the Canadas among those ministers who had so recently begun to receive supplementary stipends from the Clergy Reserves funds. Unfortunately for the Free Church ministers, the government ruled that those leaving the church in Canada would lose their claim to the moneys. The upshot was that the new colonial Free Church became unwillingly voluntarist, but eventually even those clergy who remained in the Church of Scotland also lost their stipends decades later thanks to financial mismanagement by church authorities.[13]

In the short run the Free Church interpretation of church-state relations seemed fated to disappear in the North American climate of voluntarism. Immediately after the local Disruption the voluntarist Secession Synod approached the new Free Church with a view to union. Despite the fact that the Free Church clergy had lost their government stipends, ministers such as Burns and Michael Willis, the principal of Knox College, were able to delay the union by insisting that Secessionists acknowledge that the civil magistrate is obligated to support 'true religion' because Christ is head over the nations. Their rearguard action denying the *de facto* existence of voluntarism in British North America is the more surprising in the light of the victory by the growing forces of voluntarism within the Free Church itself in 1848.

That year the government invited denominations to apply for surplus money in the Clergy Reserves Fund. The reaction in the Free Church was like Atalanta's when confronted with the golden apples. Some clergy applied for a share of the money because "endowment of the Church by the civil magistrate is lawful," but voluntarists countered with the argument that offering and accepting public funds for denominational use ought to be determined "on the grounds of Christian expediency."[14] Because Synod decided to forbid applications by either ministers or congregations, the voluntarist version of church-state relations triumphed and union with the Secessionists was possible.

The Basis of Union that created the Canada Presbyterian Church in 1861 required seven years of protracted discussion about the headship of Christ, but in the end it provided a compromise that became the official Canadian Presbyterian position on church and state for the next eighty years. The Secessionists agreed that Christ is king, but denied that He delegates power to "earthly Kings." Burns broke this log-jam with a resolution asserting that the Basis already embodied "the grand principle of national responsibility to Christ" and it should not be clogged with "an enumeration of the varied practical applications of that principle."[15] In its final form the fourth article of the Basis states that Christ is "King of the Nations" and therefore, like all men, "the Civil Magistrate . . . is bound to regulate his official procedure . . . by the revealed will of Christ."[16]

In the negotiations that led to the union in 1875 of all Canadian Presbyterians, the doctrine of Christ's headship posed no serious obstacle. The doctrine was, however, further broadened by invoking the practice of "forbearance." Article 2 concluded that nothing in the Westminster Confession or either catechism regarding the power and duty of the civil magistrate "shall be held to sanction any principles or views inconsistent with full liberty of conscience in matters of religion."[17] This produced a very Canadian formula—the headship of Christ simply means whatever you want it to mean!—a formula that satisfied all but a very few and became an enduring tradition until World War II.

In the late 1880s, Canadian Presbyterians did become vocal and involved in the Equal Rights movement when they and other Protestants accused the Jesuits of having divided loyalties that prevented them from being good Canadians. This issue certainly involved church-state relations in terms of denominational equality, expressed in the slogan "A Free Church in A Free State" that accompanied a series of resolutions on the separation of church and state by the General Assembly of 1890. At least in those day before multiculturalism and religious pluralism the solution seemed simple—keep the long arm of the Vatican out of Canada, and let the Jesuits be more like Presbyterians![18]

Although the bases of union in 1861 and 1875 had denied the right of civil government to intrude in the church's affairs, Presbyterians saw no reason why the church should not use the power of the state to achieve its own aims through legislation. Promoters of the various programmes that historians lump together under the umbrella-term "social gospel" believed that morality could be legislated into existence, or at the very least immorality could be legislated out of existence. Professor Robert Law of Knox College declared that the church is "the conscience of the community."[19] In terms of moral reform, said George Pidgeon, the welfare of the nation must override personal rights.[20] Prohibition and Sabbath observance are the two most obvious examples of campaigns to usher in the here-and-now kingdom by employing the power of the civil sword. As Brian Fraser has pointed out, social gospellers fostered a naive belief that social evils could be eliminated and instant millennium reached thanks to the simple panacea of more laws.[21]

No discussion of Canadian Presbyterianism and church-state relations (indeed no discussion of Canadian Presbyterianism) would be deemed complete without some reference to the church union of 1925, and this paper will not be the exception to prove the rule. For continuing Presbyterians the major consideration was the continuance and integrity of their church. Despite the willingness of some Presbyterians to use the civil sword for religious ends, the independence of the ecclesiastical sword had been jealously guarded in the past. The Presbyterian Church in Canada, although recognized as a legal entity by many statutes, had never been incorporated,[22] and any hint of state intrusion was as feared in Canada in 1925 as it had been in Scotland in 1843. Yet the new church was to be created not by water and the word but by legislative action of the civil state. A contemporary parody of the union process, entitled "In Lege Unitas," derided the work of Gershom W. Mason, the legal *éminence grise* of the unionist forces. Sung to Samuel Wesley's tune, "Aurelia," the parody began,

> Our Church's one foundation
> Is Mason's Union Bill,
> She is his new creation
> By legal craft and skill;
> From Parliament he sought her,
> To force into his fold
> And for law-fees to slaughter
> The Scottish kirk of old.[23]

Four more verses in the same vein attacked the Erastianism of the union, and E. Lloyd Morrow, the early archivist of nonconcurrency, summarized this perceived danger of state control in one Actonian dictum, *"An incorporated church will tend to autocracy."*[24] Ephraim Scott, probably the most vocal opponent of union, made the same point in even more purplish prose in a small pamphlet postscript to his book *Church Union in Canada*.

> In Canada, in 1925, over three years ago, as in Scotland, in the days of the Covenanters, nearing three centuries ago, came the climax and failure of a long attempt to blot out, by civil power, Presbyterian democracy, with its liberties and rights of the people, and replace it by an unpresbyterian autocracy where the rights of the people are no more.[25]

The question of defining Christ's headship over the nations might have slumbered longer among Canadian Presbyterians but for the rise of Nazism. In 1942 the issue was placed before the General Assembly by a deliverance of the Presbytery of Paris, pointing out the contradiction between the 1875 "forbearance" statement and the Westminster Confession. By that statement the church had so effectively stopped its own mouth that it could not authoritatively condemn Nazism nor affirm Christ's headship over Canada! An overture from the Synod of Hamilton and London to the same General Assembly declared that the church had thus been left without guidance as to "how to affirm their loyalty to the State; and the State . . . without assured knowledge of its powers and duties, under the Lord Jesus Christ, towards the Church."[26] The result of this episode was the appointment in 1943 of a committee on the Articles of Faith to consider the problem as it concerned church-state relations. That committee laboured long to produce the Declaration of Faith concerning Church and Nation adopted by the Assembly of 1955.[27]

As the most recent official statement of the Presbyterian Church in Canada on the question of church-state relations, the Declaration draws heavily from history but not always with harmonizing results. Reminiscent of the Free Church position, Article 1 recites that Christ is "both Head of the Church and Head of the Civil State." Article 2 recalls the doctrine of the two swords by stating that Christ has given power to both the Church and the Civil State, "entrusting to each its own distinctive function." The next three articles repeat the traditional statements that civil authority is commissioned by Christ and as a stewardship under Him civil authorities must be obedient to His revealed word. Article 6 directs the Church to denounce and resist all forms of tyranny, although a citizen's right of resistance is not so clearly stated as it was by John Knox.

Article 7, entitled "The Relation of Church and State," in part restates the earlier reference about the distinct functions of church and state but comes even closer to the concept of the two swords. Both church and state are subordinate to Christ; they must be mutually supportive but neither has a right to "domination over the other." The church therefore cannot be the religious agent of the state nor is the state the political agent of the church. The church must also not mix the Gospel with nonreligious creeds, but at the same time it is obliged to "confront the Nation with Christ's judgement and grace." This might be interpreted as acting as the conscience of the state, an implication that becomes clearer in the section on the duty of the civil government towards the church. There the state is advised that it must "pay serious attention whenever its office-bearers are addressed by the Church . . . concerning the kingdom of God and His righteousness."

Taken as a whole, the Articles of Faith concerning Church and Nation certainly do not approach the Church of Scotland's traditional position of advocating establishment and endowment, whereby whoever pays the piper has the right to call the tune. On the other hand the Secessionist insistence that the piper must not be paid with public funds is also implicitly rejected. In fact, Article 7 explicitly denies the separation of church and state : "We reject all doctrines which assume . . . that the Church's life should be or can be completely dissociated from the life of the Civil State." Of the three versions or interpretations of the church-state relation that can be found historically in Canadian Presbyterianism, the Articles come closest to the Free Church's position—the state must pay attention and perhaps money to the ecclesiastical piper, but it is forbidden to call the tune.

A modern and very real question of the application of this doctrine of church-state relations arose in 1987 when the Memorandum of Agreement between the University of

Toronto and the Toronto School of Theology was to be renewed. The changes demanded by the University threatened the independence of the church, and nonconcurrence by the churches would bring an end to government grants for the theological colleges. The University was pressing the issue of academic freedom by insisting that its rules governing hiring, discipline and firing of faculty members must be enforced in the constituent colleges of the Toronto School of Theology. Given the Canadian Presbyterian tradition of the independence of the church from state interference, this episode posed a potentially serious threat to Knox College.

The University of Toronto is state-financed and therefore ultimately state-controlled, but Knox College is the creature of the General Assembly of the Presbyterian Church in Canada. Like its sister theological colleges, Knox College's purpose, structure, requirements and rules are different from those of a secular university. Despite the limited government aid that the church receives for theological education, it cannot, by principle or tradition, admit any right of the civil power to control faculty or teaching in its college. Here was an apparent impasse in church-state relations. If the University insisted that the college submit unreservedly to the University's rules, Knox College would have to be withdrawn from any connection with the University in order to preserve the independence of the church. Such a move might also entail withdrawal from the Toronto School of Theology if other member colleges and their churches accepted this state-imposed limitation on their independence.

Long and difficult negotiations seemingly defused this crisis. The University apparently acknowledged the different and distinct nature and requirements of theological education, while Knox College moved to create a church-controlled review procedure for such cases involving its faculty. This supposedly meets the concerns of the University regarding academic freedom without impairing the independence of the church. Knox College's Bylaw 17 required the *de facto,* immediate and automatic firing of any professor removed or deposed by his/her presbytery. The compromise accepted by the General Assembly of 1989 permits, on appeal, the creation of a peer-group review committee to consider the faculty member's "competence to continue to fulfil the professorial office notwithstanding such resignation or deposition."[28] The committee reports to the College Senate, which will recommend to the next General Assembly that an appointment be continued or terminated. This formula supposedly satisfies the University's insistence on a review procedure, while meeting Presbyterian insistence on the historical independence of the church from state interference. The test of this pudding will obviously be in the eating if a conflict of interpretation ever arises between the state-controlled University and the Presbyterian Church in Canada.

This latest development of Canadian Presbyterian concern over the relation of church and state exemplifies once again the basic issue of the independence of the church from state interference and the presumption that the civil magistrate is obligated to support 'true religion', even materially with public funds. The parallel with the position assumed by the Free Church after the Disruption is self-evident in the attempt of the Presbyterian Church in Canada to reconcile secular academic freedom with ecclesiastical sovereignty while continuing to receive public funds for denominational purposes. Despite all the pressures and precedents of North American voluntarism and of secularism in the twentieth century, one Scottish tradition will be honoured by modern Canadian Presbyterianism. The piper should still be paid, but he who pays the piper is not yet permitted to call the tune.

3. ROBERT MCDOWALL
Pioneer Dutch Reformed Church Missionary in Upper Canada

In 1978 John Moir was invited to give the Third Adrian Leiby Seminar at the New Brunswick Seminary, New Brunswick, New Jersey. Because of the Seminary's historic relations to the Dutch Reformed Church, he decided to speak on Robert McDowall, an early missionary to Upper Canada. The paper was printed that year in de Halve Maen, *and in a revised form in* Presbyterian History, *the periodical of the Presbyterian Church in Canada's Committee on History, in issues spread across 1979 and 1980. The material later formed the basis of a biography of McDowall for volume 7 of the* Dictionary of Canadian Biography *(1988).*

Robert McDowall, pioneer Dutch Reformed missionary to Canada, has become so much a legend that it is difficult to separate fact from fiction. Two historical reasons for this development are easy to explain but impossible to rectify. In the first place, church records have not on the whole been well preserved in Canada. Secondly, most of McDowall's personal papers were destroyed when the family home burned in 1876, thirty-five years after his death. Nevertheless, the epic story of his missionary labours can be reconstructed in part from scattered sources, and that story must be told against the backdrop of the American Revolution and its aftermath, the Loyalist migrations which gave Canada its British character.

Two major groups of Loyalists can be distinguished. The first, coming in 1783 by ship from the seaboard colonies to the present-day Maritime provinces of Canada, was largely composed of well-to-do professional and merchant-class people, 30,000 in number. Of the second group, less than 6,000 strong who settled in present-day Ontario, many had come during the hostilities and had been formed into Loyalist regiments that spent the later years of the war in bloody raids into upper New York. These Loyalists were active participants in the war in a way that the Maritime Loyalists generally were not, and unlike the first group they were most often pioneers who had lost only backwoods farms, rather than shipping fleets, well-stocked warehouses or professional practices.

To receive this second group of Loyalists in 1784 four townships were laid out: Kingston, or the First Township, received a mixed group of settlers including several Dutch families from the Mohawk Valley.[1] The Second Township, called Ernestown, and part of the Third (which was named Fredericksburgh) were granted to members of the second battalion of Sir John Johnston's regiment, the King's Royal Regiment of New York. Nicknamed the Royal Greens, this party numbered almost five hundred on its muster roll, including some of Dutch origin.[2] The Fourth Township, named Adolphustown, was given to a mixed group under the leadership of Captain Peter Van Alstine, a Knickerbocker Loyalist. Most of this last band came from the Hudson Valley around Albany and Dutch names are again in prominence.[3] These four townships stretched some fifty miles along the "front" of Lake Ontario from Kingston to Belleville, and it was here that some 2,500 Loyalist refugees settled in 1784. To these Loyalists in 1790 came Robert McDowall, licensed to preach and officially appointed missionary of the Classis of Albany of the Dutch Reformed Church.

McDowall had been born on 25 July 1768 near the present Ballston Spa, New York, about twenty miles north of Albany.

His parents were Scottish. His father had been an officer in the British Army before he married at Dumfries and emigrated to America not long before Robert's birth. Shortly before his twenty-second birthday Robert was licensed to preach by the Classis of Albany and despatched to Upper Canada as a missionary. There is no evidence to indicate whether this journey was in response to a request from Upper Canada, or on the initiative of the Classis, or at the instigation of McDowall himself. Over a century ago an historian of the Bay of Quinte region wrote that McDowall was invited to come to Canada by Peter Van Alstine, leader of the settlers in the Fourth Township.[4] Since Van Alstine was a native of Kinderhook, a village about twenty miles south of Albany, and McDowall's home was just twenty miles north of Albany, it seems plausible that Van Alstine was somehow involved in McDowall's visit to Canada. Certainly, McDowall later baptized and officiated at the marriages of several of Van Alstine's family.

As official representative of the Classis, the young man spent that summer visiting Loyalist settlements on the north shore of the St. Lawrence and Lake Ontario and formed several congregations. "Soon after his return from the mission he received and accepted a call from three of those congregations which he had organized: Ernestown, Fredericksburg, and Adolphustown."[5] McDowall did not, however, return to Upper Canada until eight years later. Apparently desirous of obtaining ordination and an education, Robert attended Williams College in Williamstown for two years in 1793 and 1794, but left before completing his course of studies. His transcript from the college noted, "his application to study having been great, and his moral character not only good but exemplary."[6] He reputedly completed his education at Schenectady, and was ordained in 1797 by the Classis of Albany.

During this time Presbyterians in the areas adjoining the Bay of Quinte petitioned both the Church of Scotland and the Associate Reformed Church in the United States for a minister, but no permanent clergy was available. One ordained minister of the Classis of Albany, John Ludwig Broeffle (or Proeffle), had settled independently farther down the St. Lawrence towards Montreal,[7] but McDowall arrived in Upper Canada in 1798 as the official representative of the Classis which, by sending him on this mission, became the first Presbyterian or Reformed church body to respond to the spiritual needs of the Loyalists.

In 1798, when McDowall came to stay in Upper Canada, there were only five ministers in the whole colony, although three Methodist clergy and about the same number of Baptist ministers itinerated through the settled regions. At Kingston was the Anglican and Loyalist chaplain John Stuart, former missionary to the Mohawks, whose travels and labours, so reminiscent of McDowall's, earned him the title "Father of the Church of England in Ontario." At Bath, some seventeen miles west of Stuart, lived the Reverend John Langhorn, an eccentric Welsh bachelor and priest of the Church of England. Down river, near Montreal was the only Presbyterian, John Bethune, ex-chaplain to a Loyalist regiment. Not far from him were the only Lutheran, J.D. Schwerdfeger, and John Ludwig Broeffle, the Dutch Reformed pastor, who like Schwerdfeger had arrived in 1795. One other Presbyterian, Jabez Collver, ordained in New Jersey in the "Cambridge Presbyterian order," settled near Lake Erie in 1793 where he preached privately during the next quarter century, refusing to be associated with any religious body.

McDowall crossed the St. Lawrence River from Morristown, New York, to Brockville early in the spring of 1798.[8] He spent some time preaching in the Brockville area, and a contemporary letter describes him as "an excellent man, a good orator, and truly orthodox in his religious principles." After refusing a request to stay there longer, he proceeded westward to Sandhurst, on the boundary of the second and third townships, where he settled just three miles from the strange John Langhorn but a considerable distance from Peter Van Alstine who supposedly had first invited him to Canada. McDowall took the whole hundred-mile stretch of river and lake-front from Brockville to Belleville as his mission and, on 6 July 1798, he opened his first church at Sandhurst. Within two years he had formed this group into a regular congregation.

Obviously, McDowall was functioning as pastor, but as yet he had no civil authority to marry people. The marriage law of Upper Canada passed in 1793 restricted the performance of weddings to Clergy of the Church of England, but since there were only two, Stuart and Langhorn, in the length of seven hundred and fifty miles, Justices of the Peace were permitted to solemnize nuptials according to the Anglican rite. In 1798 a new law was passed that allowed Church of Scotland, Lutheran, and "Calvinist" clergy to perform weddings if they got a certificate from the local Justices of the Peace at their Quarter Sessions. This was less than equality with the established Church of England, and it deliberately excluded the Methodists from the marrying business.

McDowall applied for permission to perform marriages and apparently received authorization in 1801: his certificate was signed by the Loyalist Ebenezer Washburn and dated simply 13 July. This creates an historical problem because McDowall recorded his first wedding on 11 May 1800, fourteen months before he was licensed. Between those two dates he had in fact joined eleven couples in holy matrimony.[9] In December 1800, McDowall himself had been married at Picton in Prince Edward County to Hannah Washburn, the daughter of Ebenezer, Justice of the Peace at Kingston, who six months later authorized McDowall to perform weddings. Robert's marriage to Hannah must have been performed by a Justice of the Peace since there was no clergyman of any denomination settled within miles of Picton. Nine months later, John, their firstborn arrived, to be followed in 1804 by Sarah Washburn, in 1807 by Ebenezer (named after his grandfather Washburn), and finally James, born sometime between 1810 and 1813 (his father neglected to record the date in the baptismal register).

McDowall's baptismal register gives ample proof of his missionary travels; it records 1638 christenings in no less than twenty-four townships along the "front" and the volume has lost a number of its pages. Similarly, McDowall's fragmentary marriage register lacks pages for over fourteen years but includes 870 entries for twenty-eight years, an average of thirty-one weddings per year or more than one every two weeks. A mathematical projection suggests that he performed some 1300 marriages before his death in 1841. An examination of the entries in McDowall's marriage register confirms the impression that his flock were a mixture of English, Scottish, French, and Dutch people.

As early as 1801, John Stuart reported that the "uncouth manners and illiberal conduct" of his colleague, Langhorn, had driven some of Langhorn's flock to McDowall's ministry. Three years later Langhorn got into a controversy with McDowall regarding episcopal succession and again annoyed Stuart by demanding that Stuart as bishop's commissary report the matter to the bishop—for what purpose was never clear. On another occasion McDowall got into a theological controversy which is recorded only by his opponents. While preaching at the Adolphustown courthouse on unconditional election, McDowall offered to debate the doctrine with any disbeliever. Samuel Coate, a Methodist itinerant, reluctantly challenged McDowall who, Coate believed, had a much better education and could quote biblical texts in Hebrew and Greek.

A debate was arranged to be held in the Ernestown Presbyterian Church, a building as large as a barn. The date of the meeting is simply given as 1800. A large gathering of Methodists and Calvinists (meaning Presbyterians, Baptists, and Dutch Reformed), assembled from the region to be edified or entertained. In fact the crowd was so large that it could not be accommodated in the church, so McDowall mounted a wagon and preached "half of the day." Then Coate began his address, but he had spoken for only two hours when McDowall and his supporters walked out. This was construed by the Arminians as an admission of defeat by the Calvinists, yet even in victory Coate could not stop preaching and went on until evening. The Methodists claimed that after the McDowall-Coate confrontation, Presbyterianism declined in the Bay of Quinte region and that the Ernestown church was eventually sold. Neither claim can be verified now, and the church in question seems instead to be the same in which McDowall laboured for another forty-one years until his death.

McDowall's missionary travels were made on horseback or foot (he preferred the latter) over miserable backwood trails. Sometimes he swam rivers where no bridge had been built. Around the Bay of Quinte area he usually made his visits by canoe.[10] He certainly visited Toronto on several occasions, and Hamilton, and one contemporary reported that McDowall said he had journeyed to the site of London, Ontario, two hundred and seventy miles west of the Bay of Quinte. One unsubstantiated report claims McDowall even reached Windsor on the Detroit River, 350 miles from home.[11] Such travels can only be described as prodigious, and it is little wonder that McDowall was so widely remembered in Upper Canada. He was remembered also for his habit of calling the faithful of a neighbourhood to impromptu services by blowing a moose horn. Of several anecdotes told about him, one concerns his strict sabbatarianism. When offered biscuits at a settler's cabin on Sunday, he threw the biscuits out of the window saying, "They're much too fresh and warm to have been baked on Saturday."[12]

McDowall was the only settled Dutch Reformed Church missionary in the colony, but he did not work alone in the field at all times. When the General Synod of the Church met in 1800 it reported that five other missionaries had been sent to Canada. At this date McDowall had six organized and one unorganized mission districts, with about 425 families. The Classis of Albany had recently received more written requests for clergy to come to Upper Canada, and promises had been made to pay any clergy sent, because the Classis had already expended £150 on its six missionaries. Another volunteer was forthcoming at the General Synod, a Mr. Kirby, who was despatched to Canada but seems to have moved on to England quite soon afterwards.

Six years later, in 1806, the General Synod met in Albany and received a full report on the Canadian work from the pen of McDowall. He now was ministering to three congregations in the Bay of Quinte area. He had travelled widely and everywhere met a wish and a need for ministers. Toronto wanted a settled minister, and so did Brockville and probably Belleville. McDowall was preaching six to nine times per week and yet was unable to visit all his flock more than once every three to six weeks. As American Baptists and Methodists were sending more missionaries into Upper Canada, McDowall feared that the proliferation of denominations would soon make it impossible for the people to support all the clergy. If the Reformed Church could not help the Canadians, McDowall would have to advise the settlers to apply to the Presbyterian churches for ministers.[13]

McDowall's plea for help drew a very positive response from the Dutch Reformed Church. Three more volunteers—Bork, Ten Eyck, and Froeligh—reached Canada soon after the Synod meetings closed. At Brockville the three men held two consistory meetings with the four elders and the four deacons.[14] By 1810 McDowall had established fourteen churches and prospects for future congregational growth must have appeared good, because more settlers, mostly Americans, were flocking into Upper Canada.[15] In 1811, in fact, Ernestown alone had 2,300 inhabitants and was the most densely populated area in the colony.

In June 1812, the month that the United States declared war on Great Britain and its colonies, the Synod of the Dutch Reformed Church again reviewed its progress in Canada. In 1809, Jacob Sickles and Henry Ostrander had spent three months in Upper Canada, preaching, administering the sacraments, and receiving church members. The following year John Beattie spent eighteen weeks on a missionary tour "around Lake Ontario" and organized a church at Toronto under the care of the Classis of Albany. All of these efforts were of a seasonal nature because McDowall remained the only settled minister, and from 1810 to 1815, when the war ended, only one more missionary, John Duryee, is recorded as having been sent to Upper Canada.[16]

The war interrupted all connections with the United States for all of the denominations, but with the return of peace the mission effort of the Dutch Reformed Church was renewed. In 1817 two more missionaries visited Upper Canada, and in 1818-19 another minister and a Presbyterian licentiate were sent to the field. No less than eleven Dutch Reformed Congregations now existed in the colony, yet in 1819 that whole mission field was "quietly abandoned" by the church. Why did a missionary effort that had lasted formally a quarter of a century and had involved at least eighteen preachers, including McDowall, come to this sudden end? The answer can be simply stated as a testing time and a watershed in Canadian development.

By the beginning of the war the population had grown to about 100,000 but ninety percent of the settlers were Americans who had arrived since the Loyalist migration. The basic interest of these newcomers was the good and cheap agricultural land to be had in Upper Canada. As the risk of war between Great Britain and the United States grew after 1808, there were fears that these American settlers might side with the United States in a time of conflict. When hostilities did start in 1812 with American invasions at Niagara and Detroit, the overwhelming majority of these Americans remained loyal to Britain and even took arms against their cousins whom they viewed as aggressors and friends of the hated dictator, Napoleon.

For those religious denominations that had close contacts with the United States—the Baptists, the Dutch Reformed Church, and particularly the Methodists—the War of 1812 was the moment of truth when each was severed from its American connection. Not only did missionaries cease to enter the colony and some already there returned home to the United States, but the anti-American feeling caused by brutality of wartime experiences at the hands of the American invaders forced each group to identify wholeheartedly with the British cause. McDowall's experience must have been typical of the dilemma facing the missionaries—renounce all pro-American feelings and all connections with their motherland or leave Upper Canada.

Like most Americans in Upper Canada, McDowall did not hesitate to give his full allegiance to Britain. But the problem was institutional as well as personal. American missionaries and American influences of any kind were no longer welcome in British North America. The tie with the Dutch Reformed Church was cut by mutual agreement, and McDowall and Presbyterian ministers saw immediately the necessity of creating an indigenous Reformed Church in Upper and Lower Canada.

Because the Presbyterian churches of Great Britain still showed little interest in the religious welfare of their brethren overseas, a plan was set afoot in 1817 to draw all Presbyterian clergy in the Canadas into a Canadian presbytery to encompass five different traditions—the Church of Scotland, the secession churches (Associate and Relief) from Scotland, the American Associate Presbyterian, and the Dutch Reformed churches. In human terms, such a presbytery would bring together three national backgrounds, Scottish, Welsh and American; and soon Irish would be added as well.

Early in 1818, the last year that missionaries came from the Classis of Albany, the "Presbytery of the Canadas" was formed and McDowall joined it. The Presbytery, however, contained only half of the sixteen Presbyterian ministers in Upper and Lower Canada, and not one west of McDowall (that is, in the nearly five-hundred mile stretch from the Bay of Quinte to Detroit) had joined. McDowall had crossed his own Rubicon as a result of the decision to end the Dutch Reformed mission in Upper Canada, and to future generations he was known as a founder of the Presbyterian Church in Canada.

The remaining score of years in McDowall's career as a minister can be briefly summarized. In an attempt to attract more members and to function more effectively, the Presbytery of the Canadas reorganized itself in 1819 after only two meetings into a three-presbytery synod, of which McDowall became the first moderator. Seven more ministers joined, but the Synod did not achieve its purpose and so in 1825 it dissolved into two independent presbyteries for Upper and Lower Canada, respectively.[17] At that very moment another divisive force appeared in Canadian Presbyterianism. The Church of Scotland had ignored the colonies for two generations, but now the Glasgow Colonial Society began to send missionaries to British North America.

Local Presbyterian ministers soon found the new missionaries had no intention of co-operating; instead, their claims to religious, social and political superiority were dividing existing congregations. McDowall, as senior member of the provincial clergy, was drawn into union negotiations only to discover that his American birth and education made him unacquainted with the Presbyterian and Scottish traditions brought by the newcomers. Viewing himself as a liability to the cause of unity, McDowall withdrew from the negotiations but did join the Church of Scotland Synod when it was organized in 1831.

In his later years McDowall spent more time farming and less travelling. For two decades he was active in the Midland District Agricultural Society, and in 1835 won the Society's prize for best farm in the District. At last, after such a full and active life, Robert McDowall died on 25 July 1841, just nine days following his seventy-third birthday. His body was interred at Sandhurst, his first church in Upper Canada. Yet McDowall's story is not quite finished. On 6 July 1898, one hundred years to the day after the opening of the mission at Sandhurst, celebrations were held in the new brick church that had replaced the original wooden structure after ninety years. Two steamships were chartered to carry the crowds at "excursion rates" from Kingston and from the Bay of Quinte.[18]

After a memorial service and a church dinner, speech-making began with seven speakers in all, including the famous Canadian nationalist and principal of Queen's University, the Rev. George M. Grant, and R.J. McDowall, grandson of the pioneer Dutch Reformed missionary. Another prominent speaker was Sir Oliver Mowat, prime minister of Ontario who had been baptized by Robert McDowall seventy-seven years earlier. "Mr. McDowall," commented Sir Oliver, "was a devout, loving, and earnest missionary and a scholarship would be a fit way to express the gratitude of the descendants of the United Empire Loyalists to the pioneer missionary." This proposal had actually come from a resident of the Bay of Quinte; and before the day of celebrations ended, $500 had been subscribed. One editor commented that if every couple married by Robert McDowall gave only one dollar, the objective of $2000 would be more than half realized. Apparently those happy couples were slow to respond, because the McDowall Scholarship at Queen's University was not established for another ten years.

Seventy-seven years later, on 22 June 1975, at exactly the same place, the McDowall Memorial Cemetery at Sandhurst (the church having burned down), McDowall received that ultimate accolade from this secularized world—he was commemorated by an historical plaque erected by the provincial government.[19] If the speakers at this second ceremony were not quite so famous as those of 1898, the sentiments expressed were the same. McDowall has not been forgotten by his adopted land, nor by the Presbyterian Church in Canada, which owes much of its beginnings in Ontario to the Dutch Reformed Church and especially to the Classis of Albany that sent Robert McDowall, pioneer missionary, to Canada.

4. Through Missionary Eyes
The Glasgow Colonial Society Papers as a Source of Social History

About 1985 Moir was invited by the Champlain Society to assist with the publication of Dr. Elizabeth McDougall's transcription of letters from the missionaries of the Glasgow Colonial Society who worked in the Maritimes and Upper and Lower Canada between 1825 and 1840. The Champlain Society's volume of selected correspondence was not published until 1994, but the whole collection is a rich source of social history because the writers were educated, articulate, and keen observers. As Moir was occasionally invited to speak to historical societies, he prepared a paper for such occasions on this theme and delivered it, in several versions, at sundry meetings.

D**URING THE DECADE FOLLOWING THE END OF THE** Napoleonic Wars, large numbers of Scots escaped the depressed economy of Britain by joining other Scots who had already migrated to British North America. The new arrivals soon discovered that accustomed religious facilities were at best inadequate and at worst nonexistent in the colonies, and that repeated pleas to Scotland for familiar services from their own clergy brought little help and more often no reply. The Church of Scotland had no overseas missions and no auxiliary similar to the Society for the Propagation of the Gospel in Foreign Parts to support members in the colonies. In an attempt to fill this void, interested clergy and laity from Glasgow and vicinity, under the patronage of Lord Dalhousie, governor-in-chief of Canada and former lieutenant-governor of Nova Scotia, founded in 1825 "The Society (in connection with the Established Church of Scotland) for promoting the Religious Interests of Scottish Settlers in British North America." Understandably, that name was soon shortened unofficially to the "Glasgow Colonial Society."

The Society had two main functions: first, to raise funds and to use those funds to send and support Church of Scotland clergy in the colonies until congregations could become self-supporting, and second, to recruit and evaluate licentiates and ordained ministers who volunteered to emigrate to British North America and to put them into contact with colonists seeking to establish Church of Scotland congregations. The records of the Society reveal the many facets of the Society's operations and provide incidental insights into the religious and political issues of the day, but particularly the letters written home by the missionaries describe the physical and religious conditions encountered in the localities where they settled. As educated and articulate young men, the missionaries through their letters left posterity a valuable commentary on colonial life.

The Society's records consist of two minute books, two correspondence books (covering primarily policy matters), and seven large volumes of correspondence to its secretary, the Rev. Robert Burns, from the missionaries and interested parties.[1] In the summer of 1843 Burns had made a triumphal two-month tour through British North America that was a catalyst in transporting the Disruption to the colonies. During that tour Burns acquired many friends in the colonies, and in 1845 he accepted a call to the new Free Church congregation, Knox Church, in Toronto, with the added incentive of a professorship at the recently established

Knox College. Presumably the records of the Society were among the more than 2000 volumes donated by Burns, the Colonial Committee of the Free Church of Scotland, and interested individuals to Knox College Library in 1845. There the records lay unnoticed until, amid growing interest in the history of the Presbyterian Church in Canada, the papers were transferred shortly before World War I to a newly created archives collection. When the Church's assets were divided as a result of church union the archives (but not the college Library) were transferred to the United Church of Canada and the Glasgow Colonial Society papers found a new home in the United Church Archives.

The Glasgow Colonial Society was one product of the Evangelical party in the Church of Scotland which later gained control of the General Assembly in 1834. The Society had no official connection with the General Assembly and depended on its benevolence for permission to canvass congregations for funds and to approach the imperial government for aid from the Canadian Clergy Reserves Fund. In 1836 the Evangelical-dominated Assembly took up the cause of help for the colonies by creating its own Colonial Committee, "for promoting the Religious Interests of Scottish Presbyterians in the British Colonies." The Committee would give the Society "from time to time such sums of money as . . . may seem meet to the Committee," but the Committee had the exclusive right to raise missionary funds within the Church of Scotland. The only direct link between the Committee and the Society was Robert Burns who was appointed to a subcommittee of the Colonial Committee. In the next few years the financial condition of the Society became desperate, and at the same time the Committee successively reduced its grants to the Society. Finally, in 1840, the Committee absorbed the Society to simplify operations and to remove Burns who had proved to be stubborn and unco-operative.

The first missionaries of the Society reached British North America in 1827. Of the five British North American colonies, Upper Canada was the preferred recipient of the Society's attentions, largely because the well-established Burgher and Antiburgher communities in the Maritimes looked on any Church of Scotland missionary activities there as unwarranted and provocative. During the Society's fifteen-year life, thirty-four ministers were sent to the Canadas and twenty-five to the Maritimes. Of those fifty-nine missionaries, sixteen left the Canadas either before or immediately after the Disruption, and in the Maritimes only five remained in Pictou County and Cape Breton after 1844.

The fact that fourteen of the twenty-two still in the Canadas joined the Canadian Free Church at the Disruption reflects the Evangelical origins of the Glasgow Colonial Society.[2] The expectations of missionaries never matched the realities of life in the colonies. Letters from Upper Canada described new settlements with a mixed population of thousands, but warned of a general absence of religious interest. As for Church of Scotland ministries, Upper Canada was a near vacuum, and in Nova Scotia Horton Township Presbyterians had been settled for sixty-five years but still had no minister of their own.[3] From New Brunswick the Rev. Alexander MacLean reported that the lieutenant-governor said, "from the almost total absence of Kirks" many Presbyterians had become Anglicans, "but many more prefer Sectarianism."[4]

Some Highlanders, MacLean explained, had kept the faith by holding home services led by "the more gifted," but without Sabbath worship, a minister in Pictou added, Sunday in the colonies became "a day of mere animal rest." Do-it-yourself services as the only alternative to "animal rest" were common in Upper Canada as well.[5] Perhaps settlers found such arrangements both satisfactory and economical, for in

Lanark, where 985 Presbyterians in a hundred-square mile area had no church, a subscription for funds raised only £6 5s, and a promise of 144 bushels of wheat for four years.[6]

Even when subscriptions for ministers were raised in the colonies, attitudes in Scotland posed an additional problem. The Church of Scotland had the human and material resources, complained the Rev. William Rintoul from Upper Canada, but unlike the Glasgow Colonial Society the Church had "made no great and decisive effort to furnish this Province with Ministers."[7] For a dozen years Presbyterians of East River near Pictou had petitioned the Church for help, without receiving the courtesy of a reply. Beckwith Township in the Ottawa Valley had forwarded the necessary bond for a minister, but two years later no clergy had volunteered. Again and again, however, the missionaries in the field warned that new men must be good preachers and that the Society must lay "an absolute *interdict*" on everyone against reading sermons. That was a practice "especially abhorred" by the colonists, who assumed that a read sermon was always a borrowed sermon.[8]

Missionaries' reactions to their new environment varied widely according to conditions in their particular region. One minister found nothing but desolation around Shelburne, Nova Scotia, where some of the local roads were "impassible [sic] both on foot and horseback."[9] Physically the worst conditions were found on Cape Breton Island where some 5000 Presbyterians had arrived from the West Highlands in 1835 and 1836. Older settlements had already grown "callous" towards the lack of religious services. At least six ministers were needed, because the people were religiously ignorant and dreadfully poor. Near Whycocomagh settlers from Skye had neither food nor clothing, according to the Rev. James Fraser: "I never witnessed such utter destitution. In one house was an old man bed-ridden for two years, with but one tattered rug or covering to protect him from the cold,

& the snow drifting in between the logs."[10] A similar account came from the Rev. John Stewart: "I have baptized where neither Father, Mother or children could venture out in their tattered rags. I have seen dwellings where 6 or 8 of a Family lived for 5 weeks on the milk of a cow without any other Food. . . . I have known dozens of Families who lived on unripe Potatoes for weeks."[11] To compound their misery, as the same writer explained, many immigrants who had got their passage on credit lost their cattle or their land to the collection agent.

From every colony ministers wrote home about the religious ignorance of their flocks. A missionary in eastern Upper Canada said his people were easily swayed by "every wind of doctrine" because they were deficient in speculative religion and worse in practical.[12] Commenting on Upper Canada's religious kaleidoscope, the Rev. George Romanes suggested that the Scottish temperament seemed unhappy with sectarian groups and some persons told him that "they would rather go to hear Mass than attend a Methodist Camp Meeting."[13] From St. James, New Brunswick, newly arrived Rev. Peter McIntyre complained that half his parishioners lived five miles from the church and probably would not attend services because they refused to walk and could not afford horses.[14] Settlement in Upper Canada was rapid but in the opinion of George Romanes the scattered groups of Presbyterians would be reached only through an itinerant system, and another missionary recommended that all itinerants be celibate and remain so for a couple of years.[15]

Not all the fault for religious laxity lay with the settlers, for the missionary at Georgetown, Lower Canada, complained that the provincial Church of Scotland clergy, with one exception, practised "promiscuous baptism" and did not ask for certificates of character from communicants. Upper Canada's good lands attracted settlers with some capital, and soon the colony could boast of a high material standard of living as well as such civilizing institutions as schools, public libraries, prayer meetings and Sabbath schools. Typical of the missionaries and visitors to Upper Canada, George Romanes wrote that Upper Canada was "a magnificent and wonderful country" whose advantages surpassed the most laudatory reports common in Scotland.[16] The missionary from Richibucto, however, felt that New Brunswick was being underrated. In addition to great resources the colony had a climate more pleasant that Britain's, for "Colds and coughs are almost unknown; and there is a dryness and elasticity in the air, that gives a buoyancy to the animal spirits."[17]

In the selection of missionaries, bilingualism—English and Gaelic—was frequently mentioned by the colonists as a *desideratum,* or at least a strong advantage. The Rev. William Rintoul regretted this fact, but "the Highlanders cluster together in the same settlements, and are . . . very tenacious of their native speech."[18] Enquiring about a minister for Martintown, Upper Canada, the Rev. John Burns suggested that the Sabbath services should use Gaelic for one half of the day because "that language is generally spoke [*sic*] by the lower order of the old Settlers."[19] In 1829 the Rev. Matthew Miller, a touring missionary in Upper Canada, formed a different opinion of the bilingual question. Some Highlanders in Vaughan Township wanted a Gaelic-speaking minister although they had earlier been willing to hire an English-only preacher.

Miller believed this emphasis on Gaelic was overblown: "With a very few exceptions among the old people, they understand English." He felt Gaelic services were "quite undesirable" in a mixed population because the majority of a congregation could not understand the language. One church on Yonge Street tried the experiment and the result was "a good deal of dissatisfaction."[20] That the bilingual question in Upper Canada was a localized issue is obvious from the Rev. Alexander MacNaughton's plaintive letter to the Society: "Could you not send us *one Gaelic* Missionary of the six? In our Presb[yter]y the missionaries from want of Gaelic are in a great measure useless."[21]

In Nova Scotia, particularly on Cape Breton Island, the situation was quite different since many settlers were Gaelic unilinguals and, for many more, English was their second language. In 1829 two touring ministers preached at Pictou; one addressed a thousand people indoors in English, the other addressed between two and three thousand in Gaelic, outdoors. Writing from Lochaber in Antigonish, a spokesman for the residents told the Society how pleasing the Rev. Alexander McGillivray was to some Gaelic unilinguals who had not heard a sermon in their native tongue for twelve years.[22] Missionary James Hannay noted that the people of Black River, New Brunswick, spoke Gaelic "almost exclusively" and would be delighted to have a Gaelic-speaking minister.[23]

The missionaries of the established Church of Scotland received an ideological shock, however, when they encountered the voluntarist mood of the colonists, especially of those in Upper Canada. Alexander MacNaughton reported from Glengarry that, "A great many people here have got hold of the voluntary cant word 'that religion will support itself' & with the view, I suppose, of giving the experiment the fairest trial, refuse to put their hands in their pockets. So much for the—voluntary—principle."[24] The missionary in Beauharnois was similarly discouraged as he saw colleagues leave the colony for lack of local financial support. The voluntary principle, "however beautiful in theory," was "quite unadapted to practice."[25] William Rintoul predicted that voluntarism would turn ministers into farmers, and the history of the next two decades partly supports his prophecy.[26]

In a thoughtful letter to the Society, George Romanes also criticized voluntarism as being much worse for the colonies than for Britain. In North America the population was scattered, religiously pluralistic and often poor. Cash was so scarce that barter was the rule rather than the exception. On top of all this the settlers were so indifferent to religious ordinances that the fate of most churches seemed dismal or even desperate. The Rev. P.C. Campbell (later principal of the University of Aberdeen) informed the Society that local Yankees and others around Brockville supported voluntarism, which meant in practice hiring "a pious labourer or tradesman, who will for a day's wages, be willing to exercise the less laborious trade of preaching."[27] A collective complaint to the Society claimed that the clergy were viewed as "hired servants" without job or salary security, and that the power of the purse was exercised against them as a form of intimidation.[28]

Given the traditional importance accorded to education in forming individual and national character in Scotland, the frequent references to schools, libraries and even seminaries in the Glasgow Colonial Society papers is not surprising. As early as 1833 Burns was urging the creation of an "establishment . . . for the training up of young natives . . . to the future service of the Colonial vineyard."[29] He was convinced that Scotland was unlikely in the short run and unable in the long run to meet colonial needs for clergy. One missionary suggested a two-year theology course in Scotland for colonial volunteers.[30] Another replied that many young men who could not afford to study abroad would enter a colonial seminary, but that no one in the colonies would start such an institution as long as General Assembly refused to allow colonial presbyteries to license ministerial candidates.[31]

As for primary education, the early settlers felt that "the young have been shamefully neglected."[32] The Society did not offer direct support for education, but the extensive assistance given to teachers in Cape Breton by the Society's auxiliary Edinburgh Ladies' Association has been thoroughly described by Laurie Stanley in her excellent book, *The Well-Watered Garden*. At least many missionaries took an active interest in their local educational scene and seemed to consider their interest as a natural part of their ministry. James Morrison, writing back from Dartmouth, Nova Scotia, expressed reservations about the qualifications of the teachers in the six neighbouring schools.[33] Dugald McKichan complained from Merigomish that children of his area had no school of their own and had to travel to one of three neighbouring communities, although two schools had been built in another locality where there were no children.[34]

From Cape Breton, John Stewart advised that in his one-thousand-person parish, 376 children did not attend school, and 151 adults were illiterate.[35] At Boularderie, Cape Breton, the church doubled as a school and the new teacher collected 145 zealous pupils in a very few weeks. Four months later that number was 212, and the teacher was puzzled as to where they all came from.[36] He also had a Sabbath school with up to 130 children and thirty-five adults. Practical knowledge acquired in the day schools was in turn put to use at Sabbath schools which were often conducted by the same teacher. There praise and prayer were followed by Scripture reading and exposition. Obviously, Sunday schools were popular institutions in the colonies, for James Souter in Newcastle, New Brunswick, reported in 1831 that he had begun a Sunday school with five teachers and 84 scholars, many of them grown people.[37]

One area of education in the colonies where the Society and its auxiliaries were actively involved can be classed as "continuing education." Traditional Scottish emphasis on literacy had its complement in the promotion of good reading by means of private and public libraries. Colonial conditions enhanced interest in access to books, and as early as 1828 the Society's Report noted that an "Itinerating Library" sent to Nova Scotia was providing "an ample store of profitable reading."[38] This library of 250 volumes, "mostly religious," as well as pamphlets, magazines, reports and tracts, had been provided by Edinburgh friends of the Society. It was managed by volunteers, and each subscriber paid 2s 6d annually towards the enlargement of its holdings.

In Upper Canada the famous pioneer public library in Dalhousie received $100 and a set of the *Encyclopedia Britannica* from a patron in 1828. "I need not tell you Rev[erend] Sir," the Dalhousie correspondent continued, "that the desire of knowledge appears to be a particular inherent in Scotsmen." That library was, however, the second local Presbyterian project; the first was the St. Andrew's Philanthropic Society and the third was a "commodious house" to serve as school, church, library and meeting place.[39]

From Pictou, the Society was asked to fill a list of some twenty titles in Gaelic and the same number in English, ranging from Bunyan to Josephus and including school books, psalters, and several different printings of the Bible, although the most requested titles were poetry and sermons. Private individuals had often provided the foundations of a colonial library, but hearing that the Society had given one school £10 for a juvenile library, the Rev. Robert McGill of Niagara asked for the same "or a larger sum" to purchase books in Scotland.[40] James Souter donated to his Sunday school the library given to him by the Society. The missionary at Beauharnois had collected "the germ of a Church Library" and asked the Society for "a little addition," particularly of "Pious Biography." His flock did not expect new books: "Old ones, even odd volumes of useful reading would be very acceptable."[41]

Not all shipments of books from the Society reached the eager readers in the colonies unscathed. When one ship was wrecked on Cape Breton a neighbouring teacher bought all the water-logged books at a salvage sale. His efforts at sun-drying the bound volumes did not much improve their condition—the paper-covered items were a total loss—but the remainder were "received with transports of joy, and with the greatest feelings of gratitude to the Honourable Society, and to the pious and benevolent individuals who contributed towards the institution of a library within the reach of the most needful (I may almost say) of the British dominions in North America."[42]

The comments of the missionaries on their own working and living conditions in the colonies frequently reveal much about the colonists and the country. Partial payment of salary was the rule rather than the exception; most missionaries seem to have collected only half of their promised stipend. Dugald McKichan received less than a third of his £80 in 1830, but he blamed this on bad crops as well as the "wretched habits of the country."[43] The Rev. John McLaurin had arrived in Lochiel, Upper Canada, in 1820 and five years later had one thousand hearers in his three-point charge. Despite the fact most of his flock were considered wealthy, he warned that no minister should come to British North America "dependent upon the voluntary support of the people."[44] Hugh MacKenzie reported from Wallace, Nova Scotia, that his flock had generously promised him a horse, but only £5 had ever been raised. In two years he received £120, but half of that sum came in the form of inferior wheat or overpriced labour. For the Bibles he had brought from Edinburgh and sold, he had yet to receive one penny.[45]

Poverty was undeniably a factor in the problem of paying clergy, but the Rev. John Sprott of Musquodoboit, Nova Scotia, asked rhetorically if the settlers must be doomed to live "in a state of spiritual starvation" and perhaps lose "all relish for spiritual food" just because of their lack of means?

Sprott was convinced that only a few years of external aid would be needed to avoid this trap.[46] Peter MacNaughton, newly arrived in Upper Canada in 1833, reached a different opinion quickly when the inhabitants of Thorah and Eldon refused to give him life tenure and offered only contractually limited employment. Peter shook the dust of those townships from his feet, observing that in any case the people there were given to drinking and fighting. His next encounter with Upper Canadian Presbyterians in Vaughan Township was even more discouraging. Here he found more drinkers and fighters, who spent their Sundays either working or relaxing, were poor and ignorant, and believed that ministers did not work hard and therefore deserved less pay than labourers. "Though perhaps only a dollar is given, it is regarded as so much lost money." "This land is covered with thick moral darkness."[47] Fortunately this was not Peter's final judgement on the colony; he spent forty-three years in Upper Canada, thirteen of them in Vaughan.

The positive results of religious ministrations fortunately became more evident with the passing of time. A missionary in New Brunswick reported that wherever churches had been established there was a marked decrease of Sabbath profanation and drinking.[48] At Lancaster, Upper Canada, Alexander MacNaughton's parishioners thought that catechizing was a novelty, but he persisted with such success that they soon were convinced that non-attendance on ordinances was "decidedly disgraceful."[49] Dugald McKichan, who at first feared the Sutherlandshire people of Merigomish because of their reputation for deceit and greed, soon found his fears were groundless and he lauded their custom of morning and evening daily family devotions where a chapter of the Bible was read and all joined in worship of God. Dugald did admit that he had perhaps overdone his desire to please the Highlanders when he preached in Gaelic for an hour and twenty minutes.[50] When William McAlister gave communion to 200 people at Lanark, the church was packed and many more stood outside at the windows all day.[51] Services were governed by the agricultural calendar, so that at seeding and harvest, Sunday was the only convenient time for formal religious activities; winter, however, was the ideal season for catechising.

The advancement of true religion could not, however, disguise the fact that a missionary's life was often rough and sometimes perilous. John Sprott commented on his lack of old country comforts and on "coarse food and hard fare," but concluded optimistically that he suffered "no real want."[52] Travel, especially in winter, was probably the most difficult part of missionary life. One missionary struggled through six feet of snow for most of a forty-mile trip; two others reported that they travelled respectively forty-eight and thirty miles on foot to visit their churches in the Ottawa Valley.[53] "Trees, trees, trees continually," wrote one missionary from Lanark, with "very bad" roads that were worse in spring and autumn when a horse could be up to its belly in five feet of mud.[54] Alexander MacLean at St. Andrews, New Brunswick, was happy to have a new ministerial neighbour only thirty miles away, "a distance which, in this gigantic country, is considered trifling."[55] Travel might be trifling or broadening, but at times it could be dangerous to a missionary's health. Early one winter morning the Rev. Thomas Alexander's ship sank in half an hour on Lake Ontario, near Belleville, because of ice damage. Fortunately the water was shallow, and the half-clothed passengers who had rushed on deck to face their fate were left stranded with the icy waters lapping just two feet below them.[56]

The lack of religious ministrations, the need for education, the trials of private and public life in a mission, the danger of reading sermons, the shortcomings of voluntarism, the question of a bilingual ministry, the quality and quantity of private piety, and the independence of congregations were only some of the topics of social commentary scattered across the pages of the missionary correspondence of the Glasgow Colonial Society. Other themes include the beginnings of Queen's University, internal politics of the Church of Scotland, denominationalism in a colonial setting, extensive discussion of that perennial complaint, church-state relations, French missions and (once only) Indian missions, and the creation of presbyteries and synods. All of these topics and more can be added to the roster of historical interests touched on by the missionary correspondents of Dr. Robert Burns during that decade and a half when he assiduously preserved these letters with their insights through missionary eyes into the broad spectrum of social history in colonial British North America.

5. To Fertilize the Wilderness
Problems and Progress of the Synod of Nova Scotia in Its First Quarter-Century

The Synod of the Atlantic Provinces of the Presbyterian Church in Canada celebrated its 175th anniversary in October, 1992, and during its meeting in Truro, Nova Scotia, John Moir was invited to deliver an historical address.[1]

THE INDIGENOUS SYNOD OF NOVA SCOTIA WAS officially formed by the Burghers and Antiburghers of the province on 3 July 1817, with three presbyteries (Truro, Pictou and Halifax), 19 ministers (two of them on Prince Edward Island) and nine vacant charges. Only two Presbyterian ministers did not join the Synod—Archibald Gray of Halifax and Bruin Romkes Comingo who was by then ninety-three years old. Of those 19 ministers, 14 came from the Secession tradition, 3 from the Church of Scotland, and 2 were Congregationalists. The new Synod's first working meeting was actually held three months later, in the Truro Meeting House on 8 October 1817. The intention of this article is to describe the Synod's first quarter-century, and to assess the progress and the problems it encountered.

With the venerable James MacGregor as moderator of its first sederunt, the Synod proceeded to appoint a "Committee of Missions" to "fertilize the wilderness" as Thomas McCulloch later defined the Synod's role.[2] Synod's intention to establish a

Presbyterian theological academy at Pictou was announced, and subscriptions thereto were invited.

Transcribed into the Synod's early minutes is a letter from the Governor, Lord Dalhousie, a staunch Presbyterian but a stauncher member of the Church of Scotland. That letter thanked the Synod for its expression of loyalty and in return promised the Crown's protection for Synod equal to that protection given "other religious sects and persuasions" in the province. In retrospect, the Governor's choice of words to define the new Presbyterian Church of Nova Scotia may have been prophetic in foreshadowing the Synod's relations with the established Church of Scotland. For the moment, however, the Synod was busily and enthusiastically organizing to carry out its self-declared mission.

A decade after the Synod was formed, it had grown from three to four presbyteries and from 19 to 27 ministers, with 7 men licensed in 1825, working in Cape Breton, mainland Nova Scotia, New Brunswick and Prince Edward Island. In 1817 Nova Scotia had an estimated 93,000 inhabitants, but just one decade later that figure had risen to almost 124,000, an increase of one quarter. By the latter date 30% of Nova Scotians were Presbyterians, making them by a fair margin the largest denomination in the province. Fully one third of these Presbyterians lived in the Pictou District where they comprised more than 91% of the local population. By 1838, just eleven years later, Nova Scotia's population had passed 200,000, an increase of 61% in a single decade and an increase of 150% in the generation since the formation of the Synod. Most of this increase was, as in other British North American colonies, a result of emigration; and in the case of Nova Scotia the immigrants were predominantly Scots, who generally settled in ethnic blocks. Earlton, for instance, had 60 families, all from Sutherlandshire and all Gaelic-speaking.

The Synod's most ambitious undertakings came in 1819. That year missionaries were despatched to western Nova Scotia, to St. Mary's River and as far north as the Gulf of St. Lawrence. Equally important for the Synod's history, theology was added to the curriculum of Pictou Academy. In 1822 McCulloch reported that the King had declined the Synod's request for financial help to get a professorship of theology for the fledgling seminary.[3] Throughout the next score of years the finance, curriculum and status of that Academy became a major concern of the Synod. Much of the Synod's time, however, was still occupied with routine business. Over the years the Synod dealt with a couple of discipline cases, recommended the principle of temperance to all congregations, and complained in 1826 that dissenters in Nova Scotia "are deprived of several rights which are enjoyed by their fellow subjects who are in connection with the Church of England."[4]

In the beginning, the Synod's primary concern was to provide spiritual services for a population scattered over Nova Scotia and Prince Edward Island, and often isolated into numerous small settlements by daunting natural barriers. In 1817 the means at hand, in terms of human and material resources, could not hope to meet such a challenge, at least until a native ministry could be developed. Although the larger and more established settlements already had churches and in most cases ministers, the difficulty of finding ministers and funds to serve the pioneer population in the more isolated and poorer districts was compounded by the related problems of language and mass immigration in the years immediately after the Napoleonic wars.

The Church of Scotland, with its General Assembly in the control of the Moderate party, had shown little if any interest in the religious vacuum that swallowed those of its children who migrated overseas. Pleas from the colonies for ministers, catechists and teachers most often went unanswered, to the deep disappointment of the patient faithful who still wanted the consolation of their forefathers' religion in a new land. Help for the Synod of Nova Scotia, however, suddenly seemed at hand in the mid-1820s. Early in April 1824 a private meeting of leading Evangelical clergy of the Synod of Glasgow and Ayr was held at the Synod House in Glasgow to consider what might be done to meet the religious needs of Presbyterian emigrants, particularly those in the North American colonies.[5]

After a year of investigation and planning, this unofficial group held its founding convention as "The Glasgow Society for promoting the Interests of Religion and of Liberal Education, among the Settlers in the North American Provinces," a name soon popularly (and fortunately) shortened to the Glasgow Colonial Society. The Society's original intention was to find ministers who would accept calls to the colonies and to assist them financially for as much as three years. Later the programme expanded to include catechists, teachers, and the provision of printed religious materials, including libraries. Active auxiliaries were formed, often by ladies' groups, who raised funds for missionaries and collected materials for the emigrants.[6]

The Macedonian cry from Nova Scotia had already been heard in Scotland even before the Glasgow Colonial Society was created. The pleas from the colonies for ministers were in fact the motivation for the formation of the Society. In 1823 a resident of East River, Merigomish, wrote to Joseph Gordon, the prominent Edinburgh lawyer who, with others of his family, had assisted emigration from Sutherland to Nova Scotia. He informed Gordon that in his settlement there were eighty unilingual Gaelic-speaking families, but only four Church of Scotland ministers in all of Nova Scotia—two in Halifax and two others that "preaches gaelic." There were, however, about twenty ministers "of the Burgher

& Anti Burgher & several other Sects."[7] The next year a letter from Guysborough to the Rev. John Martin of St. Andrew's Church, Halifax, complained that for lack of ministers Presbyterians were "as lost sheep wandering without a shepherd" and drifting towards other denominations. If the faithful of Guysborough could not get a Kirk minister, they seemed ready to accept an Antiburgher who had already visited them.[8]

No sooner had the formation of the Society been announced in the Scottish newspapers (read avidly by expatriates in the colonies) than such pleading letters became a flood. Petitioners from Earlton declared, "A Minister of the Established Church is the only character for which we are desirous,"[9] and those from Horton welcomed the purpose of the Society because they had long been without a minister of their own and depended on occasional visits from the aging pastor of Cornwallis.[10] When forwarding this letter to the Society, John Martin commented, "They are very particular in requesting a Minister from the Established Church of Scotland. . . . None but Ministers from the Established church can expect the countenance of his Majesty's Government or the favour of the local authorities in these Provinces."[11]

Martin might have added that both Nova Scotia's governor, Lord Dalhousie, and lieutenant-governor, Sir James Kempt, were active members of Scotland's national church, and that Dalhousie was the patron and most generous benefactor of the Glasgow Colonial Society; but Martin had made his point that the Church of Scotland represented respectability and political influence. When writing to the Society's secretaries Kempt assured them that the Nova Scotian government was "well convinced of the benefits which would result to [Scottish immigrants] by receiving Religious Instructions from Pastors regularly educated, licensed and ordained under the Authority of the Church Establishment." Last year while they were both in London, Kempt added, he and Lord Dalhousie had impressed on the imperial government "the utility of granting an annual allowance to a few Missionaries from the Church of Scotland."[12]

Not all the petitioners who stressed their continuing affiliation to the established church were recent immigrants. From Dartmouth and neighbouring towns, some Church of Scotland people said they had been in Nova Scotia for two generations and others of Dutch and German origin had been there as much as seventy years. "We still live in a moral wilderness, without instruction, with[out] religious discipline, without Christian fellowship and consolation. We are not reminded of the return of the Lord's day by the stated ordinances of the Christian Sabbath, and our tender offspring are deprived of the friendly Ministrations of an affectionate and pious pastor."[13]

Like many other pastorless settlements, these particular petitioners were already building a church in hopes of attracting a minister. From Lochaber, settled about a generation earlier by 217 Gaelic-speaking Highlanders who were also building a church, a less literate writer complained that as emigrants they did not know they would have to "forsake that Church from whose bosom we have received the sincere milk of the word of truth." He also complained that the "Pictou Grammarian," McCulloch was apparently ignorant of Lochaber's very existence when he urged a "new Union to bring us under his Jurisdiction" and at the same time slandered "the venerable Church of our ancestors."[14]

An interested onlooker, the Rev. John Sprott, Relief minister of Musquodoboit and an acquaintance of many of the leading Glasgow Kirkmen, offered Robert Burns, corresponding secretary of the Society and a former classmate of

Sprott's, some sage if gratuitous advice on the ministerial needs of Nova Scotia where he had been living for a decade. "Hard is the lot of the Emigrant. . . . The sabbath returns but where are its wonted joys. No temple or missionary of salvation, no songs of Zion usher in that blessed day. The wind roams among the trees but he hears not the voice of devotion, his children are not Baptized except it be by a Mother's tears." The urgent need was for ministers "to go out in the spirit of the apostles," like missionaries in the primitive church. The Church of Scotland's shame was its indifference. Its sons in Scotland had grown rich on trade with North America, but Sprott asked, "Will they do nothing to enlighten her dark and destitute settlements?" "Orthodox Presbyterians are one people and they ought to be united. Let not the golden band of Brotherhood be broken by any indiscreet interference or unkind feeling."[15]

Unkind feelings had, however, already emerged by the time the Glasgow Colonial Society was just one year old. The founders of the Society may have suspected, or even expected, that their appointments of missionaries would be viewed by the Synod as an unwelcome intrusion into the Synod's "wilderness," because the Society's *First Annual Report* tried to justify or explain the Society's intention. "There need be no cause of discord and animosity," it said[16] and quoted Genesis 13:8-9: "If thou wilt take to the left hand, then I will go to the right, or if thou depart to the right hand, then I will go to the left." This olive branch of peaceable words did not, however, prevent a protracted confrontation between the Synod and the Society.

Confrontation began in the spring of 1826, when Dr. Thomas McCulloch arrived in Britain. He was raising funds for Pictou Academy but he also carried a sixty-page *Memorial,* dated August 1825, from the Synod's Committee on Missions to the Glasgow Colonial Society. This document declared that the Presbyterian Church of Nova Scotia appreciated the Society's good intentions, but unlike the Synod the Society did not understand the difficulties of pioneer people. Immigrant Scots were not numerous in Nova Scotia, and being mixed among earlier settlers they were already served by the Synod.[17] Any intrusion by Kirk ministers would therefore be both unnecessary and unwelcome.

McCulloch delivered this document to the Society at its first annual meeting on 15 April 1826, and early in May he had a lengthy and inconclusive encounter with the directors of the Society. One week later the two parties met again and exchanged angry words. The Society reiterated its policy of intrusion but no interference. McCulloch replied that the Synod and the Academy's theological branch had resources adequate to fill the spiritual needs of all Presbyterians in British North America. After this the increasingly personal debate was continued between McCulloch and Robert Burns, the Society's principal secretary, in the form of letters to the *Edinburgh Star*.

Presbyterians in Nova Scotia were kept well informed of McCulloch's clash with the Glasgow Colonial Society through their local newspapers. George Gillmore, a leading layman of the Kirk in Horton, commented to the Reverend John Martin of Halifax that McCulloch was "a Gentleman of Abilities" who deserved "much Credit" for "promoting the Interest of the Academy at Pictou," but "when I read that Doct. McCulloch has Quit his Academy at Pictou and gone Home to Scotland for the Purpose of preventing that most humane of Societies aiding or assisting the Poor people of these Colonies in obtaining either Ministers or teachers. . . . I am lost in Wonder and amazement! Is this the way to Support the Cause of Jesus? . . . And must nothing be done for these peoples Souls but what the Good Doctor can do?" Gillmore ended his letter with a serious imputation against McCulloch's motives. "Perhaps the Doctor has an eye to the Lo[a]ves and fishes and as he may not see how he can obtain them himself he is of mind to exert his Influence that others may not."[18]

The Society's answer to McCulloch and to the Synod was a defensive *Supplement* to its first annual report, which repeatedly pointed out that no less than twenty-five letters had been received from the Maritime provinces, all asking for clergymen.[19] Analysis of these letters shows that most of them came from pockets of settlement established after the War of 1812 by Gaelic-speaking Highlanders, many of whom were refugees from the Sutherland clearances. Besides providing ministers for such groups, it was the strategy of the Society and of the Church of Scotland in Nova Scotia to draw Synod congregations, in whole or in part, into allegiance to the Kirk whenever an opportunity arose.

Publicly, the controversy between the Kirk and the Synod centred on Pictou Academy, which the Kirk viewed as the presumptuous creation and continuing pawn of McCulloch's ambitions. A decade earlier, when theology was to be added to its curriculum, Lord Dalhousie had warned their Academy authorities that the Academy had been planned as "a *School* and *nothing but a School.*" "A College in Halifax, the Capital of the Province, I do think an Institution highly desireable, but not in a distant corner of it at Pictou. . . . I must, therefore, . . . oppose the extension of your Institution at Pictou beyond what was originally proposed."[20]

The Kirk's attack on Pictou Academy had, however, an ulterior motive. Dalhousie College, the creation of Lord Dalhousie, was expected to open soon, and the Church of Scotland was intent that it should be under Kirk control and have no rivals. Early in 1828 the Glasgow Colonial Society was promoting one person as first professor for the college, and supporting Marcus Dods, soon to father the renowned New Testament scholar of the same name, as its president.

"Failing Dods," Secretary Burns warned, "McCulloch must be the man."[21] When Dods was not available, the Society recommended Duncan Mearns, professor of divinity in King's College, Aberdeen, and a leader in the Moderate party. For a couple of years Mearns dallied with the proposition; but despite repeated rumours of his impending arrival in Nova Scotia, he never appeared.

The most vocal critic of the Academy was the Church of Scotland minister in Pictou, Kenneth John MacKenzie, a Highlander and a highly reputed preacher with a penchant for public controversy who had arrived in Pictou about 1823. An article in the *Scotsman* in early 1828 criticizing the Glasgow Colonial Society had, in his opinion, originated in Pictou, "the head quarters of the Antiburghers in this Country." He warned the Society that two friends of the Academy were en route to Glasgow who would "fan the flame of discord, and unsparingly vilify the characters of the Kirk Ministers in the Province. The one is a lawyer, Mr. [Jotham] Blanchard the 'Zealous Secretary' of the Pictou Academy. The other a Mr. McKay an Insolvent merchant of this place and also a Trustee of the same celebrated hot bed of discord."[22]

MacKenzie continued by quoting a letter from Blanchard to a member of the Kirk: "Your Church will never send preachers abroad who are fit to carry guts to a Bear. . . . Nor will any Established Church, it being the very nature of ecclesiastical establishments to recline in slothful indolence." At a public meeting in Glasgow, Blanchard had praised the unity of Nova Scotian Presbyterianism and blamed all the colony's religious and educational difficulties on Bishop John Inglis. MacKenzie was still convinced that government should support financially those clergy "who by their very connection with establishments are pledged and in principle bound to promote the spread and growth of loyalty and attachment to the Constitution."

Another letter to the Society, from the Kirk's minister at East River, supported MacKenzie's contentions. This writer blamed McCulloch's "selfish and exclusive views" for the Academy's failure to get government money. The Academy, he added, had few students and was not highly regarded by many Presbyterians. "As to the story of all Presbyterians in this Province being united into one church, it is just about as true as that Dr. MacGregor & Dr. McCulloch merit all the praise that Anti Burghers lavish on them."[23] In the opinion of James Morrison, the Society's missionary to Dartmouth, the conflict between the Church of Scotland and the Synod seemed to be widening: "Both parties look more fierce & determined & were it not more for civil than sacred law there would be bloodshed among them."[24]

Morrison's colleague at New Glasgow, Donald Allan Fraser, condemned the Synod clergy as "*malignant, unprincipled,* and *indefatigable,*"[25] and John Martin of Halifax, a zealot in the Kirk cause according to his own colleagues, was firmly convinced that his party was prospering despite "the most violent opposition and continued abuse from the Seceders in Pictou." "Our Ministers have proved themselves firm friends to the Government in a very trying crisis [the power struggle between the Assembly and the Council] and as they do not approve of all the revolutionary schemes of the Pictou Antiburghers they have come in for a share of their calumny."[26] Martin believed the Kirk ministers in Nova Scotia should be united in one or more presbyteries, which was achieved in 1833. Meanwhile, however, his equally vocal associate, Kenneth John MacKenzie, announced that because of the "heartless malignity of a press guided by McCulloch," he was about to publish his own journal, to be called the *Pictou Observer,* "at a very considerable expense."[27]

Suddenly this controversy, which had never been mentioned in the Synod's minutes, became equally absent from the correspondence of the Glasgow Colonial Society. A casual reference by the minister of New Glasgow to certain Presbyterians "who would rather see this country without a religion than that our Church should cultivate its waste places" stands alone in several hundred letters written by the Society's appointees,[28] and the last word on the topic came in 1838 from Burns' long-time acquaintance, John Sprott, thirteen years the Relief minister of Musquodoboit, a settlement that John Martin uncharitably described as "unprovided" with a minister "of the everlasting Gospel."[29]

After the arrival of the Society missionaries, Sprott said, "Jealousy distrust and other hateful plants speedily sprung up and poisoned the Colonial Vineyard. Our Ministers accused the Society of attempting to break up some of our Congregations. . . . War was proclaimed and fighting men threw away the scabbard. I never took any part in these bickerings. I considered them as injurious to all parties. I wrote in favour of an union of all orthodox Presbyterians: they would command more respect if they were united in one general efficient body." Sprott complained, however, that when he himself visited Scotland in 1829, the zealous John Martin had created a schism in Sprott's congregation. "I consider Mr Martin's interference as highly unbecoming. I would not invade his pulpit in his absence. It is easy to collect malcontents in any congregation."[30]

More than a decade had passed since the first Glasgow Colonial Society missionary had arrived in Dartmouth, and much had changed in that time. The province's population had expanded rapidly, but of the Society's twelve missionaries sent to Nova Scotia, five had left by 1836. Of the remaining seven, four returned to Scotland in 1844 at the time of the Disruption, one more removed to New Brunswick a year later, and only two remained in Nova Scotia until their deaths. The Society's mission to bring ministers to the spiritual wilderness of Nova Scotia can hardly be counted a success, nor can the efforts of the Church of Scotland to establish respectability, loyalty and government patronage as the exclusive and superior mark of the Kirk among Presbyterians.

Persons and institutions had been attacked by extreme voices from both the Kirk and the Synod in a display of divisive action. Perhaps in defence of the Glasgow Colonial Society it should be noted that the most active opponents of the Synod, John Martin and Kenneth John MacKenzie, were not missionaries of the Society. Equally noteworthy, in view of the Synod's claim that the Society's missionaries were invading established areas instead of "fertilizing the wilderness," only one missionary was in Halifax, as a teacher, the rest being as widely dispersed as Yarmouth, Merigomish, Wallace, New Glasgow, St. Mary's River, and two on Cape Breton.

After the formation in 1833 of the Kirk's own synod, with three presbyteries, the Kirk did grow in strength and numbers until by the early 1840s it had twenty ministers. Its primary audience was almost exclusively the more recently arrived Gaelic-speaking children of the established national church of Scotland. Nevertheless, accommodation to the new circumstances had softened attitudes in the direction of the Nova Scotian Synod's expressed goal, "to fertilize the Wilderness." Denominationalism seemed increasingly less of a duty, and unity more of a necessity. Meeting in the summer of 1838, the Synod of Nova Scotia adopted a resolution favouring union with the Church of Scotland, "could it be effected on a proper basis," and a year later it appointed a committee to find out what steps the Church of Scotland had taken.

In 1841, two more years and presumably several committees later, the Synod of Nova Scotia did hear from the convener of the Kirk's union committee, Donald Allan Fraser, the same minister of New Glasgow who had called the Synod of Nova Scotia malignant and unprincipled. Fraser announced that his Synod had passed a resolution authorizing union discussions, and had asked the General Assembly to pass legislation admitting all Nova Scotian Presbyterian ministers and congregations into full connection with the Kirk. The Synod of Nova Scotia rejected this union proposal as "a rash and inconsiderate measure" that appeared to "assume a superiority over this Synod which does not in fact exist." Obviously, it had just been reminded how slowly ecclesiastical imperialism dies.

The Disruption of the Church of Scotland just two years later hastened the Kirk's death in Nova Scotia. Effectively, that Synod became the Free Church of the region, changing its name first in 1844 to "the Synod of Nova Scotia adhering to the Westminster Standards" and later to "the Free Church of Nova Scotia." The revival of a Church of Scotland Synod in 1854, covering Nova Scotia and Prince Edward Island, created a third Presbyterian synod within the province, but one that had only ten ministers, the same number as the Kirk had forty years earlier, and of those ten, six had just arrived from Scotland.

Because of the Kirk's loss of those ministers who returned to Scotland after the Disruption and its metamorphosis into a Free Church, another blow had been struck for the cause of the institutional indigenization of Nova Scotian Presbyterianism. When a union of the Free Church and the Synod of Nova Scotia was finally achieved at Pictou in 1860, slightly over half of the ministers were from the Synod of Nova Scotia and slightly less than half from the original Kirk body. As for the Glasgow Colonial Society, it had passed from the scene two decades before this union, the victim of politics inside the Church of Scotland.

In 1836, two years after the Evangelicals won control over the General Assembly, they created a standing Committee "for promoting the Religious Interests of Scottish Presbyterians in the Colonies." Since this was an institutional duplication of the voluntary Glasgow Society, that Society was barred from soliciting funds through the church. Laymen could not serve on the Committee, and Robert Burns was the only Society member appointed to the new committee. By 1840 the Glasgow Colonial Society was effectively dead from financial starvation.

Looking back at the first quarter-century in the life of the Synod of Nova Scotia, it is obvious that real progress was made in fertilizing the wilderness despite the problems encountered in the shortage of ministers, the challenge of supplying religious services in two languages, and the distractions caused by the Church of Scotland's missionary, educational and political ambitions. If the Synod underestimated the intense loyalty of recent immigrants, particularly the Gaelic-speaking Highlanders, to the Kirk as their mother church, the Kirk itself, like other transplanted establishments from the Old World, still thought in terms of fixed parish structures and generous aid from an appreciative government. That quintessential North American aspect of indigenization, the practice of voluntarism, was slow to find acceptance by the Kirk in the New World.

Ironically, it had been the troublesome John Martin of Halifax who bridged the Atlantic by recommending a plan to reconcile parish structure and mission needs. Instead of matching ministers to congregations sight unseen, the Society should support missionaries who would travel widely before being called to a congregation already known to them. When implemented, this scheme solved a variety of pastoral problems by taking the church to the people, not the people to the church. One final element promoting change was the passing of an older generation and the consequent transfer of power to younger men, less attached to older loyalties and less active in previous conflicts. The death of McCulloch in 1843, the very year of the Disruption, seems symbolic of the Synod's first quarter-century. The fate of Pictou Academy had by then been resolved, competition from the Glasgow Colonial Society had ended, and prospects of Presbyterian unity had replaced the Synod's rivalry with the ambitious Church of Scotland. Above all, however, the spiritual wilderness had been fertilized to an extent that would have seemed like an impossible dream in 1817.

6. THE STOOL OF REPENTANCE
The Disciplinary Role of Presbyterian Courts of Session in Victorian Canada

Several years ago, while researching the history of St. Andrew's Church, Markham, John Moir discovered in the minutes of one of its first Session meetings in 1840 that a young woman had been cited for giving birth out of wedlock. Some simple mathematics, however, disclosed to the elders that the child had been conceived before the congregation had been formed. The Session immediately decided that under these circumstances it had no disciplinary authority in the case, but it warned the young woman not to repeat the offence. The author's interest in the disciplinary role of Session and its social implications was now aroused, and he began searching Session minutes for other examples of a Session acting as a court of church discipline.

It soon became apparent that this research was the physical equivalent of hunting for the proverbial needle in a paper stack. The examples were so limited in number and the process so time-consuming that the research stopped. Soon after, however, he discovered in the Presbyterian Church Archives a copy of the Queen's University 1933 M.A. thesis of the late Rev. John Robert Waldie. The article that now follows was written with the approval of Mrs. Kathy Gibson, a daughter of John Waldie and member of the Staff of Caven Library, Knox College, Toronto.

WALDIE'S 150-PAGE ESSAY, "THE INFLUENCE OF the Kirk Session on the Administration of Justice and Regulation of the Social Life of the

Community," begins with an account of the biblical and historical origins of the Session system and its powers. It then proceeds to examine the work of Session courts in Scotland, in New England and, in greater depth, in Upper Canada and Ontario between 1825 and World War I. With the permission of the author's daughter, Mrs. Kathy Gibson of Caven Library, I began editing the typescript, hoping to publish and publicize Waldie's findings on Upper Canada in an abridged form. This process, however, uncovered a methodological puzzle that I have failed to solve.

Waldie's research sources for his Upper Canada section were Session records, mostly then still held by the congregations, although four of the sets he used were in the Ontario Legislative Library and one in the Queen's University Archives. In what I assume was respect for the privacy of Session records, the author cited his authorities simply in an alphabetical sequence from A to Z, giving dates and page references but never any hint as to the congregational source. Comparing a list of these alphabetized footnotes to the list of sources in the Bibliography revealed a further dimension of the problem: thirty sets of Session records are listed in the Bibliography, but only twenty-six in the footnotes.

A lengthy attempt to match the footnotes to the Bibliography entries using the dates of each proved to be futile. Obviously, the list in the Bibliography does not follow the alphabetized sequence which has four fewer entries. The only solution will require a comparison of each footnote to the pages of the actual minutes, if these are available. By simply accepting the author's research at face value, however, one can still learn much from his analysis of the functions and powers of Session in the Victorian age of Ontario.

At the outset of his study Waldie discusses the three most important purposes of church discipline—to vindicate God's glory, to keep the Church pure, and to reclaim the sinner.

The first, by emphasizing the divine office of omnipotent judgement, requires the Church as God's earthly representative to enforce His commandments upon every living soul, in order to establish God's glory among men and defend it against attack and denial. Next, the protection of the Church's purity had an obvious internal purpose, but externally the Church's aim to do good would also be apparent to critical observers. To this end Session's careful purging of the roll and its judicatory citation of accused sinners was ordained. Discipline, whatever its form, should however be followed by reconciliation and since, in the Reformed tradition, only God can forgive, Church censures are not punishments but a means of grace to be used to recover the erring souls from sin and error.

In both the Waldensian and Bohemian pre-Reformation churches Session-like courts, based on biblical precedents, had been instituted, and Calvin in turn emphasized the ruling eldership, later suggesting that it was divinely ordained. Session courts appeared among French Protestants by 1559 and in Scotland about a year later. Because of the importance and power of a Session in relation both to the congregation and the community, the Scottish *First Book of Discipline* of 1560 defined both the qualifications desired in ruling elders and the methods of their election. At the time, however, a system of appeal courts was created as a check against tyrannical actions by Sessions.

Because the Session governs the life of the congregation, its powers refer particularly to the sphere of discipline. To preserve purity and respect within the Church, Session was given the authority to cite scandalous members to appear before them. If three summonses from Session are ignored, the obstinate party may be declared contumacious; but if the person confesses guilt or if the charges are proven, the Session has power to impose censures of several degrees. Least severe is the "admonition," a warning or exhortation often given in private. The more severe "rebuke" (also known as "lesser excommunication") may involve a suspension from church privileges; but it is the limit of Session's power because full or "greater" excommunication imposed for contumacy or for incest, adultery, triple fornication, flagrant heresy or schism can only be pronounced by a Presbytery.

Waldie closes his analysis of the powers and practices of Session with a brief discussion of privilege or immunity from charges of libel or slander arising from any case heard by Session, whether initiated by any elder or by a private communicant. He found only two cases involving privilege, both of them in Britain. In the first, involving private letters of admonition from a minister to an alcoholic elder, the judge declared the correspondence to be privileged. In the second, in 1873, the judge again defended the right of privilege. Privilege, he asserted, existed when a charge was made in *bona fide* "in the regular and becoming manner" prescribed by the law and custom of the Church, because the plaintiff is "exercising a right, and, it may be, fulfilling a duty. . . . His privilege protects him unless malice is proven."[1] Here the issue of privilege must rest, one suspects, for lack of examples or interest in a society where the disciplinary powers of Session seem to have fallen into desuetude.

In beginning his study of the judicial functioning of Sessions in Victorian Canada, Waldie notes that Session records before the 1830s are rare because most congregations developed in response to the flood of immigration that reached Upper Canada about a decade after the end of the Napoleonic wars. From an estimated 95,000 inhabitants in 1814, the colony's population grew by almost 60 percent in ten years, and by a further 60 percent in the next seven years, and by 90 percent more between 1831 and 1841, or multiplied four and a half times in a little over a quarter century.

Virtually unexplored as yet is the impact of the War of 1812 on religion and religious institutions in Upper Canada, although the parallel between the growth of a provincial political identity and political philosophy and the Canadianization of denominations has been touched on by historians of some of those pioneer churches. Waldie, however, begins his study of Upper Canadian Sessions by citing two examples from Session records concerning the effects of that War. One man denied his Session's authority, stating "I do not belong to this church—for ministers ran off and as soon as they ran off the church and Presbytery were dissolved." A second, charged with dishonesty, claimed that "he would never support another American minister. . . . You are rebels."[2]

Waldie also observes that in contrast to the harshness of a Scottish Session, in Upper Canada a moderator or committee of elders was often able to settle disciplinary issues before the case actually reached a meeting of Session. The hearing of cases in Session followed no certain pattern, however; a man accused of public drunkenness in the winter was not dealt with until the following summer, but defendants who felt they were being unfairly accused usually demanded prompt investigation of the charges.[3]

The Session rule of secrecy was almost universally honoured. Waldie records the only exception that he found—an incident when an elder disseminated gossip about a feud between two members who had already been reconciled.[4]

Waldie suggests that the evidence he had seen indicated that Sessions jealously and successfully guarded their own good name against any attack.[5] This is a conclusion that my limited research supports, but I would add that in every case where an elder was accused by a non-elder, his Session found him not guilty. Similarly, when the conduct of a Moderator was impugned, even though all jurisdiction in such affairs belonged to the Presbytery, the Session almost invariably rallied to the defence of the minister. In such cases as I have discovered, the action of Session to protect its Moderator was apparently fully justified—a good example being the Brantford minister accused of sexual misconduct with his maid. Session minutes recorded only regrets that such an accusation or *fama* had been laid, but surrogate evidence shows that his accuser was his own wife who had tired of his company and was determined to leave him whatever the outcome, which she promptly did.[6]

The variety of cases brought before Sessions is almost infinite and includes domestic disputes and family disagreements, and even property surveys. The fact that legal counsel was permitted to appear with a plaintiff or defendant implies a popular belief that justice was indeed meted out by the actions of Sessions. Purging the roll of "scandalous persons" was a regular function of Session before each communion, but as a court enforcing church discipline a Session also entertained cases concerning church attendance, neglect of ordinances, Sabbath breaking, intemperance, dishonesty, profanity, forgery and an imaginative variety of sexual sins. This, however, was obviously not the full complement of cases heard, because several categories are best described as social controls.

In the area of socio-religious problems (the adjective is hyphenated to indicate uncertainty of categorization), many could be lumped together under the Victorian title "vain amusements." These were defined by one Session to include "gambling or gaming for money, card playing, attending theatres, public balls, horse racing, circus, bowling alleys and such like." These activities, which had "the bad effect of straining the purity of the Christian character," must cease forthwith or that Session would not fail to exercise the authority or discipline with which Christ had invested it.[7] The catalogue of lesser or less common offences in this category includes profanity, gossiping, dishonesty, nonpayment of debts, and one case that I encountered, a request that Session adjudicate certain property boundaries claimed by an elder against a member.

Neglect of ordinances and church attendance were numerically the most common complaints among the major disciplinary concerns of a Session. One penitent admitted missing Sunday service because he was busy drowning a dog.[8] One Session passed a rule to deal with non-attendance—after repeated absences of any pew-holder, a part of their seat would be rented to others. In one case, when the original owner could not be appeased, his name was erased from the roll. Sessions also guarded the Sabbath by complaining to civil and ecclesiastical authorities about Sunday labour in public services, and one Moderator was ordered to report to Presbytery that the Sabbath was being desecrated during the construction of the Great Western Railway.[9]

Intemperance was another common issue brought before the Session courts.[10] In an economy based primarily on the production of grain, the distillation of alcohol allowed for the reduction of volume along with the enhancement of the price of the byproduct. When whisky, retailing for 25 cents a gallon, was commonly accepted as a preventative and a cure-all for a wide variety of physical ailments as well as a temporary escape from the chill of a Canadian winter, it is little wonder that alcoholism was endemic in society. The gospel and the machinery of temperance which appeared almost simultaneously in every colony about 1830 had limited success, and in desperation the last generation of Victorians moved on to the gospel of prohibition. For many of the preceding generations and for their Sessions, intemperance was the curse of colonial society, and the liquor traffic was its cause.

The charges were variously phrased—being guilty of the "awful sin of intemperance," "repeated intemperance," "drunk and disorderly," or more poetically, "mashed with liquor."[11] Although the Sessions seemed relentless in pursuit of excessive drinkers, they could be surprisingly tolerant, particularly if the offender confessed repentance in a convincing way. Admonition was the normal penalty in such cases, but if the offence were repeated frequently, suspension was imposed. One such offender admitted that the punishment was just, but he would "still continue to attend the public ordinances of religion."[12]

Alibis for drunkenness were seldom offered, but the commonest one recorded was that the liquor had been taken as medicine.[13] One man explained that he drank too much brandy after he took ill during a journey, whereupon his sympathetic Session restored him to good standing in the congregation. Elsewhere, two elders visited two ladies accused of intemperance. One lady claimed she only used liquor medicinally, but the other offered no excuse and instead thanked the elders for their interest and diligence and promised to reform.[14] Diligence was indeed a watchword for Session in the matter of intemperance, and when one man tried to escape the censure of his elders by joining a different Presbyterian congregation, the Moderator was instructed to write to the Session of the other congregation regarding his case.

The broader social implications of drunkenness did not entirely escape attention when the event caused a scandal in the community. The elders might individually be willing to overlook a first offence, but external pressures might explain a disciplinary action that was taken with apparent reluctance on the part of the Session. One member who had been under the influence of liquor at the Hamilton Exhibition in 1868 expressed his penitence to a committee of two elders, but when he did not come forward to get a communion token the Session directed the Moderator to "encourage him and offer him one."[15]

Although the early Presbyterian churches urged temperance at least, and teetotalism as the most desirable if difficult ideal, by the mid-Victorian period public opinion increasingly condemned the liquor trade as the root of a widespread and multifaceted evil. About 1832, the Session of a newly formed congregation resolved that total abstinence should be a "requisite for membership in this Church."[16] In another congregation when the Temperance Bill was read aloud in 1864 after worship service, there was a show of almost total approval of the bill. The agents of the liquor evil were the numerous local taverns and their keepers who were judged to be as culpable as their patrons. As early as 1834 one Session urged members individually to undertake community action to reduce the number of outlets in their town.[17]

Sessions seem to have taken a particularly vigilant interest in persons who kept hotels. One tavern keeper was refused membership in the local Presbyterian church, another was cited for non-attendance. A husband and wife were suspended for "receiving visitors and selling liquor on the Sabbath"; there is no gradation of the seriousness of the two charges in that case.[18] A malt-maker was refused the sealing ordinances because he had to work on the Sabbath.[19] When he pointed out that a Free Church minister had baptized five of his children without finding fault with his profession, the elders resolved to have nothing further to do with the malt-maker until he saw the wisdom of their criticism.[20]

There is little evidence through most of the Victorian age that elders linked the prevalent and widespread alcoholism with domestic difficulties. Waldie cites a few cases of bad feeling between family members but concludes that instances of interference in domestic matters were few and seldom successful. Unlike Scottish Sessions, Canadian ones seem to have generally avoided involvement in domestic disputes on the assumption that patriarchal rule was not only biblical, but the best and most efficient ordering of a family. Only when family unity was threatened would a Session attempt to find or impose some disciplinary solution.[21]

Waldie comments that offences against the Seventh Commandment apparently seldom occurred in some congregations, but frequently did in certain others. My own research brought me to a more general conclusion that supports Waldie's remark and broadens its base. I found that in most congregations the Session did not entertain many disciplinary cases, which may have reflected a very stable congregational and social situation. In a minority of congregations, charges before the court of Session occurred with some frequency, and often involved the same persons. My own conclusion is that certain Presbyterian congregations were litigious by nature and, perhaps for reasons not evident, even prone to quarrelsome or sinful behaviour that constituted a sort of collective recidivism.

Regarding the breaking of the Seventh Commandment, Waldie notes that the Scottish Presbyterian custom of demanding a declaration of sinlessness in this matter was required before marriage, but that this was never the practice in Upper Canada. The result here was what Waldie calls "a rather distasteful portion of the Records" devoted to "antenuptial fornication."[22] The sin usually became known when one or both partners applied for admission to membership, or when baptism was requested for their children. Postnuptial fornication was not mentioned as often as prenuptial, but both issues were dealt with by Session in a very understanding and forgiving way if the guilty party confessed with repentance. Such full and candid confessions were readily made with surprising frequency in connection with requests for admission or re-admission to membership.[23]

Historians have often noted that in a open frontier situation such as Upper Canada's, competition between denominations approached a kind of ecclesiastical free trade in which an active buyer's market seemed to encourage individuals to take a cafeteria approach to their personal religious practice.

It was easy to change allegiances to another denomination, or even to a different branch of Presbyterianism, if perfect satisfaction was not provided by one's home congregation. While desertions to Methodism were probably the most common numerically, mere temporary proximity to Roman Catholicism brought a certain precentor into trouble with his Session in 1848. The errant man had purchased tickets for himself and his son and daughter to attend the consecration of a "popish" cathedral—St. Michael's in Toronto—where he sat in a conspicuous position near the organ. The precentor admitted the charge to his Session, but claimed he had attended the function to get a better insight into the abuses of popery. The elders were not impressed or convinced by this motive, so this errant ecumenist was ordered "to abstain from the public exercise of this office till after the solemn season of Communion."[24]

From John Waldie's study of judicial functions of the Presbyterian Session in Upper Canada, it is clear that there never was any contact or collusion between the Session or presbyteries and the judicial and legislative bodies of the colony. No civil court ever turned a case over to the ecclesiastical powers, and no case was ever taken from a Court of Session to a civil court. Sessions did, however, often consider evidence that had previously been placed before a civil court. Normally, a person awaiting trial before a civil court was suspended by the Church pending the decision of the civil court; the Session minutes simply report, "suspend proceedings till it be adjudicated on by the Civil Courts." Further, there is no instance where a Session later brought in a verdict that differed from or contradicted the verdict of the civil court.[25] It is worth noting, as Waldie does, that cases heard before a Session were explicitly understood and stated to be "privileged," that is, protected from any civil action that could possibly arise from the case before Session.[26]

Waldie concludes from his investigation that in exercising its judicial authority, "The Kirk Session became in the Presbyterian communities the mightiest instrument for law and order." "The day came," he continues, "when public sentiment favoured the transference of judicial matters to secular courts; when the law of individualism began to be the predominating influence. When that stage was reached our Canadian Session willingly relinquished most of its former activities."[27] After delineating the social values that Sessions historically upheld and propagated in Canada, and which, Waldie believed, had made Canada the law-abiding sensible country that he knew, he affirms, "In this way it would appear that the type of mind cultivated and nurtured by consistorial rule in Upper Canada has been one of the chief stabilizing forces both in progress and prosperity, socially and judicially."[28] Three generations later that heritage seems to have become almost a piece of nostalgia.

John Waldie's purpose was to examine the rise and particularly the exercise of the judicial functions of the Court of Session; he did not attempt to assay in detail the causes of the gradual disappearance of those powers. From my own admittedly incomplete, even superficial research, I should like to add my brief impressions of the decline and fall of those judicial powers, with the hope that some younger researcher will find the incentive and time to pursue a broader and deeper study of the topic. To begin with, three developments in Canada during the second half of the Victorian age seem to provide the forces that slowly but inexorably caused "the stool of repentance" to be relegated to the Canadian attic. They were, in alphabetically order, industrialization, secularization, and urbanization.

My impression is that the change first became evident in the city congregations about the time of Confederation. Increasingly, persons cited to appear before the Session on whatever charge refused or simply ignored repeated summonses; in a few instances a new denominational connection is noted but most would appear to have joined the swelling ranks of the "unchurched." The same dilution or rejection of Session's authority spread into the rural congregations, but this occurred at least one generation or even two, after the phenomenon is obvious in city Sessions. No doubt there were other causes at work promoting this erosion, such as immigration, religious pluralism, increasing social instability, presumed quantitative expansion of the availability and use of alcohol, and the introduction of shift work into areas of the industrial process. Other causes will undoubtedly come to mind, and each will need to be examined after a more extensive analysis of Session records than either John Waldie or myself ever managed.

7. Loyalty and Respectability
The Campaign for Co-Establishment of the Church of Scotland in Canada

This essay was read to the Conference on Scottish Studies at the University of Guelph in 1977 and was published in Scottish Tradition, Vol. IX/X, 1979-80, *the journal of the Canadian Association of Scottish Studies. It deals not only with Scottish Presbyterianism in Canada, but also with the theme of church-state relations which had interested John Moir since he first encountered it in his undergraduate studies with Professor Bertie Wilkinson, the renowned scholar of English medieval constitutional history.*

The claims made by the Church of Scotland to be co-established in British North America along with the Church of England rested ultimately on the interpretation of the Act of Union of 1707, and of the so-called Constitutional Act (in reality an amendment to the Quebec Act) of 1791. Granted that the Church of Scotland was the national church of North Britain by the terms of 1707, just as the Church of England was the religious establishment for South Britain, did it, or did it not follow that both churches were jointly established in all British colonies? If the answer was affirmative, did the status of co-establishment extend to all British colonies or only to those acquired after the union of 1707? Such questions seem to have remained hypothetical or even unasked as far as British America was concerned until after the American Revolution, and even then the questions were certainly not put immediately or even effectively in the residual British American colonies until after the War of 1812.

It is true that even prior to that War, state support for clerical representatives of Scotland's national church had been sought and received in at least one colony, but only as a boon, never as a right. In 1791, Charles Inglis, Bishop of Nova Scotia, had been instrumental in obtaining a government salary of £75 per annum for the Reverend Andrew Brown, Church of Scotland Minister to Mather's (or St. Matthew's) congregation in Halifax, "in a province originally a fief of the Scottish Crown," but both Inglis and Brown had insisted that the grant was to Brown as an individual and not to the Church of Scotland.[1] Two decades later, £850 was given to the Church of Scotland and Pictou Academy from the £20,000 surplus raised by a special wartime excise supertax from thirsty Nova Scotians. In the other Maritime provinces, supplementary clerical stipends, grants-in-aid for church construction, or government donations of church building sites were so occasional and minuscule as to pass virtually unnoticed by historians. In effect, although the Church of England had been established in Nova Scotia since 1758, in New Brunswick since 1786, and in Prince Edward Island at least by 1793, at no time had the Church of Scotland voiced any discontent with its inferior status in those colonies because it was not legally present—all organized congregations belonged to the Secession tradition. In the longer run, the absence of any quantity of lands reserved for religious endowment explains the limited conflict over church establishment. "Happy the land without a history" might well be paraphrased in the Canadian experience as "Happy the colony without clergy reserves!"

Even before the retrenching proclivities of the reforming Whigs heralded the end of the imperial parliamentary grant to the Society for the Propagation of the Gospel in the 1830s, the question of some peculiar status and endowment of the Kirk had surfaced in New Brunswick. Governor Sir Howard Douglas proposed in 1825 that glebes be assigned to every congregation of "the established Kirk of Scotland" which built its own church and applied to the General Assembly for a minister. Colonial Secretary Lord Bathurst voiced his anti-colonialism by replying that the imperial government favoured the Canadian plan of reserving one-seventh of all future grants for the use of the Anglican clergy—but he failed to mention the Presbyterian clergy. Any move towards endowment of one or more established churches in the Maritime provinces had died before 1828, not merely because Bathurst was out of office, but also because Sir James Kempt, Lieutenant-Governor of Nova Scotia, and John Inglis, Bishop of Nova Scotia, had both opposed an endowment scheme that they were sure would only excite religious controversy in the colony.

Ironically, this acceptance of religious pluralism and the abandonment of establishment hopes in the Maritimes coincided with the very opening of the question as a major issue in the Canadas. No voice had been heard at the passing of the Constitutional Act to protest the monopoly establishment position accorded to the Church of England in the two colonies, nor to claim any status whatever for the Church of Scotland. Certainly, Presbyterians were numerous enough among the Loyalists, but the Parliament at Westminster may have recalled the too obvious involvement of American Presbyterianism on the side of the victorious rebels in the recent revolution. Again, that silence regarding the Kirk may have arisen from the visible presence of the Bench of Bishops and the greater proximity to Canterbury than to Edinburgh.

Whatever the cause, the position of the Church of England as the legally established religion of the two Canadas and as the sole beneficiary of all government largesse (which meant effectively enjoyment of the 3,000 square miles of Clergy Reserves) was apparently unquestioned and unnoticed until after the War of 1812.

Coming controversies over co-establishment in the Canadas first cast a seemingly innocent shadow in 1819 when the Presbyterian congregation of Niagara-on-the-Lake petitioned Lieutenant-Governor Sir Peregrine Maitland for financial assistance in obtaining a minister. The American invaders had burned their church in 1813 and had wasted the property of members of the congregation, so that they now asked for the charity, not the right, of £100 per annum "to a preacher of respectability; and . . . they are truly anxious to obtain one of the Established Church of Scotland, if possible."[2] The petitioners did not care where Maitland might find the money, but suggested that the Clergy Reserves fund was one possible source.

Maitland enquired of the Colonial Office if in fact "dissenting Protestants" could share in the Reserves, and the Colonial Office in turn asked the opinion of the Law Officers of the Crown. In the opinion of the Law Officers, "Protestant Clergy" in the Constitutional Act referred to ministers of both of Britain's established churches, but not to those of any "dissenting protestant Congregation."[3] Maitland's reference to the Kirk as dissenting explains his subsequent inaction on the petition, for he was always guided by the wise counsel of the redoubtable John Strachan, Anglican archdeacon of Toronto and foremost defender of his Church's unique privileges.

The precedent for government aid to ministers of the Kirk had, however, already been established. At least five individual clergymen in Lower Canada and in the Ottawa-Cornwall region were receiving up to £50, a modest sum compared with the £200 paid to Anglican clergymen. In 1820 three more ministers—two in Montreal and one in Quebec—petitioned Lord Bathurst directly for support. Their claim was based explicitly on need, respectability and political loyalty. Their respectability derived from superior education, fixed situation, and from their opposition to the "political disaffection" imported by American religious fanatics. The petitioners made much of their status as a "National Church" that deserved equal treatment with "the Sister Establishment to which they do not yield in loyalty or affection to his Majesty's person . . . but until such times as the General Assembly accepted their parallel request—to be incorporated into the Church of Scotland under its immediate Jurisdiction"—they did not and could not demand legal co-establishment in the colonies.[4]

This petition to the Colonial Office was duly forwarded by the Governor, Lord Dalhousie, himself a staunch if Evangelical Kirkman, with a covering letter that repeated all the above arguments and particularly stressed that the majority of immigrants to the Canadas were Presbyterian. Neither of these petitions—to the Colonial Office and to the General Assembly—produced positive results. The moderator, Dr. Duncan Mearns, announced to the Canadians that the General Assembly had refused to act on the request because it doubted its own authority to create a colonial connection.[5] His advice was to organize locally first and then seek incorporation. Bathurst simply agreed that the cause of the colonial Kirkmen was deserving, but the government had no money.[6]

Despite, or perhaps because of, this lack of encouragement from the mother Kirk and the home government, friends of the Church of Scotland in the Canadas began to organize a political campaign on their own behalf in 1823. Until this date the requests for aid had been based on three principles: evident need, superior respectability and undeniable loyalty. Now, in 1823, for the first time a claim was made to co-establishment by right. The bases of this new position were stated to be both legal and historical: the statutory equality created by the 1707 Act of Union between the two national churches and the Conquest of Canada in 1759 by British, not solely English forces, which had made Canada a British colony. These several points were embodied in a series of resolutions passed in 1823 by the Lower and Upper Canadian legislatures, with the precautionary additional request that if the Church of Scotland was not included in the "Protestant clergy" of the Constitutional Act, then the crown should provide a separate endowment.[7] The resolutions were passed by the Upper Canadian legislature thanks to the influence of William Morris, the prominent merchant from Perth who assumed or acquired the role of lay spokesman for the Kirk. To complete this campaign for co-establishment a petition from Church of Scotland adherents in both Canadas was sent to the home government.

Nothing came of these activities immediately, probably thanks to the effective counter-petition of Archdeacon Strachan and the Upper Canadian Clergy Corporation arguing that the Church of England was "by far" the largest body in the colony, and that all Upper Canadians would soon "conform" to Anglicanism provided no encouragement was offered to other denominations.[8] To this petition, Strachan appended an ecclesiastical chart, predecessor to his controversial chart of 1826, to show the paucity of Presbyterian ministers in the province. The mother Kirk did support its colonial children with a request from a committee of General Assembly for government stipends of £50 to £100 for its overseas clergy, and again the Colonial Secretary asked the opinion of Under-Secretary James Stephen Jr. His advice was the same in 1824 as that of the Law Officers four years earlier: the Church of

England had no right to monopolize the Clergy Reserves and "it is . . . therefore a question simply and exclusively of a political nature."[9] Accordingly, the Colonial Office instructed colonial governors that they could aid acknowledged Church of Scotland congregations if funds were available. This was a victory for the Church of Scotland, but only a partial one. The principle of co-establishment had not really been granted, but the lesson was easily read: ultimate success would depend on the political power of the Kirk at home and in the colonies. A Presbyterian counterpart of the Society for the Propagation of the Gospel was an obvious desideratum in future campaigns for co-establishment and such an organization was in fact created in 1825 under the name of the Glasgow Colonial Society, with Lord Dalhousie, ardent Kirkman and Governor General of the Canadas, as patron.

That same year, John Strachan, who was in England seeking a charter for King's College and legislation to permit the sale of some Clergy Reserves, presented the Colonial Office with a defence of his church's monopolistic establishment. He hastily produced a forty-page pamphlet to demonstrate that "Protestant Clergy" referred to the Church of England, and to that church alone. Appended to the pamphlet was an "Ecclesiastical Chart of the Province of Upper Canada" based on the one drawn up three years earlier, but this time largely from Strachan's memory. The Chart's gross inaccuracies particularly annoyed the numerous Methodists, but it also disturbed Presbyterians. The Church of Scotland's General Assembly drew the attention of the Colonial Office to the matter. Governor General Lord Dalhousie informed his superiors in London that the chart was "incorrect and erroneous to a degree that utterly astounds me."[10]

Objections from the Church of Scotland against the Anglican monopoly of the Reserves had, however, been blunted by a promise of £750 from the sale of lands to the

Canada Company. The money was for colonial ministers "acknowledged by the Kirk of Scotland" and recommended by the Kirk for such salaries. To fulfil its new responsibility the Kirk's Committee on Colonial Churches asked for detailed information about the situation in the Canadas.[11] In reply, committees of St. Gabriel Street and St. Andrew's churches in Montreal drew up a petition, to be signed by all Presbyterians in the Canadas. The next step was a meeting of the Kirk's representatives only at Cornwall in January, 1828, to work for co-establishment with the Church of England in Canada for a proportional share of the Clergy Reserves moneys, for government payment of half the stipend of Kirk ministers. To achieve these objectives the Church of Scotland in Canada again asked for the support of the mother church.

Disturbed by these efforts to topple the Church of England from its exclusive position as the legal church of the colonies, Bishop C.J. Stewart of Quebec accused the Canadian Kirkmen of sending false and misleading information to parliament, and he organized a counter-petition in defence of his church's sole possession of the Clergy Reserves.[12] The rival petitions were presented to a parliamentary committee appointed to investigate all the current political and religious controversies in the Canadas. On behalf of the Kirk, the Rev. Dr. John Lee requested aid for its Canadian members because, he said, they formed the largest Protestant denomination in the colonies.[13] This committee's report was also something less than a victory for the Kirk and co-establishment. The Church of Scotland, it said, has a right to share in the Reserves, but because neither national church was numerically strong in the colonies, other denominations might well be given some government support, too. In the determination of any colonial religious policy, however, the committee advised the imperial government to listen carefully to public opinion in the colonies.

Between 1827 and 1830 the unstable state of political parties in Britain encouraged all the Canadian contenders —Anglican establishmentarians, Church of Scotland co-establishmentarians, and Methodist and Baptist voluntarists—to deluge the Colonial Office with petitions in support of their own points of view. The locally organized United Synod of Upper Canada joined the swelling chorus late in 1829 with an offer to unite with the Kirk, and a request for recognition "as being worthy to participate equally in any provision that has or may hereafter be made for the Presbyterian ministers."[14] This was the motivation for Colonial Secretary Murray's despatch of 1 August, 1830, authorizing Sir John Colborne to promote a union of all Presbyterians. Such a union was not soon achieved, but in the summer of 1831 a synod in connection with the Church of Scotland was organized as a first step towards recognition and establishment.

As the tempo of voluntarist attacks on, and the Anglican defence of, the establishment principle increased, the Upper Canada ministers of the Church of Scotland hastened to deny Bishop Stewart's allegations that they were associated with dissenting sects, but then added, "If, however, to assert what they regard as a right, belonging as well to their Church as to the Church of England, is to be construed as 'an attack' upon the vested rights of the latter, then, indeed, Your Majesty's Petitioners must admit, that the charge is not unfounded."[15] By late 1831 the liberal-minded and reforming Whig government in Britain was prepared to accept religious pluralism as a fact of colonial life. The official policy was summed up in a confidential despatch to Colborne in 1832. In view of the difficult situation in Upper Canada, "a state of Religious peace is, above all things, essential." The following year the grant to the Church of Scotland Synod was increased to £900.[16]

Between 1829 and 1838 the position of the Church of Scotland in Upper Canada had been immeasurably strengthened by the activities of the Glasgow Colonial Society. Beginning in 1829 the Society began to send and support, modestly, missionaries to Upper Canada of whom the majority were settled in the developing western area of the colony, that is, in the Greater Niagara Peninsula region centred on London. Twenty-six missionaries arrived in the first decade, of whom nine arrived in one year alone, 1833, while twenty-one of the twenty-six had arrived by 1836. By that date there were in Upper Canada (or had spent some time there) some twenty-seven clergy identified with the Church of Scotland or in a few cases taken up by the Glasgow Colonial Society as its missionaries *in partibus*.[17]

The point of citing these statistics is twofold: to indicate that the presence of the Church of Scotland in Upper Canada was quantitatively significant, and that, however evangelical the Glasgow Colonial Society component of that total might be, all of these clergy believed that the state had a religious and moral, perhaps even political, obligation to support the cause of church establishment by material means. The popular complaint against the missionary work of the Glasgow Colonial Society (raised of course by ministers not affiliated to the national church of Scotland) was that these efforts were divisive; the Church of Scotland clergy in the colony were splitting congregations by their claims to be theologically superior, socially more respectable, and politically more loyal. In the matter of loyalty these Kirk ministers were reportedly dangling the carrot of future state financing before susceptible Scottish immigrants with the sole and selfish aim of increasing their own political influence.

After three years of fruitless wrangling by the Upper Canadian legislature, the General Assembly's Committee on Colonial Churches reported in May, 1836, that another petition regarding the Canadian Synod's claims on the Clergy Reserves had been delivered to the Colonial Office, but the imperial government had refused to take any action. The Committee recommended that the General Assembly should continue to exert pressure on the home government, and also should try to provide Scottish ministers and parish teachers to the colony. As for the Canadian request for closer association with the mother church, nothing could be done unless the colonial governments in Canada first gave legal recognition to the Canadian Synod.[18] By now, however, the practice of giving grants to religious bodies other than the Church of England had become so general that even the Church of Rome asked for a share of the Protestant Clergy Reserves.

Also in 1836, a year of economic depression in the colonies, Lieutenant-Governor Colborne created and endowed forty-four Anglican rectories (thirteen other patents were prepared but never signed) just days before his successor, Sir Francis Bond Head, arrived in the colony. Head soon clashed with his executive when the Assembly refused to pass money bills because of Colborne's "arbitrary" act in creating the Anglican rectories, and that summer, acting as his own prime minister and campaign manager, he defeated the Reformers in a general election. Although Presbyterians seem to have voted for Head's conservative candidates (so said the *Christian Examiner* of June 1838), they were not willing to let the rectories question go by default. In the spring of 1837 the Church of Scotland congregations prepared yet another petition to the King, claiming equality with the Church of England under the union of 1707 and denouncing the Anglican monopoly of the Clergy Reserves and the existence of the rectories as "an Infringement of their Rights."[19]

William Morris, member of the Assembly from 1820 to 1836, when he was appointed to the Legislative Council, was the chosen agent of the Synod of Canada to lay this complaint at the foot of the throne in the summer of 1837. Officials of the Colonial Office informed Morris that they had been "thunderstruck" to learn of the creation of the rectories and had immediately asked for a judicial opinion of their legality. They also told him that the Church of Scotland had a right to share in the Reserves and that an initial payment of £500 had been ordered in Lower Canada. Just one week later on 8 June 1837, the law officers of the Crown announced their opinion—"the Erection and Endowment of the Fifty-Seven Rectories by Sir J. Colborne are not valid and lawful Acts."[20] Morris did not actually learn the terms of the opinion until 11 July, but if the Rectories had been scotched, there still remained other questions bearing on the status of the Kirk in the colonies. The churches of Scotland and England should share the Reserves, he asserted, but if each received one-third the remaining portion could be given to other denominations, even if they were voluntarists.[21]

In Scotland, Morris' contacts with the mother Church of Scotland had been simply disheartening. The leading Kirkmen refused all assistance. Thomas Chalmers even recommended giving in to the Church of England in all matters. Morris at one point was so discouraged by "this extraordinary treatment" that he was almost ready "to bundle up my papers and return."[22] More discouraging, however, Colonial Secretary Lord Glenelg now invited the Church of England to comment on the law officers' opinion regarding the rectories. John Strachan produced such a masterly defence both of the deliberate policy behind creating rectories and of their legality, that the law officers reversed their decision and found the rectory patents valid. Strachan's arguments did not go unanswered by the Synod of Canada. The *Canadian Christian Examiner* of January 1838, published a letter from the Rev. Robert McGill accusing Strachan of adopting the disloyal style of the rebel William Lyon Mackenzie. A deputation from the Synod was shown the documents from the law officers by the Lieutenant-Governor, but they remained unconvinced of the legality of the rectories. Congregational meetings at various churches passed resolutions condemning the rectories and the Synod sent protests to the Lieutenant-Governor and the Upper Canadian Assembly. The most emotional reply, however, appeared in a printed statement by Alexander Gale, Moderator of Synod: "Is there really a just cause why Scotchmen should not enjoy equal privileges—why they should be held inferior in Canada to Englishmen? Canada is a British, not an English Colony."[23] All these protests proved vain; the forty-four Upper Canadian rectories remained as part of the Church of England establishment.

Lest anyone should misconstrue the Synod's intentions, the *Canadian Christian Examiner* of November 1838, pointed out that nine-tenths of Upper Canadians believed there was no place for an established exclusive church in the colony, and so the Church of Scotland was really only seeking equal treatment for all, not selfish co-establishment. Outsiders could be excused for doubting the Kirk's liberality in view of another petition from the Synod to the Legislative Assembly just three months later, demanding equality with the Church of England. Alexander Gale at least was sensitive to public opinion and he warned William Morris that anything that suggested sacrificing the interests of other Christian bodies to get "special advantages for our own Church" was not only morally wrong but "politically a great blunder."[24]

That the Clergy Reserves and rectories had been a major contributing factor to Mackenzie's abortive Upper Canadian rebellion in 1837 was the firm conviction of Lord Durham, the High Commissioner sent to British North America to investigate the causes and remedies of colonial unrest. At this point the Church of England in Upper Canada had twice as many members as the Church of Scotland, yet it received five times as much financial aid from the imperial and provincial treasuries, in addition to £7,000 a year from the Clergy Reserve Fund, a fruit which the Kirk was still forbidden to taste despite all government statements about legal equality of the two national churches. The hopes of the United Synod for a share of the Clergy Reserves funds did not rest on any claim for legal equality (since the Synod had none), but on the proposal of the British government to support all denominations on the so-called semi-voluntary system used in New South Wales, namely, to match from the Clergy Reserves moneys all amounts raised by the denominations themselves. This proposal was rejected by the Upper Canada legislature, which instead, after an exhausting and troubled session in 1839, passed its own solutions, to divide the Reserves and use them for religious purposes. The difficult task of making specific proposals was left to the home government.

John Strachan still believed in the necessity of an established church for any civilized state, but he was now convinced that his opponents could be bought off. "The Scotch and other Presbyterians," if formed into a single body, would be satisfied with a fifth of the Reserves and the Kirk's leaders in Scotland were "reasonable and not difficult to deal with."[25] Strachan went to Britain in the summer of 1839 but his lobbying on behalf of the Church of England monopoly of the Reserves proved unnecessary; the Upper Canadian Legislature's Clergy Reserves bill had been declared *ultra vires* on a technicality, and the whole problem of a settlement was handed over to the new Governor General of Canada, Charles Edward Poulett Thomson. Thomson's estimate of the Clergy Reserves problem coincided with Durham's, but his solution was a compromise—give the national churches of England and Scotland each one quarter of the Reserves' income and divide the remainder among all other denominations on the semi-voluntary principle.

Although the Synod's Commission passed resolutions against the Clergy Reserves bill because its division of proceeds was inequitable and the rectories had not been abolished, Thomson already had won the confidence of individual Presbyterians. His Presbyterian right hand, William Morris, was busy pushing the Synod of Canada and the United Synod towards the long-delayed union, a fate now made more attractive by the prospect of sharing in the Reserves. Both synods had agreed in 1839 to re-open the union discussions which had collapsed in 1832 because the Church of Scotland insisted that union must be on its terms. A meeting in the Legislative Chambers, engineered by William Morris, revealed a certain reluctance on the part of the Church of Scotland, and Morris suggested privately that the Governor General urge the two bodies towards union, to "simplify the duties of the Provincial Government in making provision for the support of the Ministers of both."[26] William Smart begged Morris to support the claims of the United Synod, whose ministers "may be considered as the Fathers of Presbyterianism in the province," and whose loyalty to and suffering for the British connection deserved a reward. Ten days later he had Morris' promise of help, and the union was arranged in the summer of 1840. The enlarged synod now included over seventy settled ministers, seventeen of them from the United Synod. "I should have felt better," Smart reflected, "if the courtship had not been quite so long, and if the Marriage had taken place when our feelings were youthful and warm, however, as the Union of Marriage has now taken place, it only remains for the parties themselves, and their friends to make it as happy and prosperous as they can."[27]

Thomson's powers of persuasion got his Clergy Reserves bill through the Upper Canada legislature, and he warned the Colonial Office that the bill must be supported in Britain, "for here it cannot come again without the most disastrous results." "If you will only send me back my Union and the Clergy Reserves," he pleaded, "I will guarantee you Upper Canada."[28] The shaky Whig government of Lord Melbourne could not, however, ensure delivery of Thomson's settlement. Under pressure from the bishops in the House of Lords, that government agreed to test the validity of Thomson's Clergy Reserves bill. To its surprise and political horror, the judges of England decided that the colonial legislature had no right to change the terms of the Constitutional Act. A new settlement would have to be enacted in Britain, under the hostile and watchful eyes of the Anglican bishops. Apparently the Archbishop of Canterbury dictated the new terms. All income from the quarter of the Reserves sold before 1840 would be shared by the Churches of England and Scotland in the proportions of two to one. All income from "New Sales" after that date would be divided in two, the first half going to those same two churches in the same proportions, and the remainder, three-eighths of the whole, would be divided among other denominations whenever a surplus accumulated. In the meantime the government payments to the Methodists and the Roman Catholics were also charged against the Protestant Clergy Reserves funds by the terms of the act that reunited the Canadas. If sharing in the Clergy Reserves funds made a church 'established', Canada had now not one, but four established churches, but at least it would be several years before a surplus was available to tempt other denominations to join this many-headed enemy of voluntarism.

Under the 1840 Clergy Reserves settlement the Church of England, with twenty percent of the population, received forty-two percent of the income from the Clergy Reserves, and the Church of Scotland, which now claimed almost as many adherents, got twenty-one percent. Thirty-eight percent was therefore left for the remaining sixty percent of Upper Canada's population, including those denominations sworn in the name of voluntarism to reject all public financial support. Former ministers of the United Synod had been excluded from sharing directly in the Clergy Reserves, but the Church of Scotland in Canada agreed to make them beneficiaries in the bonanza. The Church of Scotland believed it had suffered from the blatant inaccuracy of the most recent religious census. "The Scotch," Thomson warned Russell, "are however furious at having been jockeyed out of their fair share." Thomson once more used his personal charm on William Morris and reported triumphantly, "The Scotch I have in hand. . . . I have had a meeting with their principal Lay Leaders and shall keep them quiet."[29] Morris still regretted the "blunder" in the census, but he assured the Governor General, "I would most reluctantly see any attempt to agitate the public mind on the nature of the settlement now made of this tiresome subject."[30]

Unfortunately for Thomson (who had now been made Lord Sydenham), the Church of Scotland ministers, not the lay leaders, felt the injustice most. Within two weeks of Sydenham's interview with Morris, a special synod meeting sent a memorial of protest to the Colonial Office. Nothing came of their complaints—perhaps nothing had really been expected. After all, the co-established status of the Church of Scotland had been recognized. The Clergy Reserves settlement of 1840 was now a fact of life. Voluntarists still opposed the principle of establishment, the Church of England and the Church of Scotland both felt cheated, but for better or worse that settlement had seemingly ended a religious controversy that had torn at the very vitals of Upper Canadian society for a generation.

For the next seven years relative peace ensued for the Clergy Reserves, but not for the Canadian Synod in connection with the Church of Scotland. The Disruption of the Mother Kirk in 1843 was followed by a disruption in Canada a year later. While the Disruption did stem from the old issue of church-state relations in Scotland, the issues were irrelevant in Canada. Further, the Free Church which the disruptionists formed was not voluntarist; it believed as firmly as the Kirk in the establishment principle. Nevertheless those clergy who left the Kirk in Canada lost their claims to their share of the Clergy Reserves. So, regardless of their official espousal of establishmentarianism, they were in effect forced into a practical condition of voluntarism, and increasingly the laity and some of the Free Church clergy came to accept voluntarism. What would happen to the Free Church if and when public funds did become available remained to be seen. Meanwhile the residual Church of Scotland clergy in Canada rejoiced that to him who hath shall be given, for the stipends of those clergy who left for the Free Church were now added to those of clergy remaining with the Kirk.[31]

In January 1848, just after the Reform Party of Robert Baldwin and L.H. Lafontaine had gained power in a general election, the government gazette announced that the surplus of £1800 accumulated in the Clergy Reserves was to be divided according to the terms of the 1840 Act among any denominations that applied before the first day of July. The voluntarists would certainly never yield to the temptation of accepting public money for religious purposes and thus becoming a "hireling ministry"—they wanted the Clergy Reserves moneys used for general education. The churches of England and Scotland were already in possession of their shares of the Reserves funds; they could have no more. But what would be the response of the Free Church which had lost its share of Clergy Reserves because of disruption?

The Free Church Synod could not respond because it would not meet until after the July deadline. Nevertheless, five congregations in the eastern Upper Canadian Presbytery of Brockville petitioned for some of the proffered money. When the Synod did meet, a committee reported that while state endowments might be legal, their acceptance must be "determined on the grounds of Christian expediency."[32] The Synod decided to reject the overture and forbid any applications from congregations, because acceptance of such moneys would impair the Church's witness to Christ and "sow division and jealousy among our people." Government endowments were being offered "without reference to the distinction between truth and error." Their acceptance would tend to "diminish the usefulness of ministers and the liberality of the people in contributing to the support of the Gospel"; they would permit "the evil influence which an irreligious government might exert through dependence upon the State." The Free Church of Canada had accepted the voluntary principle in just four years.

This was not the end but the beginning of the last act of the Canadian Clergy Reserves drama. The Clergy Reserves question had been reopened and a "final" solution of the conflict between denominational and national interests could not be postponed indefinitely. When the next session of the Canadian parliament met in 1850 the thirty-one resolutions on the Clergy Reserves question were put forward by J.H. Price, Commissioner of Crown Lands. The first twenty-seven resolutions related the history of the question, the next one asserted that the Canadian parliament should have been allowed to settle the issue in 1840, two more declared that no denomination had any vested right in the Reserves but that present beneficiaries should be treated liberally, and the final resolution asked for the repeal of the Act of 1840 to allow a Canadian settlement to be made in Canada. The passing of these crucial resolutions, although only by two votes, seemed to win general approval from the Free Church, but the announcement that the imperial government would pass the desired enabling legislation caused the Church of Scotland Synod to send William Morris to England again, this time to defend, not demand the Kirk's share of the Reserves. Both the Synod and its mother church in Scotland asked the imperial government to reconsider its decision and to maintain the multiple establishment in the Canadas.[33]

In Scotland Morris was busy showing his petitions—sixty-two from Canadian Kirk congregations—when Bishop Strachan cut the feet from under the Church of Scotland by advocating, indirectly, a denominational division of all the Reserves. Morris was warned by the Colonial Secretary, Lord Grey, that the best that could be hoped for was a guarantee of present government salaries, and that only thanks to the efforts of L.H. Lafontaine and his Roman Catholic Reform supporters who feared that nationalization of the Reserves would invite attacks on the large Roman Catholic endowments. At least Morris learned that he could count on little or no support from the Kirk in Scotland, but the Canadian Synod was saved from "spoliation" by the decision of Britain's government to delay action for another year. Before leaving Britain Morris published in pamphlet form the arguments of the Canadian Church of Scotland for retaining its share of the Reserves, but the Rev. Alexander Mathieson had already advised him that many Canadian Kirkmen were pleased with the anti-Clergy Reserves agitation because they saw it as a prelude to a crusade against Roman Catholic power.[34]

In Canada the friends and foes of the Clergy Reserves argued their cases vehemently and occasionally attacked each other's meetings physically. In 1852 the Synod of the Church of Scotland again petitioned the Queen to uphold their establishment. This whole situation was confused by the announcement of a new Tory government in Britain that it would not honour its Liberal predecessor's promise of enabling legislation to permit a made-in-Canada settlement of the question—the Clergy Reserves must never be diverted from their pious purpose to secular uses. By the end of 1852, however, that Tory government had fallen. The respite for the Reserves was over. The next Liberal government made good the promise of enabling legislation in May 1853, and the Clergy Reserves question at last became a purely Canadian matter.

Before a Canadian settlement could be reached, a new political crisis rocked the colony. Faced with a loss of popularity for its policies, the Reform government called a snap election in May 1854, which spelled doom for the old Reform coalition. As soon as the new parliament met that September, a coalition of Upper Canadian conservatives and Lower Canadian Reformers took office, pledged to end once and for all this question that had distressed the provinces for thirty years. The driving force behind the new Liberal-Conservative government was John A. Macdonald, whose Clergy Reserves bill was introduced in Parliament three weeks later. Its terms were another compromise: the Clergy Reserves Funds would be made available to the municipalities as development loans, but the clergy now receiving stipends from the funds would be guaranteed these incomes for life. This guarantee was less than voluntarists had demanded, yet it might still have been accepted for the sake of peace had it not been for the additional provision that the life stipends could be exchanged for lump sums as a cash settlement. This commutation clause infuriated voluntarists because it allowed the four benefiting churches (including the Church of Scotland, which got £105,665, or twenty-eight percent of the total paid out) to retain these sums after the death of the commuting clergymen through investments as permanent endowments.[35]

Seventy-three ministers of the Church of Scotland commuted their stipends but eleven more who had joined the

Synod in 1853-4 were permitted by Synod to share in the funds so that each of the eighty-four received £112 per year instead of the £150 originally guaranteed to the commuters. To manage the Church of Scotland's commuted sums, a Board of Management of the Temporalities' Fund was approved by the provincial legislature, but three bank failures soon after Confederation cost the Board £150,000 of its investments. At the time of Presbyterian union in 1875 the Temporalities' Fund was ignored in the negotiations and allowed to continue as a body quite separate from the new church, despite several law suits subsequently brought against the Board by nonconcurrents in the union. After the union it became necessary to use capital to meet obligations, and by 1900 the remaining £88,731 was distributed in cash settlement to the last twelve commuting clergymen and to sixty-two widows and orphans.[36] Thus ended the Church of Scotland's search for co-establishment in Canada, a search based on claims of law, loyalty and respectability, and a search which had begun four generations earlier.

8. THE QUAY OF GREENOCK
Jurisdiction and Nationality in the Canadian Presbyterian Disruption of 1844

This paper was delivered before the American Society of Church History at Toronto, April 1975, and was originally published in Scottish Tradition, *V, 1975, 38-53.*

Lacking both racial homogeneity and a revolutionary tradition to provide the cement of nationalism, Canadians make a virtue of necessity by defining their nationality negatively as something not American and also not British. In a mixture of self-justification and self-congratulation, Canadians praise bilingualism (or multilingualism), biculturalism (or multiculturalism) and assert the superiority of all forms of cultural pluralism over anyone else's melting pot. *Unity in Diversity* is in fact the title of a Canadian history textbook, but the inevitable contrasts drawn by Canadians between their own historical experience and that of the United States are in several ways delusive, and nowhere more so than in the field of religion. Religiously Canada is almost monolithic when compared to the United States. The census of 1971 showed some ninety-two percent of the Canadian population in just six denominations. As Canadian historians delight in repeating, the thrust of Canadian religious life has seemingly always been towards union and away from diversity, as if Canadians were trying to find in a territorialized church that elusive national identity.

There have been exceptions to this unifying trend in religion, and one example was the Canadian Free Church movement—an imported old world quarrel apparently irrelevant to the Canadian situation. Why should the 1843 Disruption of the Church of Scotland be duplicated by Canadian Presbyterianism? No one suggested that the "patronage" or "intrusion" issue existed here. Nearly everyone agreed that the Presbyterian Church in Canada was independent of the mother church, that the jurisdiction of the General Assembly of the Church of Scotland, popularly called "the Kirk," did not extend beyond "the quay of Greenock."[1] Why then should this colonial Synod be torn apart by an issue entirely Scottish? The answer seems to involve such disparate factors as immigration patterns, ecclesiastical organization, theological emphases, and long-established Scottish habits of mind and life transported intact into the Canadian environment. It is difficult to discover a single element that was Canadian by its nature and origin; by every criterion, the Disruption of Canadian Presbyterianism in 1844 appeared to be a triumph for Scottishness over Canadianization.

Presbyterianism reached the valley of the St. Lawrence with the army of occupation in 1759 and was reinforced by the Loyalist refugees a generation later. Because of its Revolutionary experience Presbyterianism in Canada was characterized by Britishness and by a counter-revolutionary tradition. Few American Presbyterian clergymen were included in the small number of ministers in the two colonies, Upper and Lower Canada—most were Scottish or Irish—but taken together the clergy represented four different Presbyterian bodies and traditions. An abortive presbytery formed in 1795 never functioned, an *ad hoc* one gathered in 1803 for an ordination never met again. This lack of presbyterial supervision merely enhanced the tendency towards congregationalism bred by the isolation of the frontier.

The second American invasion of Canada, the War of 1812-14, strengthened the counter-revolutionary tradition and encouraged religious groups to form indigenous or at least quasi-independent church organizations. In 1818 a Presbytery of the Canadas sprang up, but it included only eight, or half, of the ministers then in the two colonies, none of them west of the Bay of Quinte. A year later that presbytery became a synod, but within five years it collapsed into two separate presbyteries, one for each colony. In that interval five more ministers arrived in Upper Canada and two in Lower Canada; all were independent of any external jurisdiction, and, significantly in the light of later events, five of the seven were Irish. The same year that the Synod dissolved (1825) the Glasgow Colonial Society was organized in Scotland with Lord Dalhousie, Governor General of the British North American colonies, as patron, and the energetic Rev. Robert Burns of Paisley as secretary, to promote the Kirk's interests in the colonies and provide clergy for the emigrants.

In the Canadas the Kirk's most specific interest was in obtaining a share of the three million acres of prime agricultural land reserved in 1791 to support a "Protestant clergy." The imperial government had tacitly agreed with the Tory and Anglican assumption that "protestant" meant only the Church of England, but when the great wave of post-Napoleonic immigration into Upper Canada (where eighty percent of the Clergy Reserves were located) was inflating the price of land, Presbyterians in the two Canadas cast envious eyes on the banquet of loaves and fishes which the Church of England enjoyed exclusively, *de facto*. Throughout the 1830s the Church of Scotland in Canada repeatedly claimed to be co-established in the empire and therefore entitled to share in the Clergy Reserves income. Although the Church of Scotland was granted a £750 pittance from provincial funds, the money was never given as a right until 1840.

The other and related aspect of the Society's interests was the sending of missionaries to Canada beginning in 1829. In the next fifteen years the Society (and its less Evangelical successor, the Colonial Committee of the General Assembly) despatched at least forty missionaries to the Canadas of whom twenty-five settled in Upper Canada.[2] By 1831 the stage was set for confrontation or union between these invading Church of Scotland men and the rival local presbytery. That year the Synod of the Presbyterian Church in connection with the Church of Scotland was formed on recommendation of the Colonial Secretary in the imperial government as a prerequisite to consideration of Presbyterian claims for financial support from the public treasury.[3] Those tidy civil servants' minds wanted only one Presbyterian voice, just as they dealt with only one Anglican and one Roman Catholic body in the colonies. The creation of this new Synod was, therefore, a first, albeit dictated, step towards Canadian Presbyterian unity and towards a share of the Clergy Reserves.

One week after the Kirk Synod was born, the Presbytery of Upper Canada met and re-organized its fifteen ministers into a two-presbytery synod. High on this United Synod's agenda was the church union recommended by the Colonial Office. Union, it soon became obvious, would only be possible on terms dictated by the Kirk, namely, adherence to a formula casting doubt on the validity of the Canadians' ministry; and while a few ministers of the United Synod did accept this humiliating offer after discussion with and approval by their congregations, most remained aloof until the re-assurance of also sharing in the Clergy Reserves fund brought about a union in 1840. The first-born offspring of the marriage was Queen's College at Kingston, a literary and theological institution for the enlarged Synod.

Members of this new Presbyterian Church of Canada were not the only Presbyterians in the two Canadas, but they were by far the most numerous. The next largest body was the Secessionist, voluntarist, and temperance-minded United Presbyterian Synod that had entered western Upper Canada in the 1830s. Two separate, similarly-minded minuscule groupings in the Niagara area owed their origin and their retarded growth to the American missionary enterprise, but together these three other brands of Presbyterians numbered barely 18,000 at the census of 1842, when the Church of Scotland counted 78,000. That census also showed the rapid population growth occurring in the areas west of Toronto. In 1824 the regions east of Toronto contained 80,000 persons, those west, 70,000. Eighteen years later the population had more than tripled, but the western districts, which virtually coincided with the Presbytery of Hamilton, now boasted 259,000 to the eastern district's total of 217,000, indicating a percentage increase of 365% in the west, to 275% in the east. By this date the western areas contained fifty-five percent of the Upper Canadian population, but only forty-seven percent of the Church of Scotland members in the colony.

Allowing that the population had doubled by natural increase in eighteen years, an average 10,000 immigrants must have entered the colony annually. By the same rough calculation it can be estimated that seven out of every ten immigrants into Upper Canada settled in the western half, making it the fastest growing part of British North America. It is impossible to ascertain either the number of Scots or of Presbyterians among these most recent immigrants, but it is possible to identify several communities with a predominantly, almost exclusively Scottish character. Across the province, the Church of Scotland claimed sixteen percent of the population; in the western half the percentage was only thirteen, a significant factor in the Disruption of the Kirk just two years after this census had been made.

That "marriage" of 1840 was not fated to be either happy or prosperous. Exactly four years later, the Synod of the Presbyterian Church in connection with the Church of Scotland was torn apart and mortally wounded by Canada's version of the Scottish Disruption. If the Union of 1840 can be viewed as a victory for Scottishness at the expense of the forces of indigenization and Canadianization, the Disruption of 1844 was even more clearly an example of transplanted ethnic consciousness. At first the union had seemed promising enough because the settlement of the Clergy Reserves question of 1840 by a division of funds among the four largest denominations (including the Roman Catholic church as "Protestant clergy") brought £2600 to the Kirk in Canada the next year.[4] But the Presbyterian eyes were now focused on Scotland where the conflict over the power of patrons to intrude their candidates into congregations fascinated particularly those Presbyterians who had most recently arrived in the Canadas from the "auld country." As the crisis in the Church of Scotland approached, displaced Scots in Canada began to take sides in the overseas dispute.

Events 'at home' had been reported in detail by the colonial press and no immigrant Scot could plead ignorance of the issues at stake. Short weeks before the Disruption of the General Assembly in May 1843, sympathizers in Canada moved to establish their own newspaper to promote the cause of non-intrusion. Edinburgh-born George Brown and his father, Peter, had recently begun a journal in New York for British immigrants, and while visiting Canada George was offered financial support to establish a Free Church newspaper in Toronto. The younger Brown had found in Canada congenial spirits and unlimited opportunities, and so the Toronto *Banner* came into existence in August, 1843 as the voice of those who now espoused the cause of the new Free

Church and as rival of the older *British Colonist* which was trying to avoid the importation of Disruption.

Even before the first number of the *Banner* appeared the Synod had endured the first round of open controversy in its ranks. Its meeting at Toronto in July was presented with resolutions and counter-resolutions concerning the recent Disruption of the mother church in the mother country. Discussion began with a committee report on an overture from the Presbytery of Hamilton. Its report called for the re-affirmation of the headship of Christ and expressed alarm at the conduct of the state in denying the spiritual independence of the Church of Scotland. While insisting that the Church of Scotland had no jurisdiction over this Synod, the resolutions called on Synod to defend its own independence from the state if necessary. Finally, the resolutions reached the political crux by expressing deep sympathy for the Scottish Disruptionists whose sacrifice for principle "must ever command the admiration and respect of the Christian Church."[5]

The first response came from the Rev. Alexander Mathieson of Montreal, who asserted that no action was required of the Synod because no communication had come from either church in Scotland.[6] The intrusion issue did not concern Canadians and should not be raised because it would cause "disruption and confusion" in a synod already "too much divided." Mathieson's motion to defer further consideration was supported by Peter Campbell, one of the two professors at Queen's College. Campbell charged that the whole affair was a time-wasting, impractical exercise promoted by some interested persons who now claimed that the Synod was committed to acting. He counselled against any hasty move that might, as the Canadian government had warned, lose the recently acquired share of the Clergy Reserves funds. Would not the people of Montreal and Quebec oppose such ministerial agitation? No, responded a voice from the other side, where the anti-intrusionists were ranged in a block. Kingston people would oppose, Campbell continued; and he charged that the clergy and laity were on opposite sides of this question.

Mark Y. Starke from Hamilton Presbytery spoke next for the middle position, claiming that conscience dictated action now, even if that required foregoing all government aid, but the Synod should remain in communion with both Scottish churches. Succeeding speakers generally supported the resolutions, the most interesting comment coming from John Cook, minister in Quebec, who admitted he had been converted by this discussion to support for the resolutions and avowed that even if his congregation opposed him, "he cared not for that when duty called him to act." Starke then introduced amendments mildly favourable to the Free Church, and Principal Liddell of Queen's offered a motion honouring the sincerity of the Disruptionists but condemning the Disruption. When at last the votes were taken after six hours of debate, four separate amendments were rejected and the original resolutions sustained by majorities of at least two to one, with John Cook moving the adoption of the committee's report.

The *Banner* had barely completed printing its lengthy account of the Synod's proceedings when the issue of Disruption was raised in its columns. Letters asserting that the problem was Scottish, not Canadian, were answered by calls for separation to avoid sin by association. Invariably, the conservatives tried to explain that the expression "in connection with the Church of Scotland" only meant holding the same standards. The plot thickened when the Colonial Committee of the residuary Church wrote to Canadian ministers for advice on how to provide future aid to the colonies.[7] The Presbytery of Bathurst in eastern Upper Canada replied with a fulsome expression of attachment to the Church of

Scotland, which reply was immediately denounced by Free Church supporters as a denial of Synod's resolutions and an improper answer to an improper question. At the same moment five new ministerial recruits arrived from Scotland—three of them had come from the new Free Church of Scotland, and all were received into the Presbytery of Hamilton.[8] This was hardly surprising in view of the expanding population of that region and the fact that the Synod's convener of home missions was a leading Free Church supporter and minister in the town of Hamilton.

The Presbytery of Hamilton, which had initiated the recent resolutions in synod, met in October and denounced both the interference of the Church of Scotland's Colonial Committee in Canadian affairs and any replies thereto, and then the presbytery overtured the next synod to define its relationship to the Church of Scotland. These steps were followed by a letter to the *Banner* from M.Y. Starke claiming that the Synod's sharing in the Clergy Reserves funds had nothing to do with any connection to the Church of Scotland, that he was confident the government of Canada would never interfere with Synod's privileges, and that the Synod and the Scottish Free Church held exactly the same principle regarding endowments and establishments.[9]

Suddenly, more peat was thrown on the ecclesiastical fire. In the autumn of 1843 the *Banner* discovered an unmitigated, unprecedented and unpresbyterian grab for power by those very Canadian clergy from the eastern districts who were unfriendly to the Scottish Disruption. A Temporalities bill had been introduced in the Canadian parliament to vest the church's property in presbyterial trustees rather than congregations, and to do so in the name of the Church of Scotland. The *Banner* claimed such a bill would give the state control over the church and would be a gross violation of the church's independence. More ominous still, this move was supposedly being promoted clandestinely. Eastern region clergymen tried vainly to divert popular wrath by reminding Presbyterians that the draft of this bill had been adopted by synod in 1842.[10] Still, the *Banner* would not abandon its anti-Erastian crusade, nor would at least a dozen congregations where meetings had condemned the bill in strong language.[11] Two former United Synod ministers, Boyd of Prescott and Smart of Brockville, actually withdrew their flocks from the Synod in protest.[12]

Although the Temporalities bill was ultimately abandoned, Isaac Buchanan claimed it had alienated three-quarters of the laity.[13] A number of prominent Presbyterian laymen were roused to form a committee of correspondence in Montreal and to call for a total renunciation of the Church of Scotland. "Scotchmen," said Buchanan, "when they don't like or differ with their Ministers will have an alternative besides going to the Episcopalians & losing all his weight or to sects who are in too many cases little more than political dissenters."[14] At St. Andrew's day celebrations a toast to the Free Church now usually replaced one to the Kirk. In the words of the *Banner*, "it is obvious that the question is about to be put."[15] All that Canadian Presbyterianism needed was an organizer to precipitate disruption.

The catalyst was the Rev. Robert Burns, long-time secretary of the Glasgow Colonial Society, who responded to a request from several Canadian congregations that one of the Free Church deputies then raising money in the United States should visit Canada. Burns arrived at Toronto in early April and progressed with meetings and addresses in every major centre as far east as Quebec. No copies of the *Banner* have survived to describe Burns' impact, but his own diary describes the month-long tour as a Roman triumph. Greeted everywhere by "many friends," "conveyed" from breakfast meetings to church services to long evening discussion sessions, and convoyed from Brockville to Prescott by a half-mile procession of men, women and children in carriages and on horseback, Burns injected an almost messianic note to the growing fervour for Disruption Scottish-style.[16]

Burns' only rebuff came at Kingston where the Rev. John Machar, author of the ill-starred Temporalities bill, barred Burns from his pulpit. But when Burns left Kingston six of the seven theological students at Queen's avowed their intention to join the Free Church as soon as it was organized.[17] Interestingly, in view of the final results, Burns stopped only at Hamilton in the vast Presbytery of Hamilton. Before he returned to Scotland in May 1844, the Rev. Alex Mathieson assured the residuary church of the loyalty of Lower Canada and the older parts of Upper Canada—"in the western districts I am sorry to perceive that a different spirit seems to prevail."[18] In fact, however, before Burns' departure several congregations had declared for the Free Church, and by the time Synod met at Kingston in early July, twenty-two congregations had indicated their support for disruption. The Synod resolutions of 1843 had seemed a happy compromise at the time, but on the eve of the 1844 Synod the Free Church in Scotland stirred the pot by advising the Canadian moderator that the Synod's statement was "not in all respects what we could have wished."[19]

Moderator John Clugston opened the Canadian Synod with a sermon on 2 Corinthians 4:8: "We are troubled on every side." The next morning M.Y. Starke was elected as new moderator, the third Free Church sympathizer in a row to hold that office. Various overtures on relations with the Church of Scotland were read, whereupon John Cook reported for a committee on relations with the Kirk that the Kirk in Scotland neither had nor claimed jurisdiction over the Synod, that the Synod had full liberty and expected no interference from the state, that the causes of disruption did not exist in Canada, and that correspondence with both churches in Scotland should cease.[20] Immediately, John Bayne of Hamilton Presbytery moved that every connection with the Church of Scotland be ended, and that the name of the Canadian body become simply, "the Presbyterian Church of Canada," even if that meant loss of government support. Two other conflicting resolutions were introduced and withdrawn, and after two days of discussion in synod came two days of adjournment.

In the midst of this debate the Synod was electrified by the arrival of two harbingers from the Free Church in Scotland. The first was a letter from Dr. Welsh, convenor of its Colonial Committee, who announced that, "it has pleased the Great Head of the Church to visit and support us with many and great encouragements." The second harbinger was a more corporeal Free Church deputy who was first invited to preach from Machar's pulpit but who, when Machar suddenly withdrew the invitation, preached the Disruption in a Methodist chapel. At last the votes were taken: for Bayne's version, twenty ministers and twenty elders; for Cook's report, thirty-nine ministers and seventeen elders in favour. Bayne with nineteen ministers and nineteen elders at once submitted a protest and another protest by two more ministers was also tabled. The first signature on Bayne's document was that of Moderator Starke who now became first moderator of the Free Church of Canada, or more precisely, of the "Presbyterian Church of Canada."

Who were the Canadian Disruptionists, those men who, in the name of principle and Scottishness, had smashed the Kirk in Canada? Of ninety-one ministers on the Kirk's roll, thirty-three left and twenty-nine, or ninety-six percent, of these were Scottish by birth—the residuaries' rate was only seventy-seven percent.[21] Of twenty-five Disruptionists whose degrees are known, ten came from the two Aberdeen colleges, eight from Glasgow and seven from Edinburgh. If educational origins have any relevance, however, it is more important that among the Canadian residuaries twenty-seven out of fifty-three were alumni of Glasgow. At first sight it is disconcerting to find that only fourteen of the twenty-seven Glasgow Colonial Society missionaries still in the two Canadas joined the Canadian Disruption. It is more valuable to note that seven of these fourteen were in the Presbytery of Hamilton, which had fifteen of the thirty-three Disruptionist ministers, the other eighteen being spread throughout four other presbyteries. By contrast, of the twenty-five former ministers of the United Synod only five joined the Free Church.

Of sixty-eight Church of Scotland congregations for which data is available, thirty-eight continued an uninterrupted life in the Kirk but nine other charges had not been re-established twenty-two years after the Disruption, indicating that congregations tended to leave or stay as a body rather than to split internally. Of those congregations visibly divided by the Disruption, eleven adhering to the Church of Scotland were left without ministers for an average of five years, but apparently in three instances only did the Disruption lead to legal actions over possession of congregational property.

The new Free Church was predominately Scottish, it was strongest in the newly developed areas of the provinces, and its ministers were likely missionaries of the Evangelically oriented Glasgow Colonial Society. Such an analysis is suggestive, but inconclusive. What is needed for control or balance is information regarding the Presbytery laity—the men, and women, in the pew who put (or did not put) the money on the plate. Hints of lay pressure for disruption had been dropped in the great synod debate in 1843. Allusions to lay initiative at the congregational level were scattered throughout the columns of the *Banner*. Part of this pressure was due to the tradition which one minister west of Toronto called

Ecclesiastic-phobia[22]—that ministers have their place, and should keep in it: "Vile ecclesiastics" was one layman's opinion of his spiritual advisers.[23] Certainly, the affair of the Temporalities bill had aroused resentment against the same "clerical pretensions" that Kirk laymen had noted in the constitution of Queen's University and in the management of the Kirk's income from the Clergy Reserves. Even before the Disruption those two vocal journalists and laymen, George and Peter Brown, were understood to be adamantly in favour of disruption.

Before the Disruption an outside observer, a United Presbyterian minister, remarked: "There are no indications of the ministers (except five or six) being generally in favour of any change . . . and probably (because of) the fear of losing their present pensions."[24] One of his ministerial brethren later described the seceding ministers, "They came out from popular pressure, and are kirkish enough; but they have the popular cry after them." In a reported conversation at the opening of the crucial 1844 synod, one minister stated: "If there is not a disruption of the ministers, I fear there will be one of the people; for the pressure from without is great at present,"[25] a point supported by Henry Esson, the Montreal voluntarist, who claimed a disruption between clergy and laity had occurred before the Disruption of the Church. "Scottish determination in Canada," said Principal Liddell, "was too weak to resist newly imported Scottish determination from Scotland."[26]

By the time the Free Church Synod held its first working meeting at Toronto in October 1844, it had thirty-two ministers on the roll and twenty-one congregations were listed as vacant. All the additional ministers were new arrivals. Isaac Buchanan, wealthy Upper Canadian merchant, was offering £50 to congregations joining the Free Church, if the congregation kept control of its property.[27] In succeeding years the Free Church grew by leaps and bounds: by 1846 it had forty-seven ministers; by 1856, one hundred and two. The immediate post-Disruption creation of Knox College provided a rapid and expanding supply of ministers made from local boys rather than immigrants. Knox's student body grew from the seven dissidents at Queen's to forty-four in 1847, and to fifty-two only one year later. Yet this very recruiting of young Canadians into the Free Church was one evidence that the 1844 victory of Scottishness was more obvious than real, more ephemeral than permanent. Proof of a trend towards Canadianization had begun to appear before the Disruption in the form of widespread voluntarist sentiment among the laity and some ministers.

The Free Church in Canada had accepted without demur the Scottish Free Church's avowal of continued faith in the establishment principle as embodying the public recognition by a Christian state of Christ's headship over the nations. The Scottish Disruptionists were fully agreed that the piper must be paid; their objection was against letting the payer call the tune for Christ's piper. In Canada, however, the Scottishness of the local Disruption masked a division of thought over the very propriety of establishments. The Canadian Disruption had cost the young Free Church its claim to share in the Clergy Reserves.

Should the Free Church, being *de facto* and by default voluntarist, pronounce itself voluntarist on principle, or should it maintain its support for the idea of establishment in Canada, even though the question of state aid was now seemingly as academic as the intrusion issue had been in 1844? In the late 1840s the columns of the *Banner* carried letters, articles and news items, openly stating support for voluntarism, but the moment of truth came in January 1848 when the Canadian government announced that an accumulated surplus in the Clergy Reserves fund would be divided among any interested denominations (except the four already receiving shares).

Five Free Church congregations in eastern Upper Canada (in fact in the old Bathurst Presbytery) petitioned for some of the proffered money. At the meeting of synod six months later, Brockville Presbytery overtured the synod to "secure a just proportion of said fund to the minister of this church."[28] To this a committee reported that, although state endowments might be legal, their acceptance or rejection should be "determined on the grounds of Christian expediency." Pressured by the laity, the Synod rejected the overture and forbade any congregational requests to the government. This state support, it reasoned, would permit "the evil influence which an irreligious government might exert through dependence (of the Church) upon the State." The four-year-old Free Church of Canada officially rejected endowments, and ultimately union in 1861 with the voluntarist United Presbyterians completed the transformation of the Free Church itself into a voluntarist and Canadianized Church.

For the Church of Scotland in Canada the Disruption ultimately meant a slow death despite the fact that it still contained a majority of Canadian Presbyterians. True, it had been the Kirk that protested against the introduction of Scottish issues into the Canadian scene, but the combination in the Free Church of dynamic, even aggressive expansionism with virtual voluntarism meant that within a decade of the Disruption the images of the two bodies had been ironically interchanged. Above all, their respective stands on the reopened Clergy Reserves question made the Kirk appear as the conservative and alien Scottish influence, and the Free Church the more Canadian form of Presbyterianism. By default the Free Church had inherited that leadership of Canadian voluntarist Protestant opinion which the Methodists had enjoyed a generation earlier.

By 1851, just seven years after the Disruption, the Free Church members outnumbered the Kirk's by seven to six. A decade later the membership of the Church of Scotland in Canada stood at 109,000, an increase of only seventy percent (in a generation when the Canadian population grew by 210%), but the Free Church numbered 143,000, twice as many as the undivided Kirk could claim before the Disruption seventeen years before. In 1866, on the eve of Confederation, the Church of Scotland had only 113 ministers (compared to ninety-one at the Disruption) and Queen's University had graduated only fifteen ministers in a quarter century. On the other hand, the union of Free Church and United Presbyterian boasted 248 ministers and Knox College had graduated 125 in just twenty years.

For Canadian Presbyterianism the long-term results of the Disruption of 1844 can be seen in the decline of conservative and traditional churchmanship as exemplified by the Kirk, and in the rise to dominance of a Canadianized Free Churchmanship, thanks to rapid numerical growth and aggressive, almost intolerant evangelicalism. Forced by the loss of any claim to the Clergy Reserves in 1844 and by the partial victory of voluntarism in 1849, when that contentious issue was reopened, the Free Church advanced steadily from the day of Disruption. The ultimate step was the Canadian Presbyterian union of 1875 which virtually submerged every other Presbyterian tradition and enshrined the Free Church ethos in a single Canadian denomination from ocean to ocean. In the Canadian Disruption of 1844 it had not mattered that the jurisdiction of the Church of Scotland ended at "the quay of Greenock"; what did matter was that Scots departing from that quay for British North America had carried with them a conviction of national religion which postponed Presbyterian unity in Canada for three decades.

9. On the King's Business
Canadian Presbyterians and the Laymen's Missionary Movement

In 1980 John Moir presented a paper to the Commission on Ecclesiastical History at the meetings of the XV International Congress of Historical Sciences in Bucharest, Romania. The Commission's theme was "Lay Movements in the Churches in the XIX and XX Centuries." The paper was subsequently published as "'On the King's Business': the Rise and Fall of the Laymen's Missionary Movement in Canada," Bibliothèque de la Revue d'Histoire Ecclésiastique, Fasicule 71, Miscellanea Historiae Ecclesiasticae, VII, 1985, 321-33. In 1992 it was revised to concentrate on the Presbyterians and was presented to the Canadian Society of Presbyterian History in 1993.

THE LAYMEN'S MISSIONARY MOVEMENT MAY BE viewed as the culmination of North American missionary undertakings in that "Age of Missions," the nineteenth century. The immediate roots of the Laymen's Missionary Movement lay in the sense of a divine imperative to cultural and political imperialism that took shape in the closing decades of that century. Its more distant roots lie in the vast missionary spirit and enterprise of Britain that developed after the close of the Napoleonic wars. Indeed the two common elements of the whole nineteenth-century missionary drive appear to have been a measure of prosperity engendered by industrialization and, for the first time on a global scale, a fervent response to the Apostolic "Macedonian cry," made practicable in international terms by the Pax Brittanica. In "the climactic phase of the foreign missions movement in American Protestantism"[1] at the close of the nineteenth century, Dwight L. Moody's "warm optimistic evangelism" and the channeling of enthusiasms into organized action on the model of the Young Men's Christian Association merged in 1888 as the Student Volunteer Movement which recruited the youth of North America, especially college students, for missionary service abroad. "The Evangelization of the World in this Generation" was both the aim and the motto of the Student Volunteer Movement. The Student Volunteer Movement in turn spawned the Foreign Missions Conference of North America in 1893 to co-ordinate denominational missionary work and the Missionary Education Movement formed in 1902 to promote mission enthusiasm among all church members.

As this wave of mission interest swelled it became evident that the enthusiasm of youth had outrun the financial capabilities of the denominations to support such extensive overseas work. Traditional mission fund-raising had depended on the free-will response of congregations to occasional pulpit appeals, plus the quiet but probably more effective work of women's missionary groups in the form of teas, bazaars, and church dinners. Some more lucrative and reliable way of exploiting the material resources of an opulent society was required, and the solution proposed was the Laymen's Missionary Movement. The three basic objectives of the Movement were to enlist lay support "to evangelize the world in this generation," to employ "the best business methods in all Church Missionary finance," and to promote "greater efficiency" in both home and foreign missionary effort.[2]

The Movement spread quickly from the United States to Britain and Canada, but only in the latter country did it make an impact proportional to that recorded in the United States. Nevertheless there were significant differences between Canada and the United States that affected both the organization of and the ultimate fate of the Laymen's Missionary Movement in each country. A primary difference is that Canada has never been religiously pluralistic in the same way as the United States. The 1911 census of Canada showed that fifty percent of the population belonged to just four Protestant churches: Presbyterian, Methodist and Anglican claiming about fifteen percent each and the Baptists five percent. Since another forty percent of the population were Roman Catholic, nine of every ten Canadians belonged to one of only five denominations. "Churchliness," as Robert T. Handy describes this fact and outlook, is both the organizational and psychological hallmark of Canada's religious experience.[3]

At the beginning of the century, Canada's population stood at 5.3 million, about one-tenth that of the United States. Population growth had been due to immigration, because more Canadians had emigrated to the United States than the numbers added by natural increase. In the 1890s the Canadian economy began to recover from a generation-long depression that retarded industrialization and urbanization. A central factor in the economic revival was the $800 million of new capital invested in manufacturing industry during the decade after 1900, so that the value added by manufacturing doubled in this period and Canada's urban population grew by seventeen percent.

The end of the long depression coincided with the filling up of the American West, so that immigration was now diverted towards Canada. While the majority of European immigrants settled in the farmlands of the Canadian West, a significant proportion who lacked capital and industrial skills got no further than the socially depressed areas in the eastern cities. Wherever they settled, however, the three million newcomers to Canada between 1896 and 1913 posed a serious challenge for the nation's political and religious leaders because most were completely ignorant of the Canadian lifestyle, political traditions and values. To protect the Canadian way of life as defined by "old Canadians," the new Canadians had to be Canadianized, and the churches and schools were the most conspicuous instruments for assimilation. Obviously there was need for intensive home mission work in the West and in the cities, as well as overseas missions.

As a first step to meet this perceived cultural challenge from the immigrants, Methodists, Presbyterians and Congregationalists had agreed in 1902 to seek an organic union of Canadian Protestantism. This dream of a "Canadian Church" had sprung from recognition of the similarities in theology, polity and outlook, but it was also inspired by the example of "big business" where the order of the day was mergers, monopolies, expansion, efficiency. Surely the same techniques that succeeded in the business world could create a single, powerful church to speak with authority to governments and meet the national challenge to Canadianize and Protestantize this tide of non-Anglo-Saxon immigrants. Both at home and abroad, church union would eliminate wasteful, unchristian competition, duplication in missions, and so hasten the day of the coming of His kingdom.

This same popular admiration of "big business" techniques and successes provided the rationale for creating the Laymen's Missionary Movement. Suggestions had been heard for several years both in the United States and Canada that laymen should support mission work with funds, study, and prayer. Early in 1906 at a Student Volunteer Movement meeting in Nashville, Tennessee, a Presbyterian layman, John B. Slemon, was so stirred by the sight of one hundred young people volunteering as missionaries that he conceived an idea to organize men in the churches to provide that support.[4] In November of that year, in New York City, the Laymen's Missionary Movement was organized during an interdenominational meeting celebrating the centenary of the American Board of Missions. Two months later at a conference in Philadelphia of the Foreign Missions Boards of the American and Canadian churches, S.B. Capen, one of the Laymen's Missionary Movement's founders, defined the nature and aims of the new group.

> What is it? It is a movement; it is a Laymen's Missionary Movement; it is an effort to get the denominations at home to work more closely together. The Student Volunteer Movement has to do with providing missionaries, the Young People's Missionary movement with the training of the men and women of tomorrow, and the Mission Boards are equipped for administration. The purpose of this Movement is to furnish more rapidly the money, and help push missionary work all along the line through a campaign of education among laymen under the direction of the various Mission Boards.[5]

In that audience was Dr. Alexander Sutherland, Secretary of the Missionary Society of the Methodist Church of Canada, who apparently recruited one of the most prominent Canadian Methodist laymen, Newton Wesley Rowell, to organize a Canadian branch of the Laymen's Missionary Movement. Within five months a Canadian Council had been formed with Rowell as chairman and the twelve Canadian members of the International Council as members of the Canadian Council.[6] This Canadian Council was to act in consultation with representatives of all co-operating churches, and its first step was to organize meetings in several major cities to assess the missionary needs which the Movement might fill. By November, 1907, the field had been surveyed and a second meeting in Toronto formally launched the Laymen's Missionary Movement in Canada. The next six months were spent planning a nation-wide campaign to arouse public interest. Conferences were held in larger centres, followed by visits of local groups to smaller towns and the countryside. The main meetings were addressed by the mission secretaries of the five participating Protestant denominations—Methodist, Presbyterian, Church of England, Baptist and Congregationalist—and by leading members of the Laymen's Missionary Movement Council.

The format for meetings was standardized; each opened with an evening banquet where invited laymen heard speeches from a battery of orators, each of whom gave a short talk on a specific aspect of the proposed Laymen's Missionary Movement work. The following day these speeches continued, with business sessions to allow for the establishing of local committees. Finally, on the third day, the audience divided into denominational groups, each of which was expected to establish its own local committee. The public interest aroused by this "National Campaign" was so great that J. Campbell White, general secretary of the American Movement, suggested holding an Assembly or Congress to hear reports of the progress achieved, to hear addresses by national leaders, and to consider Canada's missionary obligations and opportunities.[7] The acceptance of White's suggestion was followed in less than half a year by precisely such a Congress, held in Toronto, attended by over four thousand delegates and lasting five full days.

The Canadian National Missionary Congress opened at the end of March 1909, and after preliminary sessions addressed by White and by Robert E. Speer, the two leading American figures in the Movement, Rowell presided over the plenary sessions held each afternoon and evening. Each session began with devotions (a fifteen-page ecumenical hymnbook had been prepared for the Congress), and each session had its own theme: "The Victorious Progress of Missions," "The Place of the Church in the Making of the Nation," "Stewardship of Life," "Knowledge of Missions," and on a practical note, "How to Lead the Church to its Highest Missionary Efficiency." The closing topic was "The Unity and Universality of the Kingdom." Capen and Slemon, the founders of the Movement, spoke during the plenary sessions, and Speer and White each delivered two addresses. Other speakers represented mission work in India and Arabia, but the guest of honour was Sir Andrew Fraser, the Scottish ex-Lieutenant-Governor of Bengal, son of a missionary, past Moderator of the Presbyterian Church of India, representative of the Scottish Laymen's Missionary Movement and world leader in missionary work.

The Canadian speakers included prominent lay and clerical figures in national life, and of the 4300 delegates, more than half were laymen. Except for forty-seven Americans, all delegates were Canadian males and Protestant. Of the total of 2500 laymen, 1500 came from outside the immediate area of Toronto as did nearly 1200 of the 1500 clergy. Almost three hundred theological students were registered at the Congress. The missionary interests of Canadian women were not completely forgotten. Two sessions for women, held in Convocation Hall at the University of Toronto, drew overflow crowds.[8] Introducing the printed volume of proceedings of the Congress, Rowell praised the ecumenical spirit that pervaded the meetings and the commitment shown by the delegates.

> That active business and professional men would leave their homes and travel hundreds, some thousands of miles, at their own expense to take part in a

missionary congress was evidence of an awakened interest among the men of the churches, and an appreciation of their missionary privileges and responsibilities, such as had not hitherto been manifested. No man could look into the intent faces of these men, who, day after day, gathered to listen to a discussion of missionary problems without being deeply impressed by the remarkable possibilities of such a gathering.⁹

The programme's basic theme was "Canada's Missionary Policy—Home and Foreign," and one of the ten plenary sessions considered the problem of preserving the Canadian way-of-life. The problems of English-speaking and European settlers as well as Asians were considered, and one speaker spent his time on the problem of Canada's native Indians. In the final speech of that session, James A. Macdonald, former editor of *The Presbyterian* and now editor-in-chief of *The Globe*, summarized the motivation of the Canadian Movement: "The Christianization of our Civilization." Virtually every speech by a Canadian was permeated with Social Gospel phraseology, suggesting that the Laymen's Missionary Movement, at least in its Canadian form, was essentially another manifestation of the Social Gospel movement and one that appealed to the sense of "noblesse oblige" (as well as richesse oblige) in Canada's burgeoning and successful middle and upper classes.

One important result of the Congress was the formulation of a "National Missionary Policy" and its subsequent adoption by the five Protestant churches involved. The Policy statement acknowledged "the clear duty of the Churches of Canada to evangelize all those in the Dominion, or who come to our shores, who have not been led into the Christian life, and also to provide for the adequate preaching of the

Gospel to forty millions of souls in the non-Christian world."[10] Since Canadian church members gave an average of $1.23 annually to home missions and only 64 cents for foreign work, those givings would have to be increased to $5.00 per member and the four hundred Canadian missionaries in the field increased fourfold if the objectives of the National Missionary Policy were to be met.

At the Congress the bureaucratic structure and the methodology of the Movement also took form. A Dominion Council was created, with four laymen and the missionary secretary from each of the larger communions, and a full-time secretary to direct operations. A vice-chairman was appointed for each province, and most large cities had an interdenominational "Cooperating Committee." Rowell had refused to be secretary but agreed to chair the Dominion Council. Paralleling this national organization was an independent but co-operating national and regional Laymen's Missionary Movement for each denomination. In the months that followed, five practical steps were widely employed by the Canadian Laymen's Missionary Movement and the participating churches to implement that Policy. These steps were the wholesale distribution of mission literature, the adoption of the duplex envelope for congregational use, the organizing of innumerable local prayer meetings and regional conferences (always beginning with a church dinner to mellow the audience), the "every member canvass," which meant door-to-door visitations by teams and, finally, enlisting successful Canadian businessmen for Laymen's Missionary Movement leadership.

The first step was a continuation of the educational efforts started by the Laymen's Missionary Movement in 1907. In two years the Movement had already published two books and twenty-four pamphlets intended to enlighten laymen about the problems and challenges of missions.[11] Of these pamphlets six had been written by Canadians. This literature was sold in three packet lots, the total cost being only $2.00, or $3.00 if the Congress Report was included.[12] Head office distribution statistics for the eighteen months ending with 1910 reported 28,800 books, 7,500 charts, 1,127,000 pamphlets, and five million leaflets distributed.[13] The second measure to fulfil the National Policy, the promotion of the duplex envelope, was to make the average church member more responsive to mission needs and to encourage regular giving to missions in place of occasional special mission collections. If each congregation adopted the duplex envelope system the increased givings would enable the church to reach that goal of sixteen hundred missionaries supported and forty million heathen converted.

Thanks to the duplex envelopes Presbyterian churches in Toronto reported that mission givings increased 252 percent between 1907 and 1908, and a further 208 percent in 1909. (By 1913, 605 Presbyterian congregations were using the envelopes compared to forty-seven in 1907).[14] As a further follow-up to the Congress the Dominion Council organized 125 interdenominational conferences across Canada in 1910, and in 1911 another series of "trans-Canada" two-day conferences were held, usually with denominational sessions continuing on the third day.[15] From scattered statistics it would appear that each of the hundreds, if not thousands, of county and denominational conferences between 1909 and 1915 drew an average of two hundred and fifty persons. An example of parallel work in the annual denominational conferences were the Presbyterian Church's "Coast-to-Coast" campaigns, during which one team gave sixty-seven speeches in a thirty-two day period during 1910.[16] As for the home-to-home "every person" canvasses at the congregational level, it is impossible to estimate how many people were visited and influenced by this technique.

From its inception the Laymen's Missionary Movement was predominantly a lay-led religious movement. Clergy were involved only *ex officio* as mission secretaries for their respective churches. Among the Laymen's Missionary Movement officers, laymen outnumbered the clergy by at least three to one. More significant than their numbers was the type of laymen involved. Since the fifth step was to organize laymen with proven expertise in business and management, not surprisingly the list of leaders in the Laymen's Missionary Movement reads like a *Who's Who* of the financial, industrial, legal and political "establishment" of Canada in those prewar days. In a sample of thirty-two active office-holders in the national Movement, eighteen were Presbyterians, five Methodists, four Baptists, two Anglicans, one a Quaker, and the religious affiliation of the remaining two is uncertain. Of the thirty-two no less than fourteen were prominent in industrial and commercial life, eleven of them millionaires or near millionaires. Three men were in the public service and two more were lawyers of national reputation; only six were clergymen. The most striking social component was unquestionably the "big-business" element: five of the men were directors of no less than twenty-three major companies, another was president of six.

Canadian Presbyterian interest and involvement in the Laymen's Missionary Movement appeared early and grew rapidly. On 4 April 1907 *The Presbyterian* reported at length on the founding of the Laymen's Missionary Movement in New York and on the appointment of the Canadian executive (who were also part of the one-hundred member Central Committee). Two weeks later *The Presbyterian* recorded fully the dinner meeting of 9 April in Toronto, when three hundred "men of action" listened to White and Spear and to James A. Macdonald. This enthusiastic account covered three-quarters of a page; the only sour note was a letter from

Phineas Hophni Burton, manufacturing magnate, urging that Laymen's Missionary Movement meetings be held in the evening so that "the King's business" would not interfere with daytime profit-making. After a year of only casual references to the Laymen's Missionary Movement, *The Presbyterian* announced on 16 April 1908 that "steady and substantial progress" was being made by the Movement in eastern Canadian Presbyterian congregations, but not in the West. Ten branches were operating in Ontario and one each in Quebec, New Brunswick, and Nova Scotia. Half of Toronto's Presbyterian churches had adopted the duplex envelope and in some places mission givings had increased fourfold. One week later more statistics appeared from Toronto where forty congregations had held mission dinners and seventeen of them were using duplex envelopes. The objective now was to raise $90,700 in one year, a 225% increase over givings in 1906.

By the autumn of 1908 a "National Campaign" was under way, featuring financial goals two to three times as great as the previous year, and White was starting a seven-week, nation-wide tour supported by the Presbyterian Laymen's Missionary Movement and the boards of Home and Foreign Missions. No fund-raising was involved—the Campaign was purely educational. R.P. Mackay, Mission Board Secretary, reported weekly in *The Presbyterian* on the achievements of the Campaign, and funding-goals skyrocketed as the Laymen's Missionary Movement team lectured and ate its way across Canada. The tidal wave of statistics still rolled in as the Laymen's Missionary Movement reported 209,000 members in twenty-four cities, with Winnipeg making the highest per capita pledge—$10 compared to the $7.38 national average.[17]

The Presbyterian gave extensive advance coverage to the National Congress of which the three-and-one-half day

"Presbyterian Laymen's Convention" was a part. The Congress was intended to be "inspirational," the Convention "practical." One practical question was whether the Presbyterian Church should have a full-time Laymen's Missionary Movement secretary, as the Anglicans and Baptists did. Planning for the Convention showed how quickly Canadian Presbyterians had seized on the spirit and techniques of the Laymen's Missionary Movement. Robert Spear, Campbell White, and Charles A. Rowland of the American Southern Presbyterian Church would speak on the role of denominational Laymen's Missionary Movement organizations, a special luncheon would honour Sir Andrew Fraser, and the Women's Home Missionary Society would hold concurrent meetings for Presbyterian ladies who supported the Movement.[18] Of the nineteen Canadians who addressed the full Congress, the six Presbyterians were Knox College principal Alfred Gandier, F.B. DuVal, the social reformer from Winnipeg, C.W. Gordon (who was also listed in the programme as Ralph Connor), Robert Falconer, President of the University of Toronto, and the ubiquitous James A. Macdonald—all of them clergymen.

The follow-up to the Missionary Congress was the "trans-Canada" campaign of 1910, fully reported in *The Presbyterian* by F.W. Anderson, former secretary of the Student Volunteer Movement, the College Mission and the College Department of the YMCA, and now General Secretary of the Presbyterian Church Laymen's Missionary Movement. By his account the campaign seemed more denominational than national, and the four-man team that held 250 meetings in the West contained no laymen.[19] Although for two years after the famous Congress the Presbyterian Laymen's Missionary Movement insisted that men were "better than money," by the end of 1910 money was a diminishing resource. While Toronto Presbytery had asked for $5 per member towards missions, only $2.89 was collected.[20] In the last nine months of the year $165,675 had been spent on home missions, but only $40,623 was received.[21] By April 1911 the foreign mission deficit stood at $13,483. Only Hamilton-London Synod had increased its givings, while mission offerings from the Toronto-Kingston Synod had decreased by more than $2000.[22]

Contributions from rural areas were now larger than from urban areas. Whereas in the past, National Movement officers had made up a star-studded group of the wealthy and important, the vice-chairmen for the provinces were unknowns. Nevertheless, when the National Laymen's Missionary Movement Council met in October, its General Secretary H.K. Caskey (another Presbyterian) reported that mission givings by the major Protestant denominations had risen forty-seven percent in the last three years and Presbyterian givings were up by fifty-eight percent, the largest increase for any denomination in the period. The lesson, Caskey concluded, was that all should contribute, not just a few rich persons, and plans were again laid for another national study campaign.[23] Declining public interest, however, was already reflected in the press. The Church's official organ, *The Presbyterian Record,* whose interest was heavily mission-oriented, had reported the progress of the Laymen's Missionary Movement since 1908, but always in briefer form than did *The Presbyterian*. In the summer of 1910 coverage in the *Record* virtually ceased, both for the national and the Presbyterian Laymen's Missionary Movement. Early in 1911 *The Presbyterian* also began to show reduced interest in the Laymen's Missionary Movement, and by 1912 its references to the Movement were infrequent and perfunctory.

Despite its remarkable success in popularizing missions, as early as 1911 in the United States the Laymen's Missionary Movement was caught in a theological crossfire between liberals and conservatives. There is no evidence that this conflict arose within Canadian denominations; the Laymen's Missionary Movement seemed to advance with ever greater success. "Every person" visitations were being held widely, county conferences continued in full swing and everywhere mission givings were reportedly on the increase.[24] Certainly, these techniques were getting results. Some sixty percent of Canadian Presbyterian congregations had adopted the duplex envelope and the visitation, and in six years missionary givings had risen 134 percent compared to only sixty percent for general church givings during the same period.[25] A variation on the conference techniques was the country conference. Beginning late in 1913 over 130 such meetings were held across Canada in a twelve-month period, with an estimated total attendance of nearly 50,000.[26] By 1915, however, the Dominion Council felt that "the Movement had lost its momentum."[27]

As early as 1911 the Methodist Mission Board took over responsibility for the work of its denominational Laymen's Missionary Movement and a year later that branch of the Movement was completely absorbed by the Board in the interests of efficiency. Henceforth it had a clergyman as a secretary. The same developments occurred in the other denominational Laymen's Missionary Movement groups except for the Anglican branch. Even there, clerical participation seems to have occurred fairly early. This gradual erosion of the independence of the Movement branches as they were absorbed into denominational missionary organizations was accelerated by the outbreak of World War I. In the words of Sydney Ahlstrom, the Laymen's Missionary Movement had faltered and then failed as a crusade: "It began to appear that the foreign missions revival may well have arisen as a half-subconscious effort to divert Protestants from intellectual problems and internal dissensions by engaging them in great moral and spiritual tasks—only to have deeper problems and dissensions reappear."[28] The American Laymen's Missionary Movement survived its internal rift and the debilitating effects of World War I, but it lives on largely as the promoter of a yearly observance of Christianity's missionary mandate.

It can be argued that no comparison of the United States' experience with the Laymen's Missionary Movement is possible because the Canadian organization had disappeared by the 1920s, yet the causes of that disappearance are markedly different from the forces encountered in the United States. In the first place, the Protestant churches never interpreted mission exclusively either as home or foreign; to Canadians these terms were but two sides of a very broad definition of evangelism. Next, Canada entered World War I almost three years before the United States, and missionary organizations early faced the competing demands of a national war effort. All the denominations except the Church of England found it more convenient and efficacious to absorb their denominational Laymen's Missionary Movement structures into existing church-operated mission boards.

While a casual observer might assume that the Laymen's Missionary Movement in Canada was a victim of the War, such is too simple an answer to this story of boom or bust. Even before the War voices had been heard complaining of unnecessary duplication in mission work and also bemoaning the undeniable decline of public interest and support for the Laymen's Missionary Movement. Mission givings in all the denominations apparently peaked in the year following the Congress; thereafter the ambitious fund-raising goals were not met. The tremendous enthusiasm raised by and for the Movement, and reinforced by the famous Congress, was not sustained for more than a couple of years despite all the conferences, visitations, literature and other techniques employed. Obviously, the Laymen's Missionary Movement in

Canada was already ailing when the guns of August 1914, rendered the *coup de grâce* to this imaginative but abortive effort to enlist Canadian business men and business methods in the King's business of world evangelization.

10. A Sense of Proportion
The Presbyterian Contribution to Biblical Studies in Canada

This paper, in an expanded form, was delivered in Montreal at the 1988-1989 'symposia of two cities' described in the introduction to "Who Pays the Piper," and was based on Moir's 1982 book for the Society of Biblical Literature, A History of Biblical Studies in Canada: A Sense of Proportion.

Presbyterians have followed John Calvin in believing that the Bible is infallible—it does not lead the reader into error—but not inerrant—not free from scribal errors. Since the Reformation, however, Protestant theology has tended to treat the Bible, the *Word,* somewhat rigidly, perhaps reacting against the older emphasis on *tradition*. As a result, Protestant views of the Bible have become polarized around two opposing concepts—the Bible as *reason,* and the Bible as *authority*. For most Presbyterians, the *reason* position has been the historic norm, but the rise of modern biblical criticism since the middle of the nineteenth century has produced a minority who favour the *authority* interpretation. Officially, however, the Presbyterian Church in Canada has embraced biblical studies as a God-given support for faith.

The academic discipline of biblical studies, as opposed to the mere learning of biblical languages, involves asking questions about the Bible. The first question asks, "Is what the

Bible says true?" This presupposes an even more basic question concerning *total* truth: "Can the Bible be subjected to critical, scientific study *and* at the same time be the medium through which God speaks to us directly?" In other words, is it not a sacrilege to doubt the *total* truth of God's gift of his words? The church has always taught that the Bible is the *inspired* word of God, but does that mean God dictated his message through robot-like authors? Or could and did those authors make mistakes because they were human?

Biblical studies—combining textual, linguistic, historical and archaeological research, in addition to the learning of biblical and cognate languages—are barely a century old in Canada; yet for the first half of that century, Presbyterian scholars virtually monopolized the field, earning international renown for their academic training, teaching abilities, and research publications. This Presbyterian dominance grew from Presbyterian emphasis on the Word and from the Scottish "common sense" philosophy, but especially after 1886 from the work of one Presbyterian, James Frederick McCurdy of University College in Toronto, who set both the high scholarly standards and the moderate theological tone of Canadian biblical studies.[1]

Canadian theological students were first alerted to the importance of biblical studies by the controversies in Scotland and the United States about the views of W. Robertson Smith and Charles Briggs. Radical higher (or historical) criticism might be gaining ground in those countries, but in Canada the norm for biblical studies was always the cautious conservatism of Franz Delitzsch at the University of Leipzig. In the forty years before World War I, at least nineteen Canadians did postgraduate biblical studies abroad, and fifteen of them studied at German universities, including nine with Delitzsch. One more went to Oxford, four to Edinburgh, and a dozen completed their postgraduate work in Canada, mostly with McCurdy at the University of Toronto. Like those Canadian colleges that offered biblical studies, these young scholars found no conflict between religious truth and scientific theories.

The Canadian Presbyterian attitude to biblical studies was clearly expressed by their educational leaders. Daniel MacVicar, principal of The Presbyterian College, Montreal, commented:

> I venture to think that there is nothing very revolutionary at hand. The work of God is not about to be overthrown. The evangelical churches are not to be pulverized by the Higher Criticism.... Our age is far too practical and full of commonsense and piety to admit of this issue.[2]

Similarly, when asked if higher criticism weakened the authority of the Bible, Principal William Caven of Knox College replied:

> The permanent contributions of Criticism are not as great as some suppose, nor will its effects be as hurtful as some fear.... Higher Criticism is as legitimate as grammar or logic, and is necessary to any thorough study of the Bible.... It is not the Higher Criticism that does the mischief, but the rationalistic preconceptions, the disbelief in the supernatural altogether.[3]

MacVicar and Caven were stressing two elements of biblical studies—common sense and piety—that enabled Canadian Protestant denominations to accept higher criticism while avoiding clashes between liberal scholars and their more conservative fellow Christians. Almost all proponents of the new learning were men of proven piety and good sense, which allowed the development and popularization of higher criticism with little fanfare or opposition. Acceptable boundaries to biblical studies were defined by the moderator of the Presbytery of Montreal in 1886, at the induction of Canadian-born and educated John Scrimger to The Presbyterian College's chair of Greek and Hebrew exegesis and sacred literature:

> While you will no doubt be on your guard against the many subtle sources of misleading . . . as to the proper interpretation to be put on the Word of God, I am equally confident that you will avoid the opposite . . . extreme of striving to find startling novelties in the way of interpretation.[4]

Although Scrimger contributed articles on biblical criticism to many periodicals, he was both discrete and progressive, as the moderator had suggested. In fact, among Presbyterians the only incident concerning biblical authority involved Scrimger's colleague John Campbell, professor of church history and apologetic in The Presbyterian College. Campbell, a dilettante in biblical studies and ironically an opponent of higher criticism, stated in an 1893 address at Queen's University, "The perfect book or the perfect father," in which he stated that either God judges or Scripture is inerrant, which Campbell denied.[5]

Heresy charges followed quickly, and Presbytery found Campbell guilty of holding erroneous views on inspiration, but Synod reversed this judgement after he agreed to a compromise statement, that some parts of the Old Testament were "not the whole truth" and that God judges "in the great majority of cases." In no other Canadian Presbyterian college—Halifax, Morrin in Quebec, Queen's, Knox or Manitoba—was there any challenge to either old or new theories of biblical interpretation. Opinions on such questions, if offered as hypotheses for academic investigation, passed unchallenged, and for Canadians of any denomination who stumbled into the limelight of higher criticism debates, public reaction seemed to depend less on *what* was said than on *how* it was said.

When Scrimger became principal of The Presbyterian College in 1904, Old and New Testament studies were separated, and Richard Davidson, a former student of McCurdy, was appointed in Old Testament, only to leave a year later to join McCurdy in Toronto. Davidson's successor in 1907 was Scottish and German-trained Alexander R. Gordon, a higher critic and author of a book on Genesis. Gordon's departure to the United Church in 1925 inaugurated two decades of uninspired Old Testament teaching in the College. Daniel James Fraser had become the first professor of New Testament and principal in 1915, but even after resigning both posts in 1928 he still taught New Testament until 1948, and is best remembered as an administrator.

After the German-trained New Testament scholar, Robert Falconer, left the Presbyterian College, Halifax, in 1908 to be president of the University of Toronto, the college failed to develop a strong programme of biblical studies. Morrin College in Quebec also earned no scholarly reputation in its short life of less than forty years. At Manitoba College, the Presbyterian Church's dynamic institution in Winnipeg, Principal John Mark King, an Edinburgh graduate who had studied at three German universities, offered Hebrew exegesis and Oriental languages and literature among the many subjects he taught until his death in 1899. Andrew Browning Baird, another student of McCurdy who had gone on to Leipzig and Edinburgh, was also teaching at Manitoba College; but his only publication, in 1898, was a book opposing higher criticism.

The story of biblical studies at Queen's is different from that of its sister Presbyterian colleges. The Church of Scotland traditionally combined arts and theology in a single institution and prescribed Hebrew for all its ministers, and at Queen's all biblical instruction was entrusted to John B. Mowat who was satirized in a college song which asked,

> Does you know the gentle Rabbi who makes the critics quail?
>
> Does you know that he can demonstrate that Jonah ate the whale?[6]

One student remembered him as "a kindly old man . . . [who] would sit meditatively at our discussions, and if later on he owned that he had 'had his doubts about it at the time', he never troubled us by telling them."[7] Mowat resigned in 1899 at the age of seventy-four, having spent forty-two undistinguished years as a professor.

William George Jordan, Mowat's successor, was encouraged by Queen's intellectual climate. "I found that the soil had been prepared and the atmosphere was quite genial. Principal [George M.] Grant and Dr. [John] Watson were in sympathy with the new methods."[8] One year before Jordan's appointment, Scottish-born Ernest Findlay Scott had become Queen's professor of church history, but his real interest was biblical studies. In five years he published three books on New Testament studies which, Jordan wrote, placed Scott "in the front rank of New Testament scholars." He also published a fourth volume, *Biblical Criticism and Modern Thought*, and Jordan produced six books between 1902 and 1916. The biggest change at Queen's, however, was the secularization of arts and science in 1910, leaving only the theological department connected to the Presbyterian Church.

Among the several Presbyterian theological colleges, Knox always had the largest number of students. Its long and close connection with University College, the teaching division of the University of Toronto, was strengthened by the decision in 1905 to relocate on the University campus beside University College, and by the appointment of Alfred Gandier as principal in 1908, one year after his brother-in-law, Robert Falconer, became president of the University. In 1898 McCurdy had been instrumental in the appointment to Old Testament at Knox of John Edgar McFadyen, top-ranking theological student in Scotland in his graduating year, who had studied and married in Germany. Knox's first New Testament professor was H.A.A. Kennedy, who came in 1905 and had been at the University of Berlin with Falconer.

Kennedy left Knox in 1909, and the following year McFadyen returned to Scotland, having published nine books—two on the psalms, one on the prophetic and historical scriptures, one entitled *Old Testament Criticism and the Christian Church*, and another, *Introduction to the Old Testament*—during his twelve years at the college. W.G. Jordan praised McFadyen as

> remarkable for his soberness of judgment, his patience and tact.... There is no man who had done more to present modern scholarship in clear, persuasive style to a large circle of readers in Canada, the United States and Britain.[9]

McFadyen's liberal criticism was not challenged because of his scholarship, personal piety and sincerity of faith. His replacement in Old Testament was Richard Davidson, another protégé of McCurdy, who left University College to teach at Knox, and Kennedy was followed by another Scot, Robert Law. Law was already a renowned preacher and author, and before his death in 1919 he published two more books including a classic on the first Epistle of St. John that was reprinted as recently as 1978.

The frequency with which the name of James Frederick McCurdy recurs in these events indicates his importance in the contribution of Canadian Presbyterians to biblical studies. Born in the Free Church manse at Chatham, New Brunswick, in 1847, he was educated mostly at home before entering the University of New Brunswick at the age of sixteen. Three years later he graduated in Classics with high honours, and in 1867 became principal of Dalhousie Grammar School on the Baie des Chaleurs. After a year of successful teaching, McCurdy decided to pursue graduate studies at Princeton Seminary. There, under the conservative W.H. Green, McCurdy began his lifelong interest in biblical studies.

Upon graduation in 1871, McCurdy was ordained as a missionary by the Presbytery of New Jersey, and was also hired as Green's assistant. For eleven years he supervised the Seminary's languages programme, worked as a librarian, and learned Sanskrit, which he then taught in Princeton University. In 1878 Princeton awarded him an honorary Ph.D. for his papers on biblical languages. This research was published as *Aryo-Semitic Speech* in 1881, the same year that he married Isabella Russell, daughter of the Presbyterian minister at Dalhousie. One year later, however, McCurdy's career changed direction sharply. He was already disenchanted with the conservative tone of the seminary, and after his colleagues condemned him for modernism when he seemed to endorse evolution in a speech soon after Darwin's death, he resigned immediately.

The McCurdys spent the next three years in Germany where Fred, as he was called, studied at Gottingen and at Leipzig, where the great attraction was Franz Delitzsch. By the summer of 1885, however, the McCurdys were living in Toronto where his relative, William Henry Fraser, the French and German master at Upper Canada College, had connections to University College. At University College Jacob Meier Hirschfelder, a Jewish convert to Anglicanism who taught biblical languages for over forty years, was nearing retirement. It seemed timely to appoint a scholar who had studied in Germany, so McCurdy was soon hired by University College and an Honours Department of Oriental Languages was established.

Almost immediately the McCurdys became active in St. Andrew's congregation where Fred met a kindred soul in its minister, Daniel James Macdonnell, another New Brunswick son of the manse. A profound theologian and widely acclaimed as Canada's best preacher, Macdonnell was only four years McCurdy's senior, had studied in Germany, and a few years earlier had been the focus of a famous heresy trial. A link between the progressive Presbyterianism of McCurdy and Macdonnell was another member of St. Andrew's, Professor George Paxton Young of University College, Canada's leading philosopher, who had resigned from Knox College to escape its conservative academic environment in 1864. Young was a generation older than the other two, but all three shared one characteristic—uncompromising intellectual honesty.

When Hirschfelder retired in 1888, McCurdy was promoted to professor and head of department. By law, University College could have no religious affiliation, yet ironically this very neutrality allowed McCurdy to make Orientals a viable discipline, uniquely set within a secular institution. Because the Free Church insisted that the state should teach arts and sciences and the Church's colleges only theology, Knox College students usually did their undergraduate work, including language studies, at nearby University

College. About forty-five percent of the University's students were Presbyterians, and the proportion was probably higher in McCurdy's classes.

McCurdy, however, wanted biblical studies to be more than just a service course for future clergymen. Biblical studies could not be taught in American tax-supported colleges because of the separation of church and state, but in "Christian" Canada no such conflict existed. McCurdy was convinced that biblical studies "should form part of the curriculum of every college."[10] For him all education required an honest, respectful and enquiring pursuit of truth, without denominational or creedal bias, and scepticism about the authenticity and value of the higher religions must be unthinkable in a Christian university professor. More than two decades later when McCurdy died, his friend and colleague at Victoria College, John Fletcher McLaughlin, praised his "sane, reasonable, thorough-going, and yet reverent, application of the historical method of study."[11]

McCurdy's honours course included Arabic and Assyrian as well as the usual biblical languages. He emphasized language studies as the bed-rock of biblical research and was vindicated by the success of so many of his graduates. Already the University's Department of Orientals dominated the discipline in Canada because other institutions offered little more than skeletal programmes in biblical studies, but McCurdy was collecting resources that made both undergraduate and graduate work at Toronto outstanding. By 1890 he was lecturing seventeen hours per week to over eighty students, and when a committee examining course offerings and teaching loads recommended nine more hours of classes in Orientals, it was obvious that McCurdy must have help.

David William McGee, a Presbyterian and former student of McCurdy's who had studied at Leipzig, was hired in 1892 as his assistant, but four months after receiving his doctorate from the University of Breslau McGee drowned accidentally, aged only twenty-three. His successor, Ross George Murison, was a Scottish orphan who had put himself through the University and Knox College by working as a farm hand, teacher and railway navvy, and won a University entrance scholarship by learning Greek in six days. He too had gone to study in Germany, earning his B.D. from Knox College at the same time. In 1902 Murison received the first Ph.D. in Orientals given by the University of Toronto. After only a decade of teaching, however, Murison died of typhoid fever.

McCurdy was deeply affected by these deaths. His next choice for assistant was Richard Davidson, another Knox graduate who received his Toronto Ph.D. in biblical studies the same year as Murison. Davidson, however, was teaching at The Presbyterian College, and until he could leave for Toronto, the position was filled by yet another Knox graduate, Irish-born Thomas Eakin. Eakin too had completed a Toronto Ph.D. under McCurdy in 1905, and McCurdy called him the best biblical teacher in Canada. Also assisting McCurdy was still one more Knox graduate with German training, Calvin Alexander McRae. Five years later, when Davidson left the department to take McFadyen's place at Knox, McCurdy rehired Eakin and McRae as assistants at University College.

Recruiting faculty and improving his department was made easier for McCurdy by the support of President Falconer, New Testament scholar and former principal of the Presbyterian College, Halifax. Falconer, too, advocated liberal education and approved of teaching biblical studies in "secular" University College. Presbyterian acceptance of sensitive biblical teaching did not, however, guarantee that Christian humanism was universally welcome in a state-supported university. Soon after Falconer's arrival at the University of Toronto, criticism of the teaching in the Orientals Department emerged from an unexpected source. In 1906 a new University of Toronto Act empowered University College to teach Oriental languages, but not theology. Within two years McCurdy's department, and particularly Thomas Eakin, was accused of undermining the faith of students by teaching religion.

The University authorities defended McCurdy and his assistants, insisting that any university worth its salt "should take cognizance of literature which ranked with the most important any nation has given to man."[12] Opponents asserted that University College must by law teach only value-free languages, and must not shake "men's confidence in the Bible as being the Word of the living God." Among the books they wanted banned from use in the Department were some by John Edgar McFadyen of Knox College. A University committee reported that the charges were "not well founded," which seemed to exonerate McCurdy's philosophy of teaching biblical studies.[13]

By now McCurdy was in his early sixties, a renowned teacher and scholar, author of books and articles, especially his *magnum opus,* the three-volume *History, Prophecy and the Monuments* (1894-1901) that had won him critical acclaim and an LL.D. from his alma mater, the University of New Brunswick. Tragically, his sight was failing, and he told President Falconer that he wanted to retire soon. En route to the Holy Land, he wrote to Falconer, describing how in the past quarter-century the curriculum of the Orientals Department had broadened, "in conformity with the widening conception of the relations of the Bible to human history." Biblical studies were now recognized as an essential part of a liberal education.

Falconer asked William Robert Taylor to fill in during the coming year but Taylor, another promising scholar and graduate of University and Knox colleges, had just accepted a position in Westminster Hall, the new Presbyterian theological college in Vancouver. McCurdy wanted Taylor in Toronto permanently; but Falconer, although himself a Presbyterian, felt it "an unwise step" to hire yet another Presbyterian in a department that had been manned exclusively by Presbyterians since 1888. Eventually, McCurdy believed he had found his replacement in Immanuel G.A. Benzinger, a former professor at the University of Berlin who was now teaching Hebrew and German in a Jerusalem high school and operating tourist excursions to Egypt and the Holy Land.

Pressed by McCurdy, Falconer appointed Benzinger, and Taylor too when the latter agreed to leave Westminster Hall in 1913 for more money at University College. When McCurdy retired in June 1914, Benzinger became chairman and Taylor leaped from lecturer to full professor. Short weeks later the guns of August heralded World War I, and the University of Toronto, under public pressure, fired Benzinger and three other German nationals from its faculty. McCurdy, the Christian humanist, was confused and angered by the irrationality, violence and hatred unleashed by the war. The carnage in Europe must be the work of power-hungry nationalistic leaders, because the British and German peoples could not want it. As an emotional affirmation of his faith in western civilization and peace, McCurdy refused to stand for the singing of "God save the King" during the Sunday service at St. Andrew's Church.

In 1922 McCurdy sent Falconer a nine-page, typed account of the development of biblical studies in Canada over the previous four decades, an epistle that took the seventy-five-year-old, half-blind scholar two days to write. McCurdy shared Falconer's belief that the war had destroyed all that was best in western civilization. Christianity too, "as practised," seemed "a comparative failure," and now writers and thinkers were proclaiming that science and religion must be reconciled so that religion could be reconstructed. "In all the discussion I have seen the Bible, the ostensible basis of Christianity, has been almost entirely left out of consideration."

McCurdy recorded how his Department and its programme of biblical studies had been created on the initiative of Principals William Caven of Knox College and James Paterson Sheraton of Wycliffe College to provide religious education:

> The basal fact that religion is the mainstay of humanity, and that the Hebraistic religion of the Old and New Testament has been the chief humanizing and principal cultural influence in the history of our race, implies that the intelligent study and teaching of the *essential* Bible should be a function of every university.[14]

McCurdy believed the study of the Bible was in decline because in past the Bible had been made a "rule of faith," instead of "a way of life," and because it contained material "unspiritual or irrelevant to its main divinely human purport and message." "A sane and tactful course of Bible teaching" was needed to give young men and women "the right direction, and a sense of relative spiritual values in the most valuable single portion of their education," and its teachers must develop "communicative tact, and a sense of proportion and perspective."

This was McCurdy's *apologia pro vita sua,* yet his death did not occur until March 1935, thirteen years later. Three of his former students—William Taylor of University College, Thomas Eakin of Knox, and Richard Davidson of Emmanuel College—conducted his funeral service. Even before McCurdy's retirement in 1914, however, the decline of Presbyterian dominance in the biblical studies field was foreshadowed. Biblical scholars of other Canadian Protestant denominations were becoming more numerous and prominent, and Canadian attention was shifting from German institutions to the University of Chicago. The most important development, however, was church union in 1925, when the Presbyterian Church lost its colleges in Halifax, Kingston, Winnipeg, Saskatoon and Vancouver to the United Church.

In the next generation the two surviving colleges, Knox in Toronto and Presbyterian in Montreal, made little contribution to biblical studies. In 1925 William Manson, Knox's stimulating New Testament teacher, returned to Scotland, and the Presbyterian Church lost seven more scholars—Taylor, Davidson, T.J. Meek, Alexander Gordon, R.B.Y. Scott, Stewart McCullough and Fred Winnett—to the United Church. Those few younger scholars who stayed with the continuing Presbyterian Church found no scope for their talents because Eakin and Fraser, representing an older generation, continued teaching at the two remaining colleges but abandoned research. Only since the end of World War II has Presbyterian biblical scholarship regained that position of strength that it held before church union.

In Canada no 'schools' of biblical interpretation, centred on one person or on one institution, ever developed. Nevertheless, Canadian scholars, both Presbyterians and others, have individually made significant contributions in terms of published research, and perhaps more importantly, as teachers. The two most enduring and distinctive Canadian traditions in biblical studies have been solid language training as the prerequisite for all further studies, and a moderately conservative approach to questions of biblical interpretation. Both traditions owe much to James Frederick McCurdy, whose students filled Presbyterian pulpits and academic chairs and shared his belief that the value of biblical studies in a liberal education requires of every student and every teacher "a sense of proportion."

11. A NATIONAL VISION
The Contribution of Atlantic Presbyterianism to Canada

In 1994 John Moir was one of the keynote speakers at a Mount Allison University conference where he considered Presbyterianism's vision of Canada. Although ostensibly about the Maritimes, the address does have relevance to all of Canada. It became part of a volume, The Contribution of Presbyterianism to the Maritime Provinces, *edited by Charles Scobie and George Rawlyk and published in 1997 by McGill-Queen's University Press. It is reprinted here by permission.*

JUST TWO DAYS BEFORE THE BRITISH NORTH AMERICA Act transformed the colonies of Nova Scotia, New Brunswick and the United Canadas into the Dominion of Canada on 1 July 1867, the *Presbyterian Witness* of Halifax, unofficial mouthpiece of the Presbyterian Church of the Lower Provinces, hailed the challenge that Confederation offered for Canada's future: "Never was there a finer field than the New Dominion for the Pulpit, the Press and the Schoolmaster." The sequence in which the *Witness* listed religion, journalism, and education—those three pillars of a new nationalism—reflected the two-fold vocation of the paper's editor, the Rev. Robert Murray. More importantly, however, it was a Victorian conviction that, despite the manipulations by politicians, the confederation of the British North American colonies was essentially another mighty work of

God, and one that carried both a challenge and a heaven-given mandate to citizens of the new nation to create a Christian Canada.

Six months later, the same editor welcomed the New Year by explaining the new Canadian state and nationality in terms of the "glorious future which Providence seems to mark out for us."[1] Like church union in 1925, Confederation was widely greeted with the crusaders' battle-cry, "Deus vult!" For Maritimers the ideal of national unity presented by confederation stood in stark contrast to, but not in conflict with, the provincialism that had characterized the previous century. As for Presbyterianism in the Maritimes, its history during that earlier period had been marked by factional and denominational conflict that has been often and voluminously recorded.

Retrospectively, Nova Scotia's George Monro Grant blamed Scottish immigrants who brought old world divisions that "so blinded them to the perspective of truth that they were led to divide on petty issues . . . which had no meaning in Canada." Because of this, Grant wrote, "Presbyterianism in Canada was for some decades distracted and weakened."[2] These Maritime traditions of religious separateness are not, of course, a monopoly of the Presbyterian persuasion, but Presbyterian particularism in these provinces did enrich Canadian religious history with amusing but revealing anecdotes. Let it suffice to recall once more that sainted Anti-Burgher, James McGregor, who managed to avoid contact or co-operation with Burghers for almost a quarter-century after his arrival in Pictou.

Despite those rivalries which divided Burgher, Anti-Burgher, Kirk and Free Church for three generations, Maritime Presbyterians remained more faithful to Calvinistic principles than the Presbyterians of central Canada who began to slide into Arminianism around the middle of the

Victorian era. This development—the so-called theological revolution that broadened the focus of salvation from the individualistic to the communal—has not yet been examined in depth by Canadian historians. The conservative Calvinism of another Pictonian expatriate academic, Sir William Dawson, may be representative of the slower progress of that revolution in the Maritimes, but perhaps the rigidity of Dawson's personal theology only reflects the time gap between his generation and Grant's, even though their careers are parallel in so many other respects.

In the half-century that lay between the creations of the Synod of Nova Scotia in 1817 and the Canadian confederation in 1867, the process of Presbyterian indigenization in the Maritimes advanced despite interference by the Glasgow Colonial Society in the 1820s and by the Free Church Disruption of 1843. Addressing the Synod of the Maritime Provinces in the 1870s, a delegate from the Church of Scotland Synod offered high praise for the work of both the Free and Secession, two rivals that the Kirk had thoroughly despised short years before.[3]

Perhaps the achievement of responsible government by the Maritime provinces had brought a sense of self-assurance and an awareness of broader horizons, for even Joseph Howe, that supposedly unregenerate anti-Confederationist, had announced in 1864, "I am not one of those who thank God I am a Nova Scotian merely, for I am a Canadian as well."[4] To the Nova Scotian, comments T.C. Haliburton in *The Old Judge,* "the province is his native place, but North America is his country."[5] The attitude of Murray's friend Grant towards the Confederation movement was simple—"the sooner the better." Grant was a centralist, and he publicly opposed provincial rights.

As John Webster Grant has shown, the political unification of the colonies in 1867 was not only "the crucial moment" in the complex process of the emergence of Canada as a nation, but also a decisive factor in promoting denominational church unions to provide the necessary bureaucratic structures to meet the challenges of transcontinental territoriality.[6] A united Presbyterian Church for Canada had already been suggested before Confederation,[7] but the momentum towards union gained speed and urgency after 1867. The last hurdle in the race to territorialize Presbyterianism in the new Dominion was o'er leapt by the Presbyterian union of 1875.

The Maritime and central Canadian Presbyterian unions of the Secession and Free Churches in 1860 and 1861 had already fused two dynamic groups possessing a zealous interest in missions and in moral reform. These two theological components dominated the negotiations leading to union in 1875, and they would continue to dominate and shape the character of post-1875 Presbyterianism. The Church of Scotland, always an anomaly in the colonies and dependent on its mother church for personnel and financial support, had marked time while British North American Presbyterianism advanced rapidly in the generation before Confederation. To the union of 1875 the Kirk in the Maritimes brought thirty-five ministers, but the Synod of Nova Scotia contributed 131 ministers and six overseas missionaries, four times as many clergy as the Kirk, and in fact an even higher ratio than was the case between the two comparable bodies in the central Canadian provinces.

This union of trans-Canadian Presbyterianism was the logical corollary and religious equivalent of Confederation, and like the political confederation the event was as much a conclusion as it was a starting point in history. By the 1870s a new generation of Maritime Presbyterians had already arisen, prepared to make its particular contribution to national development. As a group, it was a clerisy—an educational (in the broadest sense) family compact—and one of the most important exports of the Maritime provinces to the rest of Canada. This was a generation that cared much less for imported Scottish divisions and quarrels of the past. For most Presbyterians Scotland continued to be the romantic subject of atavistic nostalgia, but it was a land that was not their home.

Those young Presbyterian Victorians in the Maritimes now focused their primary attention on Canada. They were ready, even anxious, to meet the challenges and capitalize on the possibilities presented by the prospect of a united and national Presbyterian Church. Their new and transcontinental church would be God's instrument to build a righteous and exalted nation. When that union of Canadian Presbyterianism was consummated in June 1875, Murray's *Presbyterian Witness* said fervently, "Thank God for it."[8] The "deep wounds made in the old fights" had too long delayed union, and if Maritime Presbyterians were not yet fully brethren, at least they were now "allies" who could march forward side by side into the promised land. Canadian Presbyterian union had ended the historic Scottish connection, noted the editor, and now, he said, "[t]here is glorious work to be done for our master in Canada."

This new generation shared more than their Maritime birthplace and their common faith in the superiority and covenanted responsibility of Presbyterianism. Products of a wealthy rural society, they shared the rich heritage of Maritime culture. They had attended the same schools and colleges, and upon graduation as many as possible made their pilgrimage to the holy land of North Britain and its universities. Summer breaks were occupied with the grand tour of those sister seats of learning in Germany. There, courses by famous and progressive scholars were attended, and other aspects of German culture were avidly absorbed at beer garden parties and hiking trips through mountain scenery.

For the youthful Canadians these shared experiences in Britain and on the continent established a fraternal bond, but many of these future Presbyterian ministers also encountered culture shock of a more drastic kind. The undersides of Europe's industrial cities were big, crowded, dirty, unhealthy and immoral. The contrast between those dark, satanic cities and the open spaces, invigorating, salubrious air, and stable, comfortable life of rural Maritimia created an indelible *crise de conscience* among the young Canadian pilgrims. The fourteen-year-old Daniel Miner Gordon reported to his family back in Pictou, "I had no idea what a stir there was in one of these large cities before; . . . thousands pass you whom you do not know." Visiting Barony Church, the young man found it crowded "as if by people just out of the workshops." Even the pleasure of ice-skating was less than at Pictou, because of the crowds.[9]

In the four decades between that 1875 union and the onset of World War I, these younger Maritime Presbyterians made a decisive contribution to the pulpits, press and classrooms of Canada. During these two generations the Maritime provinces exported their most important resource, namely, leadership in the form of their talented offspring who carried with them a moral idealism that they popularized through public life, the classroom, literature and music. Theirs was a crusade that reinforced those same concerns for mission and reform held by their brother clergymen in the central provinces, but their obvious self-dedication to the crusade for a Christian Canada earned those Maritimers recognition as the "moral tutors to the nation."[10] A quarter-century after the Presbyterian union, George Grant declared, "There has been a marked improvement in the Presbyterian Church all along the line since 1875. The union is telling powerfully on Christian life and thought. . . . The Presbyterian Church in Canada . . . is assuming something of the attitude of a national Protestant Church."[11]

Grant also alluded to those "attempts to suppress legitimate differences of opinion" which had involved him in the defence of his friend and fellow Kirkman, Daniel James Macdonnell, against the charges of heresy brought in 1877 and 1878 by the ultra-orthodox inquisitors in the Free Church wing of the new denomination. Soon after Grant became principal of Queen's University, the same former Free Churchmen who had attacked Macdonnell as the embodiment of Kirk moderation proposed to strip Queen's of its faculty of theology. This brought the comment from a New Brunswick friend that the trouble makers were "Would-be Popes." The same correspondent suggested five months later that, "it may take Centuries or Milleniums [sic] to get [rid of] Calvinism and replace it with Genuine Christianity."[12]

It was Grant's Canadianism, however, not his institutional churchmanship, that marked him out as the most influential and vocal of those Maritime Presbyterians who held a national rather than an Ontario vision of Canada's destiny. Like their central Canadian counterparts, Maritime Presbyterians were concerned with the nation's relationship to the British empire and to the United States, with the demographic and economic development of their young nation, and with the myriad issues that were later grouped under the umbrella term, Social Gospel. Differences that can be seen between the two regional groups involved relations with the Roman Catholic Church and with their giant neighbour to the south.

In the case of relations with the Roman Catholic Church, for example, Grant's eulogy of the late Archbishop Thomas Connolly in 1876 contrasted the religious peace of Halifax with the "dismal strife" in other cities, such as Toronto, thereby implying that central Canada needed more of the spirit of the Maritimes.[13] He disagreed with the violent anti-Vaticanism of central Canadian Presbyterians on the issues of the Manitoba schools and the Jesuits' estates, and in the latter case he refused to support the Equal Rights Association in which many of the Presbyterian clergy from Quebec and Ontario were leaders.

There was also apparently less fear and animosity towards the United States in the Maritimes than in central Canada. Perhaps this was because of the bloodier experience of colonial residents in the two Canadas at the hands of American invaders, a fact that explains much of the strident and exclusivist loyalism of the post-1812 era in those provinces. As a Maritimer, however, Grant's pole stars of action were always pragmatism and the potential of Canada. It was for this reason that he opposed discriminatory legislation against Chinese immigration on the grounds that "Our mission is to Christianize the world." "We have to reclaim half a continent, and throw the doors wide open that millions may enter."[14]

Thanks to a trip to the Canadian West in 1872 as secretary to Sir Sandford Fleming's railway survey party, Grant also developed a genuine interest in the development of that vast region. A transcontinental railway would, he was convinced, bind Canada into a nation, and that cross-Canada journey also gave him a greater appreciation of both the potential and problems of the West than most federal politicians, including his friend and admirer Sir John A. Macdonald, ever exhibited.

In the autumn of 1883 Grant delivered a sermon at Old St. Andrew's church in Toronto on "Patriotism" as inculcated by the Bible. The *Globe* reported that the sermon was "much admired," and it offered readers a synopsis of Grant's philosophy of nationalism. "Are we Canadians alone to be lacking in patriotism?" demanded Grant. "If so, it is not because we have not a country to be proud of." Genuine Canadian patriots were to be found in every region of British North America from Newfoundland to the Pacific coast. "In every portion of the Dominion there are ties binding the children to their native soil. What should be our aim? To make it thoroughly Christian, and be it remembered that no country can exist which has not the cohesion of faith, and that there is no faith worth having except that in Christ. . . . The Church of the future will be apostolical, historical, and National."

Underpinning Grant's nationalism lay the Maritime tradition of political and religious stability, reinforced by the Kirk's theological moderatism. Canada's mission was "to make the world the home of freedom, of justice and of peace," and the instrument to achieve this goal was, by the mandate of heaven, the British empire, "the highest secular instrument the world had ever known."[15] Grant was an enthusiastic Canadian and an enthusiastic imperialist for whom these were complementary, not conflicting loyalties. Dual loyalty, in his own words, constituted "the half-way house of the empire."[16] Imperial co-operation, rather than imperial federation or even independence, was a necessity for the exercise of stewardship over God's gifts because faith, noblesse, and richesse required it on principle. The motto of a Christian Canada was axiomatic—social justice exalts a nation.

Typical of his generation of Maritime Presbyterians, Grant was liberalizing—but not in the theological sense. At the 1880 meeting of the Pan-Presbyterian Alliance he protested against the exclusion of those churches whose declaration of faith did *not* include double predestination. The Westminster Confession was not to be taken as final and unalterable, because Christ is more important than the Church. At that same meeting Grant publicly espoused the theory of evolution and called for "a wider scholarship and a more fearless thought" on doctrinal matters.[17] Twelve years later, when the Alliance gathered in Toronto, Grant repeated on an international platform that same concern about the injustices of the wage system he had been expressing to Canadians for a generation.

As an outspoken Social Gospeller, Grant attacked the existing social order as unjust to the working class whose need for freedom of contract and freedom to organize justified the existence of trade unions and strikes. Profit sharing, fair wages and decent housing were Grant's answer to the "wage question," and looking straight at certain American ministers who preferred the "righteousness" of free enterprise, he warned them that an irrelevant church is a dead church.[18] This was a message he had often given to the merchants in his Halifax congregation a generation earlier, and one that he also delivered to his own church's General Assembly in his moderatorial sermon in that same year at Toronto.

Grant's awareness, appreciation and hope for national development had been fully awakened by that 1872 trip with Fleming, and he encapsulated his feelings the following year in his book *Ocean to Ocean,* a phrase later used by the *Maritime Presbyterian* in 1875 to describe the purpose of the union of Canadian Presbyterianism. The very first page of the book verbalizes Grant's personal dream regarding Canada's future as "the Greater Britain," and the book closes with expressions of loyalty to Canada's "distinctive mission" and gratitude to the Creator: "Thank God, we have a country."[19] The success of *Ocean to Ocean* rapidly brought Grant more opportunities to praise and popularize Canada in print. In 1879 *Scribner's Monthly* accepted his proposal to write a series of articles on Canada, to be illustrated by Notman and Sandham Company of Montreal. The publishers were so pleased with the first three articles that the series was expanded to more but shorter articles, because the illustrations of Canada were taking up so much space.

One year later Grant was approached by the Chicago publisher, H.R. Belden, with an invitation to edit a new popular illustrated periodical called "Picturesque Canada." Grant was given full control of the project and could write as much of the text as he wished, but it was to Robert Murray that he entrusted the articles on the Maritime provinces. The success of *Picturesque Canada* is today a matter of Canadian literary and artistic history. Less known than that periodical was one of Grant's last literary excursions—his overview chapter on the religious history of Canada in the two-volume study, *Christendom Anno Domini [1901]*, produced by another Canadian, W.D. Grant.

Seven years after the publication of *Ocean to Ocean*, Daniel Miner Gordon, former classmate of D.J. Macdonnell and Grant's friend and successor as principal of Queen's, became Fleming's secretary on a similar trip that changed the course of his life too. Gordon, like Grant, was native of Pictou, a graduate of Pictou Academy, a student at Glasgow University, a travelling companion of Macdonnell in Europe, a prominent actor in the 1875 union movement, and a moderator of General Assembly. "Like Grant," adds his biographer-daughter, "he had the vision of a greater Canada and an abiding faith in the beneficent influence of the British Empire."[20] He too wrote an account of his transcontinental voyage. *Mountain and Prairie,* published in 1880, is a sequel for *Ocean to Ocean*, avowedly intended to excite and enlighten Canadians about "the great Northwest."

Mountain and Prairie calls on the Presbyterian Church to extend its home missions beyond Manitoba, so it was no coincidence that James Robertson was appointed superintendent of western Canadian Presbyterian missions in 1881, the year following the appearance of *Mountain and Prairie*. For Gordon, "The call of the West . . . [was] the uncompromising voice of duty."[21] In 1882 he moved to Winnipeg, and three years later was serving as a front-line chaplain during Riel's second rebellion. In that tragic episode, Gordon's sympathy lay entirely with the Indians misled by Riel. That rebellion, Gordon hoped, would awaken the Christian churches to their duty to native North Americans.

The Maritime vision of a greater Canada assumed a more institutional form when the Round Table group was formed in 1894 by some members of the Synod of New Glasgow. The club included George Monro Grant, Robert Falconer, Walter Murray, Clarence Mackinnon—all Maritimers—plus Trinidad-born but Maritime-rooted Arthur Silver Morton, later professor of church history at Pine Hill and Knox Colleges, and finally Alfred Gandier, Maritimer by adoption because he served a Halifax church and had married Falconer's sister. Their meetings, three or four per year, were supposedly more social than intellectual affairs, but most members already shared numerous characteristics including postgraduate education in Scotland and Germany, university teaching experience and, in the case of Grant, Falconer, and Murray, university or college appointments which the other three received in later years.

These modern knights of the Round Table also shared Grant's liberal view of theology. Mackinnon, for whom evangelism was a social crusade, espoused evolution and higher criticism, and his orthodoxy was further suspect because of an article he published in The Presbyterian College's journal, *The Theologue*, in 1899. Robert Falconer and his brother James, whose father was a friend of Grant, had studied at Edinburgh with Mackinnon. Robert was also Daniel Gordon's colleague and next-door neighbour for seven years at the Presbyterian College, Halifax, where Falconer displayed that same dedication to duty that carried first Grant and then Gordon to Queen's.

Falconer's sense of national mission was intensified when his subsequent appointment as president of the University of Toronto provided him with a public platform far larger than

Halifax could offer.²² Like his fellow-Maritimer James Frederick McCurdy, founder of biblical studies at the University of Toronto, he was both a nationalist and internationalist—"a citizen of a larger world" for whom that citizenship itself carried a Christian obligation. Falconer was the vocal opponent of every social evil and the founder of a settlement house where student volunteers could fulfil their moral obligations. His planned programme of Canadian Studies at Toronto constituted for him, to use his own words, "a national service."

The founding of *The Theologue* in 1889 had already provided Maritime Presbyterian leaders an opportune sounding board from which to promote their vision of Canada's future. During the next quarter-century that periodical carried articles by Daniel Gordon, Walter C. Murray, Alfred Gandier, A.S. Morton, Clarence Mackinnon, and Robert Falconer, who had been instrumental during his student days in founding the journal. All of them held teaching positions in the College at some time, but with few exceptions all surprisingly confined their contributions in *The Theologue* to matters of ministerial training and the ministerial life, seldom venturing into the politico-theological sphere.

A new feature in *The Theologue* in 1902 was an anonymous occasional column entitled "The Round Table," but the writer limited himself to comments on the goings and comings of faculty members and church leaders. An unsigned 1906 article entitled "Our Forests" (environmental issues were a popular theme in Murray's *Presbyterian Witness)* turns out to be a plea for a mission to lumberjacks. Over the years Falconer contributed numerous book reviews which display his liberal theological leanings, and his theologically progressive colleague John Currie provided an encomium for Ritschlism.²³ By the end of the century, however, *The Theologue* was becoming excited about the church union movement. As early as 1899 Gandier defended denominationalism against organic union. He based his argument on the proposition that "nature abhors uniformity,"[24] words he may have regretted when he led the staff and most of the students of Knox College across the Toronto campus to the United Church's new Emmanuel College after church union in 1925. Brother-in-law Falconer later suggested in *The Theologue* that, as a "new people," Canadians needed a "national Evangelical church" to meet the challenge of the peopling of the West.[25]

Another proponent of a broader Canadian nationalism was Robert Murray, poet laureate of the new national vision but never a member of the Round Table. Born in Earltown in 1832, he moved to Halifax in the early 1850s to study theology at the Free Church College, but while still a student was made editor of the *Presbyterian Witness* in 1856. He occupied that post until his death in 1910, and during those years made the *Witness* into the Maritime voice of the new national vision. His theologically-based editorials supported the gamut of Canadian concerns—home missions for Canada's West, temperance, sabbatarianism, conservation of resources, prison reform and votes for women. Murray had high praise for Grant's brand of patriotism embracing loyalty to both Canada and Britain, and for Gordon's demand that the nation's schools inculcate patriotism in the heart. His insistence that Canada welcome "the homeless of every nation under Heaven" is, however, circumscribed by his explanation that the exclusion of Asians was neither Christian nor wise because Asians were needed for "servile purposes" to free Canadians "for duties that may require loftier minds and better education."[26]

Today Murray is remembered primarily as a writer of hymns, including an additional verse for "God save the Queen." That verse reads, "Our loved Dominion bless/ With peace and happiness/ from shore to shore;/ And let our Empire be/ United, loyal, free,/ True to herself and Thee/ for evermore." His addition can be found in the United Church-Anglican 1971 *Hymn Book,* but inexplicably it was omitted from the 1972 Presbyterian Church's *Book of Praise.* Both hymnals include Murray's better-known composition, "From Ocean unto Ocean," inspired by his own train trip across Canada, a hymn that blends nationalism and covenant theology in such phrases as "Our land shall own thee Lord" and "Thyself in us reveal." Again, however, the *Book of Praise* inexplicably omits the third verse which combines evangelization and multiculturalism in the lines, "Till all the tribes and races/ that dwell in this fair land,/ adorned with Christian graces/ within thy courts shall stand."

In the last decade of Queen Victoria's imperial rule, Grant's espousal of symbiotic imperial and national loyalties brought him front and centre on the Canadian public stage. He could not remain silent after 1891 when Goldwin Smith propounded his Darwinian continentalist heresy, predicting the inevitability of Canada's annexation by the United States in his volume *Canada and the Canadian Question.* Before the publication of Smith's book, however, one small incident offers a foretaste of the clash of personalities between the two men. In a letter to Grant late in 1879, D.J. Macdonnell discussed the possibility of Smith becoming chancellor of Queen's University. In two pages of minuscule scribbled queries, Smith had commented adversely about the university, calling it "a completely relig.[ious] College." Macdonnell warned Grant against such an appointment, concluding, "After all, perhaps, it is as well to have some one else, for you are not always sure where you will find Goldwin Smith."[27]

Donald Creighton has described Grant's writings as "the most effective rejoinder" made to the continentalism of Goldwin Smith,[28] and Frank Underhill, who once called

Smith's *Canada and the Canadian Question* "the most pessimistic book that has ever been written about Canada," characterized Grant's response as "temperamental as much as intellectual."[29] After Grant's death a friend recounted an incident in Kingston when a person, unnamed but certainly resembling Smith, made a fervent pro-annexation speech. At the end of that oration Grant rose and made a short and scornful rebuttal. "Can there be [any defence] for the man who would prostitute the honor of his country for gain?" he demanded. Immediately the whole audience rose spontaneously and sang the national anthem.[30] Smith, nevertheless, had the last if feeble word in his controversy with Grant about the nation's destiny under God. When Grant published a highly critical article about Smith in *The National Review*, Smith told Grant it constituted "a portrait of a man drawn by an evidently unfriendly hand." "I am content to share with the University of Oxford the burden of your reprobation and contempt. We go henceforth different ways."[31]

It is debatable whether Smith and Grant had ever travelled in the same direction when discussing Canadian identity and freedom. Grant's sudden death in 1904 produced a wave of appreciative eulogies for this Nova Scotian who had been the adviser of prime ministers and politicians—Mowat, Tupper, Bowell, D'Alton McCarthy and Laurier—and the confidant of lords Lorne, Stanley, Devonshire, and Aberdeen. It was Aberdeen who embraced Grant's concept of imperial co-operation and Canadian nationalism by supporting Canada's claims against the American "bully" in the Alaska Boundary dispute.

Among the tributes to Grant, Kingston's Board of Trade remembered him as "a Kingstonian, a Canadian, and an Imperialist," and as "the man who might himself have well claimed the motto, 'Canada First'."[32] The Synod of Toronto and Kingston hailed the late Principal as an advocate of Confederation and Presbyterian union whose greatest monument was "the men who received from him their mental and spiritual enfranchisement . . . and who will seek to perpetuate what was best in his work for Church and Country." "His pen and voice have helped to break down racial, political, and religious walls of partition which divide men who should dwell together in unity," said the Toronto Presbyterian Association.[33]

Such high praise was fully deserved by Grant, but his passing was certainly a major event in the westward dissemination of that Maritime vision of Canada because it initiated a series of academic promotions with lasting consequences of national and denominational importance. At Queen's Grant was replaced by D.M. Gordon, and Gordon's place at The Presbyterian College, Halifax, was now filled by Robert Falconer. Five years later Falconer became president of the University of Toronto and Clarence Mackinnon replaced him as principal in Halifax, while in 1914 A.S. Morton moved from Knox College to the new University of Saskatchewan. The network of Maritime Presbyterian influence—a clerisy of nationalist educators—reached new frontiers just before Canada was plunged into the Armageddon of World War I.

Perhaps the last word on the contribution of Maritimers to a new vision of Canada can be left to that remarkable apostle of Canadian nationalism, the late Frank Underhill. "It has struck me," he wrote, "how often the best exponents of the imperial idea in Canada have come from the Maritime provinces: men such as Grant and Parkin among intellectuals; such as Howe, Tupper, Foster, Beaverbrook among the men of affairs."[34] That clerisy of Presbyterians who articulated, expounded and defended the concept of undivided and indivisible loyalties to province, to Canada and to Empire during the half-century preceding World War I, had first announced their vision of Canada in those Atlantic provinces previously racked by sectarian rivalry. Then, through the public forum, the press, the pulpit and the classroom, they carried their message westward to the rest of Canada. The full extent of their influence in the process of nation-building has yet to be thoroughly examined and to be acknowledged by their intellectual heirs.

12. Loyalties in Conflict
Scottish and American Influences on Canadian Presbyterianism

In the 1970s, Old Dominion University at Norfolk, Virginia held a centre for Scottish studies. An annual conference each spring saw John Moir in attendance and in 1977 he spoke at the conference banquet. He delivered a very popular paper on "Scottish Influences on Canadian Presbyterianism" later printed in the conference's journal. In 1984, Moir was invited to address the annual joint meeting of the local Canadian and American presbyteries of the two national Presbyterian bodies meeting in Ogdensburg, New York. He gave an overview of the relations between Presbyterianism in the two countries, hoping to exemplify both differences and similarities and to explain their origins. Observing the two presbyteries in operation separately was a learning experience, because the observable differences were obviously both wider and more subtle than he had realized when preparing the address. His later printed paper, "Loyalties in Conflict: The Historic Relations between Canadian and American Presbyterians" drew upon the same sources and came to the same conclusions as "Scottish Influences." They have been brought together into this new overview for this collection.

NEITHER AMERICANS NOR CANADIANS ARE strangers to the challenge of loyalties in conflict, whether those loyalties are political, economic, social or religious. Both know the conflicting loyalties of regionalism *versus* nationalism, and Canadians have faced and reconciled quite readily the apparent but largely unreal conflict of loyalty between Canadianism and membership in the British Empire and the British Commonwealth of Nations. Some Canadians and some Americans do share a loyalty to Presbyterianism, but because of historical developments they have shared little else. The explanation for this lack of close ties between Canadian and American Presbyterians can be found in the way that divided loyalties have shaped the Canadian outlook in general and, in particular, in how Canadian Presbyterians have tried to cope with their own peculiar identity crisis, which is bound up with loyalty to Scotland.

Among the clergy of the Christian denominations in Canada, sons, and more recently daughters, of Scotland have played a very prominent part. The English-speaking Roman Catholic Church, particularly in the Maritime provinces, can justly boast of many famous Scottish priests and bishops. The Anglican (Episcopal) Church of Canada, which has had close connections with the Episcopal Church in Scotland, has also received some Scottish clergy but proportionally more Scottish bishops, including the multi-talented John Strachan, first Anglican bishop of Toronto, and Charles James Stewart, cadet of the house of Argyle and second bishop of Quebec. The Canadian Baptist communion still displays a strong Scottish influence, and among the numerous small religious groups in Canada there still exist a few Cameronian congregations in the Ottawa Valley. Scottish influences on Canadian Presbyterianism is a subject so vast in extent that this can be no more than an overview, particularly with reference to the more subtle and psychological aspects such as folk religion.

"We are too Scotch—our habits, our brogue, our mode of sermonizing are all too Scotch. The thistle is everywhere seen . . . our mission is a foreign affair."[1] The speaker was William Proudfoot, Secessionist minister at London, Ontario, and the date was 1846. "[Our Church] prides herself on continuing a Presbyterian tradition that looks to Scotland as the Mother Country. See how often we call ourselves 'the Kirk' and talk of the Kirk Session and exalt St. Andrew and Robert Burns. All this adds up to a specific style, a type symbolized beautifully by the old-fashioned Scottish lace which our Assembly Moderators wear at throat and cuffs."[2] This speaker too is a Canadian Presbyterian minister, but he made these comments on the Scottishness of Canadian Presbyterianism in 1965—one hundred and twenty years after Proudfoot's similar complaint. The fact is that Canadian Presbyterianism began as an ethnic church and continues so to a noticeable degree even today. According to the 1971 decennial census of Canada, the Presbyterian Church was the most British in composition of any major denomination,[3] and for this fact Americans deserve a fair measure of the credit, or blame.

The earliest Scottish Presbyterians to settle permanently in Canada were disbanded soldiers from Fraser's Highlanders who fought for Wolfe at Louisbourg in 1758 and at Quebec in 1759. Robert McPherson, battalion chaplain to the Frasers, held the first recorded Presbyterian service in present-day Canada amid the ruins of Louisbourg and he held services at Quebec for men of the 78th and of the other Highlanders—the 42nd or Murray's Regiment, more popularly known as the Black Watch. Soldiers from these two units stayed in Quebec after the Peace in 1763, and in 1765 they formed there the nucleus of the First Presbyterian congregation under another chaplain, George Henry.[4] Other Presbyterians arrived in group migrations in Nova Scotia and Prince Edward Island, and those at Quebec were joined by American Presbyterians of Scottish and Scots-Irish background who entered the lucrative fur trade after the British Conquest. In Nova Scotia Presbyterianism came from Ireland and the Thirteen Colonies as well as from Scotland, but the majority of the clergy that they imported came from Scotland and brought with them the ecclesiastic divisions of home. Not only was the Kirk represented, but also the Burgher and Anti-Burgher wings of the Secession movement, an early evidence of the exportation of a Covenanter tradition to British North America.

For the long range development of Presbyterianism in Canada, the American Revolution was a watershed, just as it was for the history of Canada in so far as the Revolution stamped both church and nation with a strong strain of anti-Americanism as part of the general counter-revolutionary heritage. In reaction against the Revolution, Canadians espoused loyalism—a loyalty to and veneration of all things British—and for Canadian Presbyterianism this meant a total repudiation of any connection with or influence from American Presbyterianism. Had not the Revolution in fact been called a Presbyterian revolution by the Loyalists? Canadian Presbyterianism for the next century had no alternative but to identify with Scotland, with loyalty and with respectability, which of course was the Loyalists' antidote to all 'democratical tendencies,' as American habits were called. Like those earlier children of the covenant, the Israelites, these later exiles also thought of themselves as God's chosen people, leaving their Egypt—the rebellious American colonies—to seek the promised land where they could enjoy their British birthright.

Among the Loyalist refugees from the Revolution were some Presbyterians—their numbers can only be guessed at. The Revolution also brought the first Presbyterian minister to the Scottish fur traders of Montreal in the person of John Bethune, chaplain to the Royal Highland Emigrant 84th Regiment.[5] In the three decades between the Revolution and the War of 1812 more Presbyterians arrived in Canada from Britain, but few heard the call to serve under the hard and unrewarding conditions of the British North American frontier. Those ministers who did come, at the request of settlers rather than as part of any church outreach from home, were Scottish or Irish, although both were necessarily educated in Scotland. Of 336 ministers connected with the Church of Scotland in the old provinces of Canada before 1865, 228 or 68% were Scots, 41 or 12% were Irish, and 42, that is another 12%, were born in Canada. Only 2 men, half of 1%, can be identified as American, leaving 7% unidentified according to national origin.[6]

The War of 1812 was the next testing time for Canadian loyalism. That second invasion confirmed and magnified existing anti-Americanism. For Canadian Presbyterianism the war led to increased Scottishness despite two brief countervailing influences, namely an indigenous Canadianism and American Presbyterian mission work in the region of Niagara. To dispose of this last element first, it will be sufficient to note that these American missionaries created a short-lived presbytery that died soon after the abortive Rebellion of 1837 because the presbytery was too revivalist, too temperance-oriented, and especially too American in its connections.[7]

As for the other influence, Canadianism, both in Upper and Lower Canada (now Ontario and Quebec) and in Nova Scotia, indigenous presbyteries were at last created by 1820, only to face almost instant competition from Scotland. After turning a deaf ear for decades to the settlers' request for spiritual support, the Church of Scotland, so long dominated by the Moderate party, responded indirectly in 1825 when its evangelical wing established the Glasgow Colonial Society to provide clergymen for the colonies. What at first appeared to be a generous gesture of trans-Atlantic Scottish solidarity soon proved to be the very opposite. The Society's missionaries claimed to represent the only true, loyal and respectable

Presbyterian church and wherever they went congregations were split by these assertions of Church of Scotland superiority. Local clergymen tried to compromise with the newcomers, only to be told that the price of co-operation must be their total submission to the dictates of the Church of Scotland.[8]

One might expect that such presumptuous claims would be rejected by the colonists, but that expectation would be historically wrong. After all, the Church of Scotland was the national church, the orthodox church, the respectable church, the loyal church of North Britain. All other Presbyterians therefore must be schismatic, inferior and perhaps even democratic. Reinforcing the Church of Scotland's prestigious position was the more convincing argument that, as one of the two established churches of Britain, the Kirk could expect by right to receive financial support from the state.[9] In the Maritime colonies that support had been forthcoming spasmodically in the form of small land grants, donations towards church construction, and salary supplements for some Church of Scotland clergy. In the two Canadas the loaves and fishes took the form of the Clergy Reserves, three million acres (eighty percent of them in Upper Canada) of prime agricultural land to be sold or rented for the benefit of the Protestant clergy.[10] The Church of England had already been recognized as the only state Protestant Church in 1791,[11] but the Church of Scotland insisted on its right to equal status—and equal endowment—with its sister establishment. Had not Scottish soldiers, as much as English, assured the Conquest of Canada in 1759 and its preservation from the Americans in 1776 and again in 1812?[12] The opportunity of sharing in those Clergy Reserves caused the Church of Scotland to organize a Canadian synod in 1831, and similarly caused the local indigenous Synod to accept union on the Kirk's terms in 1840.[13] Scottish influences were again predominant in the founding of that still ever-so-Scottish university, Queen's, at Kingston, along the lines of a totally Scottish model, including imported Scottish professors.[14]

By 1840 Scottishness was on the advance in Canadian Presbyterianism in terms of education, clergy personnel, theological and liturgical influences, co-establishment with the Church of England (which in 1840 had been forced to share the Clergy Reserves),[15] and dependence, almost subservience, to the mother church in Scotland. Then two developments occurred that changed the direction of Canadian Presbyterianism away from this particular Scottish orientation. The first factor was the modest growth of a Secession tradition church with a strong voluntarist doctrine and desire to identify with Canada.[16] The church was led, even created, by William Proudfoot whose complaint was against the hyper-Scottishness in the Kirk, namely, the importation into Canada of the Great Disruption which created the Free Church in 1843. The issues involved in the Great Disruption had nothing directly to do with the colonies in British America, but what was good enough for Scots at home was good enough for Scots abroad. Therefore the Church of Scotland in the colonies had to undergo a disruption in 1844 to please the most recently arrived wave of Scottish settlers.[17]

The new Free Church in Canada drew heavily on the Covenanter tradition, or at least on those parts of that tradition which suited its own purposes. Most obvious was that sense of divine selection, of moral superiority, and of doctrinal rigour, particularly adherence to the ideal of Christ as head over the nations. Although the Free Church was not opposed to church establishment, it did demand that a godly prince should never interfere with God's church, and that he must always heed the voice of the Church as the conscience of the state to ensure godly rule over a godly nation. The whole position stemmed of course from theocratic

Calvinism, which starts and ends with the supremacy of omnipotent God over every facet of human life. Like the Covenanters before them, the Free churchmen insisted that the state had its well defined if circumscribed position, and that it must be kept in that place.

In Canada, however, the Free Church Synod was not entitled to share in the Clergy Reserves and therefore, in the name of 'Christian expediency', that Synod decided that the Clergy Reserves should be nationalized.[18] In one decade of furious politicking this new and expedient church led the true voluntarists to total victory; in 1854 the Reserves were secularized and thus the only substantial historical evidence of religious establishment disappeared from Canada.[19] From its inception the Free Church grew rapidly in numbers in its slow shift of emphasis from Scottishness to Canadianness until it far outstripped both the residual Church of Scotland and the Secessionist body of Presbyterians.

From the moment of the Disruption in 1844, union negotiations between the Secessionist church and the Free Church were opened, but all talks foundered on the Free Church's insistence on its own interpretation of one doctrine, namely a necessary belief in Christ's headship over the nations as opposed to the Secessionist faith in the separation of church and state. At last in 1860 and 1861 two regional unions of the two churches for the Maritimes and for the Province of Canada were achieved by a typically Canadian compromise. Everyone was left free to define church-state relations as their conscience dictated. This was called "forbearance"—in present-day parlance it might be termed a 'cop-out'. In either case it created a dilemma from which the Presbyterians were forced to extricate themselves a full century later.

Forbearance was again the accepted principle in 1875 when all Canadian Presbyterians were united in a single church which soon became the largest Protestant denomination in Canada. This refusal or failure to reach any consensus on the old Scottish issues of church-state relations was at last brought home to roost in Canada by Adolf Hitler. In 1942 a Canadian Presbyterian minister issued a pamphlet entitled *King of Kings* in which he pointed out quite correctly that the principle of forbearance made it impossible for the Presbyterian Church in Canada to denounce authoritatively the abomination of Nazism.[20] Faced with this unpleasant consequence of an ancient compromise, the Church redefined its faith during the 1950s and '60s in such a way that its creed has now returned precisely to the Free Church's position—Christ is head over the nations, and the civil magistrate is therefore subject to ecclesiastical direction.[21] This amounts in fact to a kind of spiritual ultramontanism if pushed to its logical conclusion, as Presbyterians are sometimes wont to do.

The domination of Canadian Presbyterianism, both in terms of numbers and attitudes, by the Free Church tradition and ethos cannot be denied, and the gradual Canadianization of the Church never meant a complete break with Scotland. Canadian Presbyterians, especially the clergy, still went to Scotland in considerable numbers for post-graduate training, and Scottish ideas and personalities still had a large influence on Canadian academic and religious life. One important feedback from this Scottish connection was the concern of Canadian Presbyterianism with the so-called "social question" that beset late Victorian industrial and urban society. Early in the nineteenth century the Presbyterian churches had taken up, in varying degrees, the causes of temperance and Sabbath observance. Now first-hand experience in the slums of Glasgow and Edinburgh sent young Canadians home to Canada with a fervent desire to prevent such horrors in their own country and through the expression of this search for social justice, Canadian Presbyterianism became a leading force in the Social Gospel movement.[22]

While the first interest in the Social Gospel did come from Scotland, it was the United States that was the major continuing inspiration in this area for Canadian Presbyterianism. Canadian Presbyterian leaders toured American cities and learned at first hand from persons such as Jane Adams and Graham Taylor about the American settlement movements, inner city missions, sociological surveys and other programmes to combat the de-humanizing effects of city and factory life. In the light of the earlier strong anti-American and pro-Scottish orientation of Canadian Presbyterianism some explanation is necessary for this change in outlook and relations. The answer lies in the American Civil War and the new Canadian view of its neighbours which that tragic conflict engendered.

Even after the Canadian fear of further American aggression and American-style democracy began to wane in the 1840s, Canadians still were consciously estranged from any and all neighbours who condoned slavery. Canadian Presbyterians and especially the Free Church type were foremost in supporting anti-slavery. In 1849 the Free Church had officially supported a settlement in western Ontario as a refuge for slaves escaping via the underground railway. The principal of Knox College was the first president of the Anti-Slavery Society of Canada, a society formed one year before *Uncle Tom's Cabin* was circulated in Canada.[23] In 1856 the Canadian Free Church made the holding of anti-slavery principles a prerequisite for membership in its ministry, and in 1859 it even refused to exchange fraternal delegates with the liberal American New School Presbyterian Church.[24] Canadian Presbyterians joined in a boycott of all American Presbyterian publications; all imported tracts, books, Sunday School lessons, etc. were purchased from Scotland. But emancipation changed all this—purged of their sin of contamination with slavery, Americans in general and American Presbyterians in particular were acceptable once more as fellow-Christians. An equally influential contact grew up in the post-bellum period through the medium of Princeton Theological College. Canadian students still went to Scotland, but more and more did theological studies under the Hodges and Warfield (and later under J. Gresham Machen) at Princeton.[25]

It was the Social Gospel movement that drew Canadian Presbyterians even closer to their American co-religionists, and the same was true for other Protestant denominations as well. Distressed by the destructive results of urbanization, industrialization and massive ethnic immigration, Canadians turned to the United States to learn from the American experience. For a few short decades North America seemed united in a shared concern for creating His Kingdom here and now and for spreading the Good News to the non-Christian world. In their search for the here-and-now Kingdom of God, Canadians visited and studied such social experiments as Hull House in Chicago, and Americans toured Canada consulting and advising on the challenges of the new age. A multitude of international organizations grew up, usually American-inspired but involving extensive Canadian participation. The YMCA, the Laymen's Missionary Movement, the WCTU, the Student Volunteer Movement, the Prophetic Bible conferences, the International Sunday School conventions, the Foreign Missions Conference of North America, the International Council of Religious Education—the list seems endless. For a moment in history North American evangelical Protestantism seemed to overcome its conflicting loyalties.

To this day Canadian Presbyterianism feels this double-pull—towards Scotland, the mother country, and towards the United States, the sister country—yet for the last half of the twentieth century, the pull of Scotland was much the stronger. American-Canadian rapprochement was disrupted by World War I and then destroyed by the consummation of organic church union in 1925. The Presbyterian Church in Canada had in 1902 entered into negotiations with the Methodist Church, and later the Congregationalists as well to form an organically united church. Unions within a common religious tradition were well-known in Canada but this union was breaking new ecclesiastical ground by bringing together three very different denominations and traditions. Behind this church union movement lay two integrally related ideas—the Social Gospel and the concept of a godly Christian nation.

At the turn of the twentieth century Canada's vast western region was filling with new Canadians—a thirty-three percent increase in the nation's population in ten years. In addition to the problems of urbanization and industrialization old Canadians were now faced with assimilating waves of new Canadians who brought differing cultures, languages and religions. What kind of Canada did Canadians want? A Canada that would be British and Christian? A United Protestant church was seen as a prime means of bringing about this kind of messianic nationalism.[26]

From the beginning of the church union movement to the consummation of union in 1925, a solid block of Presbyterians, approximately one third of the members of the church, opposed the idea of organic union. The opponents' relations with the United States became chilled because that country continued to support the ideas which influenced the church union movement so greatly. The opponents of church union had many reasons—theological, social, political—for taking the stand they did, but Scottishness seems to have been one specific cause of their opposition. As the moment of truth—the union—approached ever closer (it took twenty-three years because of Presbyterian problems), the resistance movement among Presbyterians became more openly ethnic, even to the point of expressing a crude racism.[27] Opinions were heard about the superiority of all things Scottish and of people raised on oatmeal. Canada was, they proudly announced, what Scots, loyal Scots, had made it, and the dissidents were determined to preserve those distinctive Scottish characteristics and distinctive loyalty. One Toronto minister, a recent arrival from Scotland, declared, "Those who come from good Anglo-Saxon stock" (presumably he meant to include Celtic stock too) could never forget their native land—to forget one's roots was "allright [sic] for those who come from Poland" but real Britishers would not and should not ever be fully Canadianized.

The day after church union became a fact (10 June 1925) the nonconcurring Presbyterians met in Toronto and signed a covenant to preserve Presbyterianism in Canada. This appeal to the Covenanter heritage was based on the nineteenth century Canadian Free Church custom of extolling the steadfastness and sacrifice of conventiclers, and especially the Wigtown martyrs, in the face of oppression and adversity. Etchings depicting an outdoor conventicle baptism were to be found in many Canadian Presbyterian homes, and the "killing times" provided seemingly endless material for Canadian Presbyterian magazines, newspapers and Sunday school materials. The signing of another covenant in 1925 was as natural to Canadian Presbyterianism as the Shorter Catechism.

In the wake of the union the continuing Presbyterians officially renamed their church sessions "kirk sessions." If such demonstrations of Scottishness were emotional, excessive and of questionable historicity in 1925, they were nonetheless representative of a segment of those Presbyterians who stayed out of the church union, and they were popularly accepted as typifying all continuing Presbyterians in Canada.

Part of this proclamation of Scottishness had a deliberate political purpose, namely, to attract public support to the dissident cause from outside Canada. In the case of Scotland it is questionable whether Scottish Presbyterians felt more sympathy for those Canadian brethren who stayed out of union or for those who went in. In the case of American Presbyterians there is much more certainty about their attitude towards the Canadian union. Generally Americans accepted the new United Church of Canada as the legitimate successor of the Presbyterian Church in Canada and ignored the claims of the continuing Presbyterians to be the only true Presbyterian Church.[28] Presbyterian relations with the United States became chilled.

In the decade after 1925 the Canadian Presbyterian Church waged an all-out legal and ultimately successful battle for the right to retain the name "Presbyterian Church in Canada" as proof of its continuity and legitimacy. Nevertheless the traumatic effects of 1925 are still evident in its garrison mentality and its distrust of any ecumenical effort that might jeopardize its identity. One Canadian church historian says the older Presbyterians still believe the union was "ecclesiastical rape." Unlike the United Church of Canada, the Presbyterian Church has failed in the public mind to make itself distinctively Canadian; like the Anglican (Episcopal) Church of Canada the Presbyterian Church is still eighty percent British stock.

This identity problem is compounded by some Canadians who transfer to the Presbyterian Church from other denominations on the debatable assumption that because it opposed organic union in 1925 it must now be "conservative" and anti-modernist. Often such persons gravitate into the Christian education department, where they soon discover that in fact the Canadian Presbyterian church is an unleavened (and perhaps unleavenable) lump; and after having disturbed the tranquillity of that congregation, these religious wayfarers move on to some other apparently greener pastures.

Since World War II there has been some rapprochement by Canadian Presbyterians with Americans, but it seems to be more on the personal than institutional level. Honorary degrees are awarded to American Presbyterians, American Presbyterians sometimes are visiting lecturers, and Canadian Presbyterian students do occasionally enrol in American colleges; but American Presbyterians seem also to relate more easily to the United Church of Canada because of its more vocal stand on social and international issues.

Canadians, who pride themselves on being better acquainted with the United States and American affairs than Americans are with Canada, remain woefully ignorant of the real nature of American Presbyterianism. Reaganomics and American involvement in the internal problems of the Near East and Central America were viewed with distrust by many Canadians who retain a subcutaneous suspicion of much that emanates from our southern neighbour, be it acid rain or brinkmanship. But Presbyterianism is another matter. Until Canadian Presbyterianism finds, adopts and feels comfortable with its own identity, it will be distracted by loyalties in conflict. That larger, catholic loyalty to Presbyterianism which it might share with its American neighbours is likely to remain rather low on the church's docket.

While the Presbyterian Church in Canada survived church union, it has not grown with Canada. Its membership remains numerically the same as in 1925, but as a proportion of the Canadian population it continues to fall. From eight percent after the union it had fallen to four percent in 1975 and two percent in 1991. Perhaps it is as part of a defence mechanism that the Presbyterian Church in Canada still exhibits marked affinities with Scotland and Scottish ways.

Scottish clergy are welcome in her pulpits and her colleges; Burns' nights, St. Andrew's banquets and Scottish country dancing find a happy home in Presbyterian congregations; Gaelic services and the kirking of the tartan are still occasionally held as part of the apparatus of nostalgia. In the March 1977 issue of the Church's official magazine, a feature article retold once again the story of the Wigtown martyrs,[29] and every visitor to Toronto's Knox College is greeted in the foyer by a semi-nude marble statue of the supposed martyr, Margaret Wilson. To paraphrase William Proudfoot, "Today we are still too Scotch, the thistle is nearly everywhere seen." The motto of Ontario reads "Ut incepit fidelis, sic permanet"—Loyal she began, loyal she remains. Since four of every ten Presbyterians in Canada now reside in the province of Ontario, it may be fair to suggest that the motto of the modern Presbyterian Church in Canada could equally well be, "Scottish she began, Scottish she remains."

Endnotes

NEC TAMEN CONSUMEBATUR

1. D.B. Quinn, ed., *New American World* (New York: Arno Press, 1979), IV, 299.
2. Quoted in Marcel Trudel, *The Beginnings of New France, 1524-1663* (Toronto: McClelland and Stewart, 1973), 56.
3. *Dictionary of Canadian Biography (DCB)* (Toronto: University of Toronto Press, 1966), I, 520.
4. Trudel, 60.
5. Quinn, IV, 311.
6. H.P. Biggar, ed., *The Works of Samuel de Champlain*, 6 vols. (Toronto: Champlain Society, 1922-36), III, 311.
7. *DCB*, I, 294.
8. Marc Lescarbot, *The History of New France*, trans. by W.L. Grant, 3 vols. (Toronto: Champlain Society, 1907-14), II, 232.
9. Gabriel Sagard-Theodat, *Histoire du Canada*, 4 vols. (Paris, 1866), I, 26.
10. R.G. Thwaites, ed., *The Jesuit Relations and Allied Documents*, 73 vols. (Cleveland, 1896-1901), I, 135.
11. Robert Le Bant and M. Delafosse, "Les Rochelais dans la Vallée du Saint-Laurent, 1599-1616," *Revue d'Histoire de l'Amerique Française*, X (1956-7): 333-63.
12. Champlain, *Works*, IV, 357.
13. *Ibid.*
14. Sagard, *op. cit.*, II, 92; Christian Le Clerq, *First Establishment of the Faith in New France*, trans. by J.G. Shea, 2 vols. (New York, 1881; reprint AMS Press, 1973), I, 111ff.
15. Champlain, *Works*, V, 15.
16. *DCB*, I, 433.
17. Robert Le Bant and René Baudry, eds., *Nouveaux Documents sur Champlain et son époque*, I, *1560-1622* (Ottawa: Public Archives, Publication No. 15, 1967), 429.
18. Trudel, 132, gives the fullest and most critical account of Le Baillif's operations.
19. Le Clerq, I, 253; Champlain, *Works*, V, 194-5.
20. Champlain, *Works*, V, 85-6.
21. J.B. Conacher, ed., *The History of Canada or New France by Father François du Creux, S.J.*, 2 vols. (Toronto: Champlain Society, 1951), I, 33; Champlain, *Works*, V, 194-5.
22. Champlain, *Works*, V, 206-7.

23. *Ibid.*, 207.
24. *Ibid.*, 258-9.
25. Du Creux, I, 31.
26. Sagard, III, 788.
27. Du Creux, I, 33-6.

'WHO PAYS THE PIPER...'

1. James Bryce, *The Holy Roman Empire*. 2nd rev. ed. (New York: A.L. Burt, 1887), 103.
2. Bryce, 105.
3. Walter Ullmann, *A History of Political Thought: The Middle Ages* (Harmondsworth: Penguin, 1965), 75.
4. David Laing, ed., *The Works of John Knox*. 6 vols. (Edinburgh: Wodrow Society, 1846-64), IV: 506; W.C. Dickinson, ed., *Knox's History of the Reformation in Scotland*, 2 vols. (London: Nelson, 1949), I: 136-7.
5. In two of a series of lectures delivered during World War I, Harold Laski first drew the parallel between the anti-Erastianism of the Free Church and Oxford movements. Historians have generally not followed up this line of analysis as applied to religious history of the first half of the nineteenth century. See Harold Laski, *Essays in the Problem of Sovereignty* (New Haven: Yale University Press, 1917).
6. J.S. Moir, ed., *Church and State in Canada 1627-1867: Basic Documents* (Toronto, 1967), 144.
7. Moir, *Church and State*, 146.
8. Moir, *Church and State*, 161.
9. See "Loyalty and Respectability: The Campaign for Co-establishment of the Church of Scotland in Canada" in this collection.
10. J.S. Moir, *Church and State in Canada West* (Toronto, 1959), 38.
11. See "The Quay of Greenock: Jurisdiction and Nationality in the Canadian Disruption of 1844" in this collection.
12. R.F. Burns, *Life and Times of the Rev. R. Burns, D.D., Toronto* (Toronto: James Campbell, 1871), 133-5.
13. *Historical Report of the Administration of the Temporalities' Fund of the Presbyterian Church in Canada . . . 1856-1900* (Montreal, 1900).
14. Moir, *Church and State in Canada 1627-1867*, 213.
15. A.F. Kemp, ed., *Digest of the Minutes of the Synod of the Presbyterian Church of Canada, with a Historical Introduction and an Appendix of Forms and Procedures* (Montreal: John Lovell, 1861), 309.
16. Kemp, *Minutes of the Synod*, 307.

17. *Acts and Proceedings of the General Assembly of the Presbyterian Church in Canada,* 1875, 5.
18. J.F. McCurdy, ed., *Life and Work of D.J. Macdonnell, Minister of St. Andrew's Church, Toronto, with a Selection of Sermons and Prayers* (Toronto: William Briggs, 1897), 259-74; J.R. Miller, *Equal Rights: The Jesuits' Estates Act Controversy* (Montreal: McGill-Queen's University Press, 1979), 63, 106. By the terms of the Quebec Act, Roman Catholic canon law forms part of the *code civile* of the Province of Quebec, a fact that excited Protestant concern in the early decades of the twentieth century over the implementation of the *Ne Temere* Decree. See J.S. Moir, "Canadian Protestant Reaction to the *Ne Temere* Decree," *Study Sessions,* Canadian Catholic Historical Association, 48 (1981): 78-91.
19. *Pre-Assembly Congress of the Presbyterian Church in Canada, 1913* (Toronto: Board of Foreign Missions, 1913?), 44-45.
20. George Pidgeon, "Problems of Moral Reform," in W.R. McIntosh, ed., *Canadian Problems* (Toronto: Committee on Young People's Societies, Presbyterian Church in Canada, 1910), 66.
21. B.J. Fraser, *The Social Uplifters: Presbyterian Progressives and the Social Gospel in Canada, 1875-1915* (Waterloo: Wilfrid Laurier University Press, 1988), 173-8.
22. G.W. Mason, *The Legislative Struggle for Church Union* (Toronto: Ryerson, 1956), 7; because relevant statutory and legal references were so scattered as to be virtually inaccessible, Thomas Wardlaw Taylor had collected and published all these materials after the union of 1875. See T.W. Taylor, *The Public Statutes relating to the Presbyterian Church in Canada: with Acts and Resolutions of the General Assembly, and By-laws for the Government of the Colleges and Schemes of the Church* (Toronto: Willing & Williamson, 1879).
23. Presbyterian Church Archives, Daniel Strachan Papers, file 2.
24. E.L. Morrow, *Church Union in Canada: its History, Motives, Doctrine, and Government* (Toronto: Thomas Allen, 1923), 205.
25. Ephraim Scott, *Postscript to "Church Union and the Presbyterian Church in Canada"* (Montreal: John Lovell & Son, 1928), 1. The appeal to the Covenanter tradition has little historical basis in the Canadian experience, but it is such a recurrent theme in both religious and secular life that it deserves closer examination.
26. *Acts and Proceedings,* 1942, 112-13; 1943, 130-31. G.A. Peddie, *"The King of Kings": The Basis of Union of the Presbyterian Church in Canada and its relationship to the present need of the Church for a Confession of Faith in Jesus Christ as Lord of the Church and State, together with The Petition of a Memorial of the Presbytery of Paris in the General Assembly, 1942* (Toronto: Age Publications, 1942?), unpaged.

27. *An Historical Digest of the Work in Articles of Faith 1942-1967* (Don Mills: Presbyterian Church in Canada, 1967?), 97.
28. For the full text of the Agreement see *Acts and Proceedings,* 1989, 292-94.

ROBERT MCDOWALL

1. William Canniff, *History of the Settlement of Upper Canada (Ontario) with special reference to the Bay of Quinte* (Toronto, 1869), 425-6.
2. *Ibid.,* 440, 442-3, 449, 667-9.
3. *Ibid.,* 449.
4. *Ibid.,* 275.
5. *Acts of the General Synod of the Reformed Protestant Dutch in North America, convened at Albany, June 3rd, 1806,* 352-3.
6. Presbyterian Church Archives (PCA), Toronto, McDowall Papers, certificate from Ebenezer Fitch, President, Williams College, 2 March 1795, photocopy.
7. William Gregg, *History of the Presbyterian Church in Canada . . . to 1834* (Toronto, 1885), 169.
8. Family tradition sets the date as 1796, but 1798 is accepted by historians because the General Synod's appointment was made that year. See Gregg, 172.
9. McDowall's register was published by the Ontario Historical Society in its *Papers and Records,* Vol. I (1899).
10. Canniff, 275.
11. *The Canadian Presbyterian,* 18 October 1878, letter from R.J. McDowall.
12. PCA, McDowall Papers, undated article from *Kingston Whig Standard* by Deane Van Luven.
13. *Acts of the General Synod of the Reformed Protestant Dutch . . . 1806,* 353.
14. Gregg, 177-8.
15. PCA, McDowall Papers, typed biography by Stuart Woods, January 1947, 3.
16. Gregg, 178-80.
17. Isabel Skelton, *A Man Austere, William Bell, Parson and Pioneer* (Toronto, 1947), 189 *et passim.*
18. *The Westminster,* 23 July 1898.
19. Ontario Heritage Foundation, press release, 13 June 1975.

THROUGH MISSIONARY EYES

1. *DCB*, IX, 104-8; see also R.F. Burns, *Life and Times of the Rev. R. Burns, D.D. Toronto* (Toronto, 1871), 152. R.F. Burns claims that his father started the Glasgow Colonial Society.
2. See "The Quay of Greenock: Jurisdiction and Nationality in the Canadian Disruption of 1844" in this collection.
3. John Taylor *et al.* to John Scott, York, UC, 16 March 1825, Glasgow Colonial Society Correspondence, I, 3. Unless otherwise indicated, all letters were addressed to Robert Burns. This paper is based on the transcriptions prepared by Mrs. Elizabeth McDougall. Reference numbers are to the bound volume-and-letter numbers of the original manuscripts in the central Archives of the United Church of Canada; Samuel Avery *et al.* Horton, NS, 27 June 1825, I, 1.
4. Alexander MacLean, St. Andrews, NB, 26 September 1825, I, 25.
5. Kenneth Jno. Mackenzie to John Scott, Pictou, NS, 9 December 1825, I, 30; John Crichton to Thomas Crichton, Caledon, UC, 24 October 1826, I, 36.
6. Matthew Leech, Lanark, UC, 13 June 1828, I, 158.
7. William Rintoul, Williamstown, UC, 22 September 1835, V, 181.
8. Kenneth Jno. Mackenzie to David Welsh, Pictou, NS, 19 November 1829, II, 104.
9. Gavin Lang, Shelburne, NS, 24 December 1829, II, 111.
10. James Fraser, CB, to Isa Mackay, 31 January 1837, VI, 125.
11. John Stewart, CB, to Isa Mackay, March and April 1835, V, 206.
12. Alexander Ross, Aldborough, UC, 30 December 1829, II, 116.
13. George Romanes, Hamilton, UC, 25 June 1833, IV, 159.
14. Peter McIntyre, St. James, NB, 7 March 1834, V, 112.
15. George Romanes, Smith's Falls, UC, 24 November 1833, IV, 215; Walter Roach to James Henderson, Beauharnois, LC, 24 October 1834, V, 80.
16. George Romanes, Hamilton, UC, 25 June 1833, IV, 159.
17. James Hannay, Richibucto, NB, February 1834, Glasgow Colonial Society, 5th Report.
18. William Rintoul, Streetsville, UC, 10 October 1835, V, 202.
19. John Burns, Montreal, LC, 23 May 1825, I, 17.
20. Matthew Miller, Perth, UC, 29 September 1832, III, 65.
21. Alexander MacNaughton, Lancaster, UC, 12 July 1834, V, 61.
22. Donald Henderson *et al.*, Antigonish, NS, 25 March 1833, IV, 74.
23. James Hannay, Miramichi, NB, 15 November 1833, IV, 214.
24. Alexander MacNaughton, Lancaster, UC, 12 July 1834, V, 61.

25. Walter Roach to James Henderson, Beauharnois, LC, 24 October 1834, V, 80.
26. William Rintoul, Streetsville, UC, 10 December 1835, V, 202.
27. Peter Colin Campbell, Brockville, UC, 3 May 1836, VI, 52.
28. Memorial of the Committee of the Presbytery of Quebec, 7 August 1835, V, 158.
29. Queen's University Archives, William Morris Papers, Robert Burns to William Morris, 23 March 1833.
30. James Ketchan, Belleville, UC, 16 March 1836, printed in the 9th Report of the Glasgow Colonial Society.
31. John Fairburn, Ramsay, UC, 19 January 1837, VI, 121.
32. John Crichton to Thomas Crichton, Caledon, UC, 7 July 1826, I, 136.
33. James Morrison, Dartmouth, NS, 28 April 1829, II, 62.
34. Dugald McKichan to David Welsh, Merigomish, NS, 18 June 1830, II, 176.
35. John Stewart to Isa Mackay, 16 December 1836, quoted in Isa Mackay to Robert Burns, March 1837, VI, 154.
36. Hugh Munro to Isa Mackay, Boularderie, CB, 2 October 1837, quoted in Isa Mackay to Robert Burns, 2 November 1837, VI, 203; Hugh Munro to Isa Mackay, CB, 27 February 1838, VII, 52.
37. James Souter, Newcastle, NB, 11 January 1831, III, 3.
38. Glasgow Colonial Society Report, April 1828.
39. John McIntyre, Dalhousie, UC, 23 October 1828, I, 178.
40. Robert McGill to David Welsh, Niagara, UC, 6 April 1830, II, 153.
41. Walter Roach, Beauharnois, LC, 26 May 1836, VI, 38.
42. Glasgow Colonial Society, 4th Report, Robert MacDonald to ?, New Laird, Pictou, NS, 24 July 1829.
43. Dugald McKichan to David Welsh, Merigomish, NS, 18 June 1830, II, 176.
44. John McLaurin to John Scott, New Longueuil, Ottawa District, UC, 5 July 1825, I, 19.
45. Hugh Mackenzie, Wallace, NS, 15 December 1834, V, 189.
46. John Sprott, Musquodoboit, NS, May 1827, I, 90.
47. Peter MacNaughton, Vaughan, UC, 27 August 1833, IV, 189.
48. James Souter, Newcastle, NB, 26 January 1836, VI, 8.
49. Alexander MacNaughton, Lancaster, UC, 7 March 1837, VI, 140.
50. Dugald McKichan to David Welsh, Merigomish, NS, 18 June 1830, II, 176.
51. William McAlister, Lanark, UC, 3 July 1832, III, 121.
52. John Sprott, Musquodoboit, NS, May 1827, I, 90.
53. Donald Henderson *et al.*, Lochaber, NS, 25 March 1833, IV, 74; Memorial of the Committee of the Presbytery of Quebec, 7 August 1835, V, 158.

54. William McAlister to David Welsh, Lanark, UC, 25 May 1831, III, 36.
55. Alexander MacLean to John Geddes, St. Andrews, NB, 22 February 1833, IV, 29.
56. Thomas Alexander to James Gibson, Cobourg, UC, 1 April 1835, V, 122.

TO FERTILIZE THE WILDERNESS

1. The origins of the Synod had already been traced in detail by the late Charles Bruce Fergusson in 1967 when the Synod celebrated its sesquicentennial. Fergusson, then provincial Archivist of Nova Scotia, had written an article published in the *Dalhousie Review* (Vol. 48, 1968-69) about the events and personalities involved in the creation of this first Presbyterian synod in Canada's history. The materials from the Glasgow Colonial Society papers were drawn from the transcripts by Dr. E.A. McDougall that subsequently were the basis of Elizabeth Ann Kerr McDougall and John S. Moir, eds., *Selected Correspondence of the Glasgow Colonial Society 1825-1840* (Toronto: Champlain Society, 1994). See also the article "Through Missionary Eyes" in this collection.
2. *A Memorial from the Committee of Missions of the Presbyterian Church of Nova Scotia to the Glasgow Society for promoting the Religious interest of the Scottish Settlers in British North America; with Observations on the constitution of that Society and upon the proceedings and First Annual Report of the Committee of Directors* (Edinburgh: Oliver and Boyd, 1826), 61.
3. Minutes, PCNS, 29 June 1826.
4. Minutes, PCNS, 29 June 1826.
5. *Society for Promoting the Religious Interests of the Scottish Settlers in British North America*, 3-page foolscap pamphlet, Maritime Conference Archives, United Church of Canada.
6. For an excellent account of the work in Cape Breton by the Glasgow Colonial Society and its auxiliaries see Laurie Stanley, *The Well-Watered Garden: The Presbyterian Church in Cape Breton, 1798-1860* (Sydney: University College of Cape Breton Press, 1983), 49ff.
7. Glasgow Colonial Society Papers (hereafter CGS), Vol. I. 2, United Church Central Archives, William Mackenzie to Joseph Gordon, East River, Merigomish, Pictou County, NS, June 1823. Spelling and punctuation in all quotations have been left unchanged from original form.
8. CGS, I. 7, Duncan McColl to John Martin, Guysborough, NS, 12 October 1824.

9. CGS, I. 9, John Sutherland *et al.,* To Robert Burns, Halifax, 22 August 1825.
10. CGS, Correspondence Book I. 1, Samuel Avery *et al.,* Horton, NS, 27 June 1825.
11. CGS, I. 29, John Martin to Robert Burns, Halifax, NS, 22 August 1825.
12. CGS, I. 53, Sir James Kempt to A. Beith and R. Burns, Halifax, NS, 19 June 1826.
13. CGS, Correspondence Book, I. 2, John Farquharson *et al.,* Dartmouth, Preston, Lawrencetown, Cole Harbour, and Porters Lake, n.d.
14. CGS, I. 78, Donald McKenzie to Robert Burns, Lochaber, NS, 16 December 1826.
15. CGS, I. 90, John Sprott to Robert Burns, Musquodoboit, NS, May, 1827.
16. *First Annual Report of the Glasgow Society . . . for Promoting the Religious Interests of the Scottish Settlers in British North America* (Glasgow: The Society, 1825?).
17. *Memorial,* 5-8, 11, 18-19.
18. CGS, I. 65, George Gillmore to John Martin, Horton, NS, 16 October 1826.
19. *Supplement to the First Annual Report . . . containing a Reply to the Memorial of Dr. M'Culloch* (Glasgow: Andrew Young, 1826).
20. CGS, II. 104, The Earl of Dalhousie to Edward Mortimer, Halifax, NS, 12 March 1819.
21. CGS, I. 141, Robert Burns to David Welsh, Paisley, Scotland, 21 March 1828.
22. CGS, I. 173, Kenneth John MacKenzie to Robert Burns, Pictou, NS, 27 June 1828.
23. CGS, II. 9, Donald Fraser to Robert Burns, East River, Pictou County, NS, 13 January 1829.
24. CGS, III. 16, James Morrison to Robert Burns, Halifax, NS, 4 March 1831.
25. CGS, I. 169, Donald Fraser to Robert Burns, Pictou, NS, 28 August 1828.
26. CGS, III. 17, John Martin to Robert Burns, Halifax, NS, 4 March 1831. Besides his regular duties in Halifax, Martin conducted a widespread mission centred at Truro.
27. CGS, III. 34, Kenneth John MacKenzie to David Welsh, Pictou, NS, 6 May 1831.
28. CGS, V. 204, Donald A. Fraser to Robert Burns, Pictou, NS, 29 December 1835.
29. CGS, VI. 210, John Martin to Robert Burns, Halifax, NS, 19 December 1836.

30. CGS, VI. 221, John Sprott to Robert Burns, Musquodoboit, NS, February 1838.

THE STOOL OF REPENTANCE

1. John R. Waldie, "The Influence of the Kirk Session on the Administration of Justice and Regulation of the Social Life of the Community," M.A. thesis, Queen's University, 1933. Unless otherwise indicated, all succeeding notes refer to pages in this thesis.
2. 99.
3. 105.
4. 106.
5. 107.
6. John S. Moir, *The Labour Not in Vain: A History of Alexandra Presbyterian Church, Brantford, Ontario 1845-1995* (Brantford: Alexandra Presbyterian Church, 1994), 36. I am indebted to Professor Marguerite Van Die of Queen's Theological College, Queen's University, who discovered in other sources an explanation for the vaguely worded minutes of the Session.
7. 113.
8. 115.
9. 115.
10. 120.
11. 120.
12. 120.
13. 121.
14. 121.
15. 120.
16. 121.
17. 122. For instance, the village of Markham on the plank road for farmers taking grain to Toronto had eleven taverns on its Main Street, typical in a rural society that complained that there was a tavern on every concession.
18. 36.
19. 122.
20. 122.
21. 117.
22. 118.
23. 117-9.
24. 117.
25. 137.

26. 138.
27. 139.
28. 140-2.

LOYALTY AND RESPECTABILITY

1. J.S. Moir, ed., *Church and State in Canada, 1627-1867: Basic Documents* (Toronto, 1967), 46, 52-5.
2. Moir, 161.
3. Moir, 162.
4. Moir, 162-3.
5. Queen's University Archives, Church of Scotland Synod Papers, Box 1, D. Mearns to H. Esson, 6 June 1821.
6. National Archives of Canada (NAC), G1, II, 217-20, Lord Bathurst to Lord Dalhousie, 19 August 1821.
7. A.G. Doughty and N. Story, *Documents relating to the Constitutional History of Canada, 1819-1828* (Ottawa, 1935), 205 and n.1.
8. Moir, 165-6.
9. *Report of the Canadian Archives, 1899* (Ottawa, 1900), 5.
10. NAC, Q, 179: 361, Lord Dalhousie to Wilmot Horton, 23 October 1827.
11. W.S. Reid, *The Church of Scotland in Lower Canada, Its Struggle for Establishment* (Toronto, 1936), 80; *Report of the Canadian Archives, 1899*, 25-7.
12. T.R. Millman, *The Life of the Right Reverend Charles James Stewart, D.D., Oxon., Second Anglican Bishop of Quebec* (London, ON, 1953), 75.
13. Reid, 85-90.
14. Moir, 79.
15. Moir, 182.
16. Toronto Reference Library, Scadding Collection, Strachan Papers, Lord Goderich to Sir J. Colborne, 5 April 1832, copy; Queen's University Archives, Church of Scotland Synod Papers, W. Rowan to Synod, 15 March 1833.
17. *A Historical and Statistical Report of the Presbyterian Church in Canada in connection with the Church of Scotland, for the Year 1866* (Montreal, 1867), 165-72.
18. *Report of the Committee of the General Assembly on Colonial Churches, 30 May 1836* (Glasgow, 1836), 3, 7.
19. Moir, 203.
20. Moir, 204.

21. E.C. Kyte, "Journal of the Honourable William Morris' Mission to England in the Year 1837," *Papers and Records of the Ontario Historical Society* XXX (1934): 230, 234.
22. Kyte, 239.
23. Queen's University Archives, Church of Scotland Synod Papers, printed statement of A. Gale, July 1838.
24. Queen's University Archives, Clergy Reserves Collection, A. Gale to W. Morris, 19 April 1839.
25. Ontario Archives, Macaulay Papers, J. Strachan to J. Macaulay, 21 May 1839.
26. Queen's University Archives, Morris Papers, W. Morris to T.W.C. Murdoch, 4 January 1840, copy.
27. Morris Papers, W. Smart to W. Morris, 7 January 1840; 13 July 1849.
28. Paul Knaplund, ed., *Letters from Lord Sydenham, Governor-General of Canada, 1839-1841, to Lord John Russell* (London, 1931), 45, 44, 48.
29. Knaplund, 91; 95.
30. Morris Papers, W. Morris to Lord Sydenham, 2 October 1840, draft.
31. A.F. Kemp, *Digest of the Minutes of the Synod of the Presbyterian Church of Canada* (Montreal, 1861), 12.
32. Kemp, 413-4.
33. J.S. Moir, *Church and State in Canada West: Three Studies in the Relation of Denominationalism and Nationalism, 1841-1867* (Toronto, 1959), 66.
34. Moir, 59-60.
35. Moir, 77-9.
36. *Historical Report of the Administration of the Temporalities' Fund of the Presbyterian Church of Canada . . . 1856-1900* (Montreal, 1900).

THE QUAY OF GREENOCK

1. Robert McGill, *Brief Notes on the Relation of the Synod of Canada to the Church of Scotland* (Niagara, 1844), 21.
2. James Croil, *Historical and Statistical Report of the Presbyterian Church of Canada in Connection with the Church of Scotland for the Year 1866* (Montreal, 1867), 165-72.
3. J.S. Moir, ed., *Church and State in Canada 1627-1867: Basic Documents* (Toronto, 1967), 179-80.
4. J.S. Moir, *Church and State in Canada West: Three Studies in the Relation of Denominationalism and Nationalism, 1841-1867* (Toronto, 1959), 38, 188.
5. *Banner*, 18 August 1843.

6. *Ibid.*
7. *Ibid.*, 22, 29 September 1843.
8. *Ibid.*, 27 October 1843; J.A. Johnston, "Presbyterian Disruption in British North America," unpublished B.D. thesis, Presbyterian College, 1953, 59.
9. *Banner*, 27 October 1843.
10. *Ibid.*, 17 November 1843.
11. *British Colonist*, 9, 14 November 1843.
12. *Banner*, 17 November 1843.
13. *Ibid.*, 5 July 1844.
14. Queen's University Archives, Morris Papers, I. Buchanan to W. Morris, 5 July 1844.
15. *Banner*, 15 December 1843.
16. R.F. Burns, *Life and Times of the Rev. R. Burns, D.D.* (Toronto, 1871), 196 et passim.
17. J.S. Moir, "Confrontation at Queen's: A Prelude to the Disruption in Canada," *Presbyterian History* xv(1), May 1971.
18. *Banner*, 29 March 1844; Burkhard Kiesekamp emphasizes this regional disparity of response in terms of economic and political interests as well political and religious beliefs, see "Response to Disruption: Presbyterianism in Eastern Ontario, 1844," *Canadian Society of Church History Papers, 1967*, 30-51.
19. Quoted in Robert Burns, *A Letter Addressed to the Ministers and Elders of the Synod of Canada* (Montreal, 1844), 8.
20. *Minutes of the Synod of the Presbyterian Church in Canada in connection with the Church of Scotland, . . . at Kingston, 1844*, 15.
21. Croil, 165-72.
22. National Archives of Canada (NAC), Isaac Buchanan Papers, W. Rintoul to I. Buchanan, 7 April 1845.
23. Queen's University Archives, Morris Papers, I. Buchanan to W. Morris, 17 August 1844.
24. *United Secession Magazine,* August 1844.
25. A.M. Machar, *Memorials of the Life and Ministry of the Rev. John Machar, D.D., Late Minister of St. Andrew's Church, Kingston* (Toronto, 1873), 86-7.
26. *Report on a Discussion of the Late Disruption in the Presbyterian Church* (Galt, 1845), 59-60.
27. NAC, Isaac Buchanan Papers, various items, 1845.
28. A.F. Kemp, *Digest of the Minutes of the Synod of the Presbyterian Church in Canada . . .* (Montreal, 1861), 413-15.

ON THE KING'S BUSINESS

1. S.E. Ahlstrom, *A Religious History of the American People*, 2 vols. (Garden City, N.J., 1975), II, 343-7.
2. General Synod of the Church of England in . . . Canada, *Journal of Proceedings, Seventh Session, 1915*, 289; *The Presbyterian*, 4 April 1907, 2.
3. R.T. Handy, *A History of the Churches in the United States and Canada* (New York, 1977), *passim*.
4. Ahlstrom, *loc. cit.*; United Church of Canada Archives (UCCA), Stephenson Collection, Box 1, File 2, Methodist Church General Board of Missions, Young Peoples' Forward Movement for Mission, 17.
5. UCCA, Stephenson Collection, *loc. cit.*, 19.
6. Methodist Church of Canada, *Journal of the Methodist General Conference 1910*, 284.
7. UCCA, Stephenson Collection, *loc. cit.*, 20-1.
8. *Ibid.*, 21. The verbatim proceedings of the congress were published as a 368-page volume entitled *Canada's Missionary Congress* (Toronto, 1909?).
9. *Canada's Missionary Congress*, vii.
10. Canada's National Missionary Policy, adopted at National Missionary Congress, Toronto, 3 April, 1909, unpaged.
11. *Ibid.*
12. *Ibid.*
13. General Synod of the Church of England in . . . Canada, *Journal of Proceedings, Sixth Session, 1911*, 259.
14. *The Presbyterian*, 8 April 1909.
15. UCCA, Stephenson Collection, *loc. cit.*, 22; *The Missionary Outlook*, October, December 1911.
16. *The Presbyterian*, 5 May 1910.
17. *The Presbyterian*, 6 November 1908.
18. *The Presbyterian*, 11 March 1909.
19. *The Presbyterian*, 29 December 1910.
20. *The Presbyterian*, 5 January 1911.
21. *The Presbyterian*, 12 January 1911.
22. *The Presbyterian*, 13 April 1911.
23. *The Presbyterian*, 12 October 1911.
24. *The Presbyterian*, 21 March 1912, 1 May 1913, 23 October 1913, 12 February 1914, 27 November 1913, 16 April 1914.
25. *The Presbyterian*, 23 July 1914.
26. General Synod of the Church of England in . . . Canada, *Journal of Proceedings, Seventh Session, 1915*, 290.

27. General Synod Archives of the Anglican Church of Canada, Anglican Laymen's Missionary Movement, Executive Minute Book, 53, 7 October 1915.
28. Ahlstrom, II, 346 and n. 5.

A SENSE OF PROPORTION

1. For a fuller account of McCurdy's contribution to the discipline of biblical studies see Moir's two articles, "James Frederick McCurdy: Christian Humanist," in Canadian Society of Presbyterian History, *Papers 1981,* and "Frederick McCurdy," in J.S. Moir, ed., *Called to Witness,* Vol. 3 (Hamilton: Committee on History, Presbyterian Church in Canada, 1991).
2. John H. MacVicar, *Life and Work of Donald Harvey MacVicar, D.D., LL. D.* (Toronto, 1904), 219-20.
3. *The Westminster,* New Series, Vol. 1, no.4, October 1902, 201.
4. *Presbyterian College Journal,* Vol. 3, no.1, October 1882, 30.
5. *Presbyterian Review,* 15 March 1894, 635.
6. T.R. Glover and D.D. Calvin, *A Corner of Empire: the Old Ontario Strand* (Cambridge: Cambridge University Press, 1937), 135.
7. Glover and Calvin, 136.
8. W.G. Jordan, "The Higher Criticism in Canada: II, The Canadian Situation," *Queen's Quarterly,* Vol. 36, 37-8.
9. University of Toronto Archives, Loudon Papers, M 25, J.F. McCurdy to James Loudon, undated.
10. *University Monthly,* Vol. 15, 1914-15, 206.
11. United Church Archives, Printed Order of Service for the funeral of J.F. McCurdy, unpaged.
12. Wycliffe College Archives, O'Meara Papers, quoted by S.H. Blake to John Hoskin, Chairman, Board of Governors, University of Toronto, 22 December 1906.
13. *Report of Special Committee to the Board of Governors, the University of Toronto, adopted 20th December, 1909* (Toronto: University of Toronto Press, n.d.), 4.
14. University of Toronto Archives, Falconer Papers, Box XI, J.F. McCurdy to Sir R.A. Falconer, 3 February 1910, and enclosure.

A NATIONAL VISION

1. *Presbyterian Witness,* 1 January 1868.
2. William D. Grant, ed., *Christendom Anno Domini [1901],* 2 vols. (Toronto: William Briggs, 1902), "Canada," 1, 91-92.
3. Alexander Maclean, *The Story of the Kirk in Nova Scotia* (Pictou, NS: Pictou Advocate, 1911), 94.
4. *Morning Chronicle,* 16 August 1864, quoted in J. Murray Beck, ed., *Joseph Howe: Voice of Nova Scotia,* Carleton Library No. 20 (Toronto, 1964), 272.
5. T.C. Haliburton, *The Old Judge* (London, 1849), II, 228.
6. "Canadian Confederation and the Protestant Churches," *Church History* 38, 3 (September 1969): 327-37. In August 1857, the *Christian Instructor and Missionary Register* of Halifax informed its readers regarding a proposal to unite the Kirk and Free Church in a single body "independent of any foreign body," that the Kirk was not attitudinally ready for union, and that in Nova Scotia politics impinged on many aspects of religious life.
7. *The Presbyterian,* October 1866.
8. 19 June 1875.
9. Wilhelmina Gordon, *Daniel M. Gordon: His Life* (Toronto: Ryerson, [1941]), 42, 46; see also Barry Mack, "George Monro Grant: Evangelical Prophet," unpublished Ph.D. dissertation, Queen's University, 1992, 66-67, and "Grant, George Monro," *DCB,* 13 (1994), 403-408.
10. *Halifax Herald,* 2 January 1907.
11. *Christendom Anno Domini* [1901], I, 92-3.
12. Grant Papers, J. Melville, Nashwaak, NB, to G.M. Grant, 31 July and 29 December 1879.
13. Grant Papers, 28 July 1876.
14. W.L. Grant and Frederick Hamilton, *Principal Grant* (Toronto: Morang, 1902), 372, 250.
15. Carl Berger, *The Sense of Power* (Toronto and Buffalo: University of Toronto Press, 1970), 229, 218; *The Pictou News,* 30 November 1883.
16. Grant and Hamilton, *Principal Grant,* 514.
17. *Report of Proceedings of the Alliance of Reformed Churches, at Philadelphia, 1880,* 238-39, 231, 298-300.
18. *Proceedings of the Alliance of Reformed Churches, 1892,* 351-62.
19. *Ocean to Ocean* (Toronto and London, 1873), I, 367, 366.
20. Gordon, *Daniel M. Gordon,* viii.
21. *Ibid.,* 97.

22. James G. Greenlee, *Sir Robert Falconer: A Biography*, (Toronto, Buffalo, London: University of Toronto Press, 1988), 157.
23. For example, *The Theologue*, VI (5), April 1895, 133-38, calling for a more open-minded approach to the findings of science. Currie's lengthy article appeared in VII (1), November 1895, 1-14.
24. *The Theologue*, X (4), March, 1899, 109-16, 115.
25. *The Theologue*, XVI (3), February 1905, 59-63.
26. *Presbyterian Witness*, 23 September 1893, 5 April 1902, 28 February 1903, 2 May 1903.
27. Grant Papers, D.J. Macdonnell to G.M. Grant, 8 December 1879, "Private."
28. D.G. Creighton, *Canada's First Century*, (Toronto: Macmillan of Canada, 1970), 77.
29. Frank Underhill, *Images of Confederation* (The Massey Lectures, 1963), (Toronto: Canadian Broadcasting Corporation, 1964), 30, 31.
30. Grant Papers, ? to W.L. Grant, 26 February 1903.
31. Grant Papers, Goldwin Smith to G.M. Grant, 19 August 1896.
32. Grant Papers, resolution of the Kingston Board of Trade, 14 May 1902.
33. Grant Papers, copy of a resolution, May 1902.
34. Underhill, *Images of Confederation*, 30-31.

LOYALITIES IN CONFLICT

1. Presbyterian Church Archives (PCA), Proudfoot Papers, William Proudfoot to David Anderson, 13 July 1846.
2. Joseph McLelland, *Why Our Pond Is Lukewarm, or Forty Years in the Wilderness* (n.p., 1965), unpaged.
3. *Census of Canada*, 1971, Vol. 1, Part 3, Table 9-1.
4. J.S. Moir. *Enduring Witness: A History of the Presbyterian Church in Canada* (Toronto, [1974]), 47.
5. Ibid., 38 et passim. See also Robert Campbell, *A History of the Scotch Presbyterian Church, St. Gabriel Street, Montreal*, 1877, and A.H. Young, "The Bethunes," *Papers and Records of the Ontario Historical Society*, Vol. XXVII (1931).
6. *A Historical and Statistical Report of the Presbyterian Church of Canada in connection with the Church of Scotland for the Year 1866*, (Montreal, 1867), 165-72.
7. John Banks, "American Presbyterianism in the Niagara Peninsula, 1800-1840," *Ontario History*, September 1965.
8. Moir, *Enduring Witness*, 62-3, 77-8.

9. J.S. Moir, ed., *Church and State in Canada, 1627-1867: Basic Documents* (Toronto, 1967) 162-3 *et passim.*
10. Alan Wilson, *The Clergy Reserves of Upper Canada,* Canadian Historical Association Booklet No. 23, 1969; J.S. Moir, *Church and State in Canada West: Three Studies in the Relation of Denominationalism and Nationalism, 1841-1867* (Toronto, 1959), 26ff.
11. Moir, *Church and State in Canada, 1627-1867,* 108-10.
12. A.G. Doughty and N. Story, eds., *Documents relating to the Constitutional History of Canada, 1819-1828* (Ottawa, 1935), 205 and n.1.
13. Moir, *Enduring Witness,* 93.
14. *Ibid.,* 95-9.
15. Moir, *Church and State in Canada, 1627-1867,* 192-5.
16. Moir, *Enduring Witness,* 84-5, 106, 117, 122.
17. See "The Quay of Greenock: Jurisdiction and Nationality in the Canadian Presbyterian Disruption of 1844" in this collection.
18. Moir, *Church and State in Canada, 1627-1867,* 213-5.
19. *Ibid.,* 212-45; Moir, *Church and State in Canada West,* Chap. 3.
20. Moir, *Enduring Witness,* 253-4.
21. *An Historical Digest of the Work in Articles of Faith, 1942-1967* (Toronto, 1967), no pagination.
22. Moir, *Enduring Witness,* 192-6; Richard Allen, *The Social Passion* (Toronto, 1972), Chap. 1.
23. A.L. Farris, "Willis, Michael," *DCB* x, Toronto, 1972.
24. A.F. Kemp, *Digest of the Minutes of the Synod of the Presbyterian Church of Canada . . .* (Montreal, 1861), 354-5, 347-9.
25. Moir, *Enduring Witness,* 159, 226-53.
26. *Ibid.,* 164-9.
27. *Ibid.,* Chap. 10.
28. *Ibid.,* 226, 231-5.
29 *Presbyterian Record,* March 1977.

A Select Bibliography of Early Canadian Presbyterianism

THIS BIBLIOGRAPHY IS BY ITS NATURE UNFINISHED because new titles are continually becoming available. Furthermore, the present bibliography is only a selection, because several thousand items were left out to avoid burdening the present book. We hope that, despite omissions, this bibliography will be useful to students of early Presbyterian history in Canada. The complete bibliography is available at the Presbyterian Church Archives.

One feature of the bibliography, namely its division into subject categories, is inevitably subjective, and users are advised to use imagination in searching for relevant material beyond the main entry title. Historical articles from *The Presbyterian Record* or the *Canadian Society of Presbyterian History Papers* have been omitted by the fact that these publications contain myriad articles and have their own indices. Published works of authors and a section devoted to individual biographies have also been omitted; readers are asked to seek out the *Dictionary of Canadian Biography,* the *Dictionary of Hamilton Biography,* or the more general works listed below for further details about individual Presbyterians. Lastly, local histories have been omitted, although regional histories have not, since they should include many local histories in their own bibliographies.

Users should be aware that "Mac" is separated from "Mc". Note also that two periodicals carry the title *Presbyterian History*—one is the American quarterly, the other the semi-annual, leaflet-size publication of the Committee on History of the Presbyterian Church in Canada which, in this bibliography, carries the volume and number, *e.g.,* 14, 2. In general, pagination has been included for pamphlets, manuscripts, and the rarer nineteenth century monographs.

In conclusion we wish to record our thanks to our colleagues, the Reverend Doctors T. Melville Bailey, John A. Johnston, and Brian Hogan for their assistance and encouragement.

SUBJECT CATEGORIES

1. Guides 209
2. Sources 210
3. General Works 215
4. Church History-Philosophy and Principles 217
5. Regional History, Synods and Presbyteries 218
6. Biography—General and Collective 225
7. Religious Practice and Pastoral Care 228
8. Missions 231
9. The Arts 236
10. Education 240
11. Migration and Settlement 243
12. Politics, Labour and Social Thought 244
13. Church and Society 248
14. Women and Religion 249
15. Ecumenism and Inter-church Relations 250
16. Religion, Ethics and Health 258
17. Theological Thought 258

1. Guides

Boyle, George. "Sources for the Study of Presbyterianism in Canada." United Church Archives, *The Bulletin,* No. 10 (1957), 10-18, and No. 11 (1958), 18.

Gillette, G.W. "A Checklist of Doctoral Dissertations on American Presbyterian and Reformed Subjects, 1912-1965." *Journal of Presbyterian History* 45 (1967): 203-221.

Johnston, John A. "The Presbyterian Press." *Presbyterian History* 3, 2, June 1959. Unpaged.

King, G.B. *Church History Resources in Manitoba.* Historical Society of Manitoba, 1944. Pp. 8.

Kyte, E.C. *A Note on the Manuscript Collection in the Douglas Library, Queen's University.* Kingston, 1943.

Laverdure, Paul. "Twentieth Anniversary Index of Papers 1975-1995." The Canadian Society of Presbyterian History, *Papers 1996,* 43-58.

Moir, John S., comp. *Handbook for Canadian Presbyterians.* Toronto: Record Books, 1996.

———. "Reassessing Presbyterian Record Sources." In *Readings in Ontario Genealogical Sources,* Toronto: Conference on Ontario Genealogical Sources, 1959. Pp. 159-166.

Pierce, Lorne, ed. *The Chronicle of a Century 1829-1929 . . . Publishing Concerns of the Methodist, Presbyterian and Congregational Churches in Canada.* Toronto: United Church Publishing House, 1930?

Ray, Margaret. "Canadian Denominational Periodicals in Victoria University Library." United Church Archives, *The Bulletin,* No. 6 (1953), 29-33.

———. "The Presbyterian Archives Collection of Victoria College." United Church Archives, *The Bulletin,* No. 4 (1951), 4-9.

2. Sources

Acts and Proceedings of the General Assembly of the Presbyterian Church in Canada. *1875–* .

Banner. Toronto, 1843-1850. [Unofficial newspaper of the Free Church in Canada.]

Blue Banner. Sydney: Blue Banner Company, 1903-1907.

British American Presbyterian. [Weekly.] Toronto, 1872-1875.

Canada Presbyterian. Toronto, 1872-1897. [Unofficial newspaper of the Canada Presbyterian Church.]

Canadian Christian Examiner and Presbyterian Review. Niagara, 1837-1840.

Canadian Presbyter [Free Church]. Montreal, 1857-1858.

Canadian Presbyterian Magazine [United Presbyterian Church]. Toronto, 1851-54. [Continues as *Canadian United Presbyterian Magazine.*]

Canadian Society of Presbyterian History. *Papers.* Toronto, 1975– . [Annual.]

Canadian United Presbyterian Magazine (formerly *Canadian Presbyterian Magazine*). Toronto, 1854-61. Ontario Legislative Library, Presbyterian Church Archives, United Church Archives.

Christian Instructor and Missionary Register of the Presbyterian Church of Nova Scotia. Halifax, 1856-60. Presbyterian Church Archives, United Church Archives.

Christian Messenger. 1854-1856.

Constitution and Procedure of the Presbyterian Church in Canada. Toronto, 1879. Pp. 86.

Croil, James. *A Historical and Statistical Report of the Presbyterian Church of Canada in connection with the Church of Scotland, for the Year 1866.* Montreal: The Synod, 1867. 2nd ed. 1868.

Ecclesiastical and Missionary Record for the Presbyterian Church of Canada. 1844-61. [Official periodical of the Free Church in Canada.]

Fox, Michael, ed. *Queen's Quarterly, A Canadian Review: 90th Anniversary Special Issue* 90, 3 (Autumn 1983): 607-932.

Glad Tidings. Toronto: Women's Missionary Society, 1925- .

Historical Report of the Administration of the Temporalities' Fund of the Presbyterian Church of Canada in connection with The Church of Scotland. 1856-1900. Montreal, 1900.

Historic Sketches of the Pioneer Work and the Missionary, Educational and Benevolent Agencies of the Presbyterian Church in Canada. Toronto: Murray Printing, 1903.

An Historical Digest of the Work in Articles of Faith 1942-1967. Toronto, 1967?

A Historical and Statistical Report of the Presbyterian Church of Canada, in Connection with the Church of Scotland, for the Year 1866. 2nd ed. Montreal: Synod of the Presbyterian Church of Canada, 1868.

Histories of local Canadian Churches (Evangelical United Brethren; Methodist; Presbyterian before 1925; Congregational), compiled on the occasion of the 50th Anniversary celebration of the founding of the United Church of Canada. The Collection includes some 300 monographs and pamphlets. Toronto: United Church Archives, 1975-76. Unpublished.

Home and Foreign Record of the Canada Presbyterian Church. Toronto, 1861-1875.

Home and Foreign Record of the Presbyterian Church of the Lower Provinces of British North America. Halifax: J. Barnes, 1861-1875.

Juvenile Presbyterian. Montreal, 1856-? [Sunday School magazine.]

Kemp, Alexander F. *Digest of the Minutes of the Synod of the Presbyterian Church of Canada, with an Historical Introduction, and an Appendix of Forms and Procedures.* Montreal: Lovell, 1861.

———. *Handbook of the Presbyterian Church in Canada.* Ottawa, 1883.

Knox College Monthly. 1887-1895.

Legislation as to Presbyterian Union. 1873.

Legislation as to Presbyterian Union, 1873, a Comparison.

Legislation sought and secured in connection with the Union of 1875.

Minutes of the Synod of the PRESBYTERIAN CHURCH OF CANADA. At Kingston. Kingston, 1841. Pp. 42.

Missionary Register of the Presbyterian Church of Nova Scotia. 1851.

Missionary Record and Ecclesiastical Intelligencer of the Free Church of Nova Scotia. 1851-60.

Monthly Record of the Church of Scotland in Nova Scotia, New Brunswick and adjoining Provinces. Pictou, 1876-188?

Monthly Record of the Church of Scotland in Nova Scotia. Halifax, 1861-1868.

Pre-Assembly Congress Addresses . . . also a Report on the Men's Missionary Convention . . . . Toronto: Board of Foreign Missions, Presbyterian Church in Canada, 1913.

Presbyterian. Montreal, 1852-1860.

Presbyterian. Toronto, 1902-1915.

Presbyterian Advocate. St. John, NB, ?

Presbyterian, a Missionary and Religious Record of the Presbyterian Church of Canada in connection with the Church of Scotland. Montreal, 1848-1875. [Incorporated into *The Presbyterian Record.*]

Presbyterian and Evangelical Protestant Union. (microform) Vol. 1, No. 1 (Jan. 7, 1875) - Vol. 12, No. 26 (June 25, 1885). Charlottetown: Public Archives of PEI, 1980.

Presbyterian and Westminster. Toronto, 1872-1925.

Presbyterian Church in Canada. *An Historical Digest of the Work in Articles of Faith: 1942-1967.* Don Mills: Presbyterian Church in Canada, [1967?].

Presbyterian Church in Canada. *The Book of Forms.* Don Mills: Presbyterian Publications. [Revised annually.]

Presbyterian Church of Canada in connexion with the Church of Scotland. *Minutes of Synod,* 1837-57. United Church Archives.

Presbyterian Church of Canada, in connection with the Church of Scotland. History of individual congregations in Canada as requested by church authorities in 1831. MS, United Church Archives.

Presbyterian Church of Canada. *Synod Reports,* 1855- . United Church Archives holds 1857-65.

Presbyterian Church of Nova Scotia. *Minutes of Synod.* 1849-55. Presbyterian Church Archives.

Presbyterian Church of the Lower Provinces of British North America. *Minutes of the Synod of the Presbyterian Church of the Lower Provinces of British North America.* Halifax, ?-1875.

Presbyterian Church of the Lower Provinces of British North America, Synod of. *Rules and forms of procedure of the Presbyterian Church of the Lower Provinces of British North America: Approved by Synod, 1873.* Halifax: A. & W. Mackinlay, 1874.

Presbyterian College Journal. Montreal, 1881-1908.

Presbyterian Magazine (United Secession Church, Missionary Presbytery). Ed. William Proudfoot. London, UC, 1843.

Presbyterian Record. Montreal and Toronto: General Assembly of the Presbyterian Church in Canada, 1875- .

Presbyterian Review (microform). Québec: Université Laval, Bibliothèque, 1952. Vol. 1, No. 36 (September 3, 1885).

Presbyterian Witness and Evangelical Advocate. Halifax, 1848-1875.

Presbyterian Student. Montreal: Presbyterian Theological Colleges of Toronto and Montreal, 1935-1937.

Protestant Union (microform). Vol. 1, No. 1, (July 2, 1885) - Vol. 2, No. 28 (December 30, 1886). Charlottetown: Public Archives of PEI., 1985.

PYPS. Presbyterian Young People's Society, Presbytery of Toronto, 1937-1939.

Queen's College Journal. Kingston, 1873-1875.

Reid, Elspeth M. "Women's Missionary Society Records in the Presbyterian Archives." *Archivaria* 30, 1 (Summer 1990): 171-9.

Reports concerning an Act to incorporate congregations outside the Presbyterian Church in Canada, 1882.

Robinson, C. Blackett. *Prospectus of the British American Presbyterian.* Toronto: C.B. Robinson, 1871.

Stevenson, E.M. "The Witness." *Nova Scotia Historical Quarterly* 10, 1 (March 1980): 41-58.

Taylor, Thomas Wardlaw. *The Book of Forms.* Toronto: N.A. MacEachern, 1933.

———. *The Ruling Elder, His Office, and His Duties.* Toronto: Presbyterian Publications, 1947.

———. *The Public Statutes Relating to the Presbyterian Church in Canada: with Acts and Resolutions of the General Assembly, and By-Laws for the Government of the Colleges and Schemes of the Church.* Toronto: Williamson, 1879.

United Church of Canada. Joint Committee on Church Union. *Basis of Union of the United Church of Canada as prepared by the Joint Committee on Church Union and approved by the Presbyterian Church in Canada, the General Conference of the Methodist Church, the Congregational Union of Canada, also, a brief historical statement.* Toronto: The Committee, 1924.

Westminster. Toronto, 1896-1916.

3. General Works

Bailey, Thomas Melville. *The Covenant in Canada; Being Four Hundred Years History of the Presbyterian Church in Canada.* Hamilton: The MacNab Circle, 1975.

Balfour, R.G. *Presbyterianism in the Colonies, with special reference to . . . the Free Church of Scotland.* Chalmers Lectures. Edinburgh, 1900. Pp. 1-17 re Canada.

Burns, R.F. *Our United Church.* Montreal: A. Stevenson, 1875.

——. *The Presbyterian Church in Canada.* Halifax: Nova Scotia Printing, 1876.

Clark, S.D. *Church and Sect in Canada.* Toronto: University of Toronto Press, 1948.

Croil, James. *Genesis of Churches in the United States and the Dominion of Canada.* Montreal, 1907.

Farris, A. L. "Presbyterianism in Canada, 1600-1957." *Journal of Presbyterian History* (1966): 156-77.

Grant, John Webster. *The Church in the Canadian Era* (Vol. 3 of *A History of the Christian Church in Canada*). Toronto: McGraw-Hill Ryerson, 1972. 2nd ed.,"Updated and Expanded." Burlington, 1988.

Gregg, William. *Short History of the Presbyterian Church in the Dominion of Canada: from the earliest to the present time.* 2nd ed. rev. Toronto: The Author, 1893. Pp. viii, 248.

——. *History of the Presbyterian Church in the Dominion of Canada: from the earliest times with a chronological table of events to the present time, and map.* Toronto: Presbyterian Printing, 1885. Pp. xv, 646.

Handy, Robert T. *A History of the Churches in the United States and Canada.* Oxford History of the Christian Church. New York, NY: Oxford University Press, 1977.

Historical Sketches of the Pioneer Work and the Missionary, Educational and Benevolent Agencies of the Presbyterian Church in Canada, edited by a

Committee of the Executive of the "Twentieth Century Fund." Toronto: Murray, 1903. Pp. 128.

Johnston, J.A. "Early Presbyterianism in Ontario." *Families,* 21, 4 (1982), 300-8.

Kemp, Alexander. *A Reply to the "Review Reviewed" of the Rev. D. Inglis: and a vindication of a Review of the State and condition of the Canada Presbyterian Church since the Union of 1861.* Sarnia: Observer, 1867.

———. *A Review of the State and Progress of the Canada Presbyterian Church since Union 1861.* Windsor, 1867.

Kilbourn, William. *Religion in Canada.* Canadian Illustrated Library. Toronto: McLelland and Stewart, 1968.

Klempa, William, ed. *The Burning Bush and a Few Acres of Snow.* Ottawa: Carleton University Press, 1994.

MacBeth, R.G. *The Burning Bush and Canada.* [Toronto]: Westminster, c. 1912.

———. *Our Task in Canada.* Toronto: Westminster, 1912; Vancouver: Cowan Brookhouse, 1925.

MacNab, John. *Our Priceless Heritage.* Presbyterian Church in Canada: 75th Anniversary Committee, 1950.

Mark, Malcolm A., and Kenneth G. McMillan. *Canadian Presbyterianism in Action 1761-1961.* Toronto: Synod of Toronto and Kingston, 1961.

McNeill, John Thomas. *The Presbyterian Church in Canada 1875-1925.* Toronto: General Board, Presbyterian Church in Canada, 1925.

Moir, John S. *Enduring Witness: A History of the Presbyterian Church in Canada.* Toronto: Presbyterian Publications, 1974. 2nd ed. Toronto: Committee on History, The Presbyterian Church in Canada, 1987.

———. *The Church in the British Era* (Vol. 2 of *The Christian Church in Canada).* Toronto: McGraw-Hill, Ryerson, 1972.

Oliver, Edmund H. *The Winning of the Frontier.* Toronto: United Church Publishing House, 1930.

Parker, C.S. *Yet Not Consumed: a short account of the history and antecedents of the Presbyterian Church in Canada.* Toronto, 1946.

Pearson, S.C. "Presbyterianism in America." *Journal of Presbyterian History* 46 (1968): 139-44.

Pollok, Allan. *Presbyterianism in Canada.* Halifax: McNab Press, 1875.

Smith, David A. "Fifty Years Ago and Now: The Presbyterian Church in British Columbia." *Presbyterian History* 1 (3), December 1957, 1-4.

Smith, Neil G., A.L. Farris and H.K. Markell. *Enkindled by the Word: Essays on Presbyterianism in Canada.* Toronto: Presbyterian Publications, 1966.

———. *A Short History of the Presbyterian Church in Canada.* Toronto: Presbyterian Publications, 1966.

Vaudry, Richard W. *The Free Church in Victorian Canada, 1844-1861.* Waterloo: Wilfrid Laurier University Press, 1989.

Walsh, H.H. *The Christian Church in Canada.* Toronto: Ryerson, 1956; reprint, Ryerson Paperbacks, 1968.

Wilson, D.J. *The Church Grows in Canada.* Toronto: Ryerson, 1966.

4. Church History: Philosophy and Principles

Davison, Marion. "A Monument of Faith in Action: Covenanter's Church." *Bluenose Magazine* 4 (Summer 1979): 30-33.

Gill, Stewart D. "'A Coat of Many Colours': Some Thoughts on Canadian Religious Historiography." *Bulletin of Canadian Studies,* 9, 2 (1985).

Honeyman, David. *Giants and pygmies (geological): earth's order of formation and life, and harmony of the two records.* Rev. and corr., with synoptical table. Halifax: [Provincial] Museum and Booksellers, 1887.

Longfield, J. *The Presbyterian Controversy: Fundamentalists, Modernists, and Moderates.* New York: Oxford University Press, 1994.

Marshall, David Brian. "The Clerical Response to Secularization: Canadian Methodists and Presbyterians, 1860-1940." Ph.D. thesis, University of Toronto, 1988. Ottawa: National Library of Canada, 1988. ISBN 0-315-36101-8.

———. *Secularizing the Faith: Canadian Methodist and Presbyterian Clergy and the Crisis of Belief,* 1850s-1930s. Toronto: University of Toronto Press, 1992.

Moir, John S. "Coming of Age, but Slowly, Aspects of Canadian Religious Historiography since Confederation." Canadian Catholic Historical Association, *Study Sessions, 50th Anniversary Edition.* 2 vols., 50 (1983). Vol. 1, pp. 89-98.

Moir, Kim M. "The Politics of Records Acquisition: a Study of the Presbyterian Church in Canada Archives, 1875 to the Present." The Canadian Society of Presbyterian History, *Papers 1984,* 87-105.

Reid, Allan S. *A Bird's Eye View of the Activities of the Presbyterian Church in Canada.* Montreal, n.d.

Schlenther, B.S. "The Presbytery as Organ of Church Life and Government in American Presbyterianism from 1706-1788." Ph.D. thesis, Edinburgh University, 1964-1965.

Schriver, G.H. "Philip Schaff as a teacher of Church history." *Journal of Presbyterian Church History* 45 (1968): 74-92. [Schaff was first president of the American Society of Church History.]

Vorpahl, B.M. "Presbyterianism and the Frontier Hypothesis." *Journal of Presbyterian History* 45 (1967): 180-92.

5. Regional History, Synods and Presbyteries

Angus, Murray. "'Living in the World of the Tiger': Methodist and Presbyterian Churches in Nova Scotia and the Great War, 1914-18." M.A. thesis, Dalhousie University, 1993.

Archibald, Frank. "Contribution of the Scottish Church to New Brunswick Presbyterianism from its earliest Beginning . . . 1784-1852." Ph.D. thesis, University of Edinburgh, 1932-33.

Archibald, Tim F. "Opposing Voices: Church Union in Pictou and Truro Presbyteries." *Presbyterian History.* 36, 2 (October 1992): 1-5.

Atlantic Provinces, Synod of. *Focus on Atlantic Canada (Centennial Magazine of the Synod).* Pictou: Advocate Printing, 1975.

Bailey, Thomas Melville, ed. *'Wee Kirks and Stately Steeples': a history of the Presbytery of Hamilton, The Presbyterian Church in Canada 1800-1990.* Burlington: Eagle, 1990.

Ballantyne, Francis. "Historical Sketches of the Congregations in the London Presbytery of the Presbyterian Church in Canada." *Western Ontario Historical Note* 21 (1965): 51-87. [Continuation of an account dealing with fourteen churches in the London area.]

Banks, John. "American Presbyterians in the Niagara Peninsula 1800-1840." *Ontario History* 57 (1965): 135-40.

Barker, Kenneth S. *Contending for the Faith: Presbyterianism in Owen Sound.* N.P., 1991. Pp. 66.

—. "Presbyterianism in Grey and Bruce Counties: The Presbyterian Church of Canada (Free) Experience." *Presbyterian History.* 38, 2 (October 1994): 1-5.

—. *Response to Challenge: Presbyterianism in Grey and Bruce.* Owen Sound: Austin Graphics, 1996.

Best, C.M. *Development of the Methodist and Presbyterian Church in Western Canada, prior to Union.* James Robertson Memorial Lecture, 1956.

Beveridge, Thomas. "An Account of the First Mission of the Associate Synod to Canada West." Transcribed and ed. by Andrew W. Taylor. *Ontario History* L, 2 (1958): 101-11.

Binnington, Alfred Fernes. "The Glasgow Colonial Society and its Work in the Development of the Presbyterian Church in British North America. 1825-1840." Victoria University, 1960.

Bishop, James Harvey. *Church of Scotland in Prince Edward Island.* [Charlottetown,] 1990.

Boyce, Gerald E. *The St. Andrew's Chronicles: An Account of Presbyterianism Before 1879 in the Belleville-Hastings County-Quinte Area.* Belleville: St. Andrew's Presbyterian Church, 1978.

Bryce, George. *The Presbyterian Church in Canada and the Canadian North-west.* Toronto: British American Presbyterian, 1875.

Burton, R.J., ed. *Growth.* Alberta: Synod of Alberta History Committee, 1968.

Bush, Peter. *Western Challenge: the Presbyterian Church in Canada's Mission on the Prairies and North, 1885-1925.* Winnipeg: Watson-Dwyer, 2000.

Butcher, W.F. "Presbyterian Beginnings in Quebec." *Presbyterian History* 4, 1 (October 1959): 3-4.

Campbell, Douglas F., and Gary D. Bouma. "Social Conflict and the Pictou Notables." *Ethnicity* 5 (1978): 76-88.

Cameron, James. "The Garden Distressed: Church Union and Dissent on Prince Edward Island, 1925." *Acadiensis* 21, 2 (Spring 1991): 108-31.

———. "The History of the Presbyterian Church in Prince Edward Island." *The Abegweit Review* 8, No. 1 (Fall 1994-Spring 1995): 85-102.

Carnochan, Janet, ed. "Early Churches in the Niagara Peninsula, Stamford and Chippawa, with Marriage Records of Thomas Cummings, and Extracts from the Cummings Papers." Ontario Historical Society *Papers and Records,* Vol. 8 (1907): 149-225.

Chernoff, Lee. "Fort Steele's Presbyterian Church." *British Columbia Historical News* 27, 3 (Summer 1993): 14-17.

Church in the Kootenay; the story of the United Church of Canada in Kootenay Presbytery. Trail, British Columbia, 1965.

Crawford, David. "Blue Flame in the Foothills: Presbyterian Activities in the Calgary Region." In *The Search for Souls, Histories of Calgary's Churches.* Calgary: Century Calgary, 1975. Pp. 435-520.

Crerar, Duff Willis. "Church and Community: The Presbyterian Kirk-Session in the District of Bathurst, Upper Canada." M.A. thesis, University of Western Ontario, 1979.

Croil, James. "Story of the Kirk in the Maritime Provinces." *The Presbyterian* 38 (1875): 214-22, 237-47, 261-69, 285-96.

Duncan, K.J. "Aspects of Scottish Settlement in Wellington County." *Scottish Colloquium Proceedings*. Guelph, 1972.

Dunning, R.D. *A Century of Presbyterianism in Saskatchewan, 1866-1966*. Prince Albert, Saskatchewan: St. Paul's Presbyterian Church, 1967.

Ferguson, C.B. "The Sesquicentennial of the First Synod of the Presbyterian Church in Canada." *Dalhousie Review* 48 (1968-1969): 215-21.

General Associate Synod of Scotland. *Address to the Congregations under the Inspection of the General Associate Synod, regarding Nova Scotia*. Paisley, Scotland: J. Neilson, 1815.

Hay, Eldon. "Covenanter Worship and Religion: Chignecto Practice." *Presbyterian History*, Part I, 32, 1 (May 1988): 1-7; Part II, 32, 2 (October 1988): 1-7.

———. *The Chignecto Covenanters: a Regional History of Reformed Presbyterianism in New Brunswick and Nova Scotia, 1827-1905*. Montreal: McGill-Queen's University Press, 1996.

Johnston, George A. *Northwest Above Sixty: the story of the Presbyterian Church in Canada in the Yukon Territory and the Western Third of the Northwest Territories following Church Union in 1925*. N.P., 1989.

———. "Northwest above Sixty." *Presbyterian History* 35, 1 (May 1991): 1-4; 35, 2 (October 1991): 1-6.

Johnston, Harcourt T. *History of Presbyterianism in Thunder Bay and District (1869-1980)*. N.P., 1980.

Johnston, John A. "Our Church in French-speaking Canada." *Presbyterian History* 1, 1 (March 1957): 1-3.

———. "Early Presbyterianism in Ontario." *Families* 21, 4 (1982): 300-308.

———. "Early Presbyterianism in Ontario." *Presbyterian History* 29, 1 (May 1985): 1-4.

King, George B. "Presbyterianism in Western Canada." United Church Archives, *The Bulletin*, 1956.

Kitzan, Lawrence. "The London Missionary Society in Upper Canada." *Ontario History* 59 (March 1967): 39-45.

Lennox, Harry. "A Short History of the Presbyterian Church in the Synod of British Columbia." In Charles P. Anderson, ed., *Circle of Voices—a history of the religious communities of British Columbia*. Lantzville, British Columbia: Oolichan Books, 1983. Pp. 149-161.

Levine, G.J. "In God's Service: The Role of the Anglican, Methodist, Presbyterian and Roman Catholic Churches in the Cultural Geography of Kingston." Ph.D. thesis, Queen's University, Kingston, 1980.

Lucas, Calvin Glenn. "Presbyterianism in Carleton County to 1867." M.A. thesis, Carleton University, 1973.

MacBeth, R.G. *The Selkirk Settlers in Real Life*. Toronto, 1897.

MacKinnon, Archibald D. *The History of the Presbyterian Church in Cape Breton*. Antigonish: Formac for the Presbytery of Cape Breton, 1975.

Mackinnon, Ian F. *Settlements and Churches in Nova Scotia, 1749-1776*. Halifax: T.C.Allen, 1930?

Maclean, Alexander. *The Story of the Kirk in Nova Scotia*. Pictou: Pictou Advocate, 1912. Pp. 102. Drawn from James Croil in *The Presbyterian*, 1875.

MacLeod, John M. *History of Presbyterianism on Prince Edward Island*. Chicago, 1904.

MacMillan, Donald Neil. *The Kirk in Glengarry*. Finch, Ontario: The Author, 1984.

Manson, Ian M. "Serving God and Country: Evangelical Piety and the Presbyterian Church in Manitoba, 1880-1900." M.A. thesis, University of Manitoba, 1986.

McColl, H. *Some Sketches of the Early Highland Pioneers in the County of Middlesex*. Ottawa, 1979.

McDougall, Elizabeth Ann. "The Presbyterian Church in Western Lower Canada, 1815-1842." Ph.D. thesis, McGill University, 1969. Canadian Theses on Microfilm, No. 5174. *Dissertation Abstracts* 31 (1970): 1171-A.

McKellar, Hugh. *Presbyterian Pioneer Missionaries in Manitoba, Saskatchewan, Alberta and British Columbia.* Toronto, 1924.

McMillan, Donald. *History of Presbyterianism in Cape Breton: with brief memorial sketches of the lives of Rev. Hugh McLeod, D.D., Rev. Matthew Wilson, Rev. Alexander Farquharson and other pioneer ministers of Cape Breton.* 3rd ed. Inverness: Inverness News, 1905.

McMullen, W.T. "History of Presbyterianism in the County of Oxford." *Papers and Records of the Ontario Historical Society* 17 (1919): 22-24.

Mills, Thora McIlroy. *The Contributions of the Presbyterian Church to the Yukon During the Gold Rush, 1897-1910.* Archives of the United Church of Canada. *The Bulletin* 25 (1976). Pp. 94.

Moncreiff, Wilfred M. "A History of the Presbyterian Church in Newfoundland, 1622-1966." B.D. thesis, Knox College, Toronto, 1966.

———. "A History of the Presbyterian Church in Newfoundland 1842-1967. . . ." *Presbyterian History,* Part One: 1842-1925, 11, 2 (December 1967): 1-4; Part Two: 1925-1967, 12, 1 (June 1968): 1-3.

More, Robert. *Aurora Borealis: A History of the Reformed Presbyterian Church in Canada (Covenanter), 1820-1967.* Philadelphia: Board of Education and Publication, 1967.

Morris, John Joseph Harold. "The Presbyterian Church in Edmonton, Northern Alberta, and the Klondike 1881-1925." M.Th. thesis, Vancouver School of Theology, 1974.

Murray, John. *The History of the Presbyterian Church in Cape Breton.* Truro: New Publishing, 1921.

Oliver, E.H. "The Presbyterian Church in Saskatchewan, 1866-1881." *Transactions of the Royal Society of Canada,* Section II, 1934, 61-94.

Parker, H.E. "Early Presbyterianism in Western Ontario." *Transactions of the London and Middlesex Historical Society,* Part XIV, 1930, 5-72.

Patterson, George. *A History of the County of Pictou, Nova Scotia.* Montreal: Dawson, 1877.

Pauley, Frederick. "Pictou County Churches, Nova Scotia." *Presbyterian History* 10, 2 (October 1966): 1-4.

Report of the Church of Scotland Missionary Association in Nova Scotia. Halifax: Wesleyan Steam Press, 1860.

Rioux, Georges. "Les Presbytérians à Québec de 1760-1890." Thèse M.A., Université Laval, 1987. ISBN 0-315-39097-2.

Robertson, James. *History of the Mission of the Secession Church to Nova Scotia and Prince Edward Island: from its commencement in 1765.* Edinburgh and London: J. Johnstone, 1847. Pp. 292.

Runnalls, Rev. F.E. *It's God's Country: A Review of the United Church and Its Founding Partners, the Congregational, Methodist and Presbyterian Churches in British Columbia.* N.P., 1974. Pp. 247, 17, 4. Toronto: United Church Archives.

Russell, P.A. "Church of Scotland Clergy in Upper Canada: Culture Shock and Conservatism on the Frontier." *Ontario History* 73 (June 1981): 88-111.

Schissler, J.P. "The Conference of Western Synods 1945." *Presbyterian History* 12, 2 (December 1968): 1-4.

Scobie, Charles H.H., and G.A. Rawlyk, eds. *The Contribution of Presbyterianism to the Maritime Provinces of Canada.* McGill-Queen's Studies in the History of Religion. Series Two. Montreal: McGill-Queen's University Press, 1997.

Smith, Neil Gregor. "By Schism Rent Asunder: A Study of the Disruption of the Presbyterian Church in Canada in 1844." *Canadian Journal of Theology,* October 1955.

Stanley, Laurie Catherine Christina. *The 'Well-Watered Garden': The Presbyterian Church in Cape Breton, 1798-1860.* Sydney: University College of Cape Breton Press, 1983.

Stinson, Thomas Andrew. "A Kind of Question that Raises Feeling: Nova Scotia Presbyterians and the Formation of the United Church of Canada." M.A. thesis, Dalhousie University, 1991.

Synod History Committee. *Growth: A History and Anthology of the Synod of Alberta of the Presbyterian Church in Canada.*

A Tale of Two Centuries: Truro Presbytery, oldest in Canada. Sackville, NB: Tribune Press, 1993.

"The Highland Pioneers of the County of Middlesex." *Papers and Records of the Ontario Historical Society,* Vol. 9 (1910): 26-32.

Tour Guide: church historic sites: the United Church of Canada, the Presbyterian Church in Canada, the Methodist Church, Canada, the Congregational Churches, Canada, the Evangelical United Brethren: Atlantic Provinces and Bermuda. [Toronto: United Church Archives, 197?.]

Walker, John C. "The Early History of the Presbyterian Church in Western Canada, from the earliest times to the year 1881." Ph.D. thesis, University of Edinburgh, 1928.

Wallace, Malcolm. "Pioneers of the Scotch Settlement on the Shore of Lake St. Clair." *Ontario History* 41, 4 (1949): 172-200.

Young, M. *Reminiscences of the Early History of Galt and the Settlement of Dumfries.* Toronto, 1879.

6. Biography-General and Collective

Betts, E. Arthur. *Our Fathers in the Faith: Being an account of Presbyterian ministers ordained before 1875.* Halifax: Oxford Street Press for Maritime Conference Archives Committee, 1983. Pp. 140. [Maritime clergy.]

Bryce, G. *The Scotsman in Canada.* Toronto, n.d.

Campbell, Malcolm. *Cape Breton Worthies: life sketches of notable men in the early Presbyterian Church, eminent for piety and talent.* Sydney, 1913.

Campbell, W. *The Scotsman in Canada.* 2 vols. Toronto, n.d.

Careless, J.M.S. *Brown of the Globe.* 2 vols. Toronto: Macmillan, 1959, 1963.

Davin, Nicolas Flood. *The Irishman in Canada.* Toronto, 1879.

Dent, John Charles. *The Canadian Portrait Gallery.* 4 vols. Toronto: John B. Magurn, 1880-81.

Dictionary of Canadian Biography. 14 vols. + index, 1966-   .

Dictionary of Hamilton Biography. 3 vols., 1982-   .

Dictionary of National Biography. 1908-   .

Fraser, Brian J. *The Christianization of our civilization: Presbyterian reformers and their defence of a Protestant Canada, 1875-1914* [microform]. Ottawa: National Library of Canada, 1984.

Galbraith, John Kenneth. *The Scotch.* Toronto: Macmillan, 1964.

Gibbon, J. Murray. *Scots in Canada.* Toronto, 1971.

Mack, Barry. "George Munro [Monro] Grant: Evangelical Prophet. Ph.D. thesis, Queen's University, Kingston, 1992.

MacPhie, R.P., ed. *Pictonians at Home and Abroad.* Boston: Pinkham, 1914.

MacTavish, W.S., ed. *Missionary Pathfinders; Presbyterian Labourers at Home and Abroad.* Toronto: Musson, 1907.

McKellar, Hugh. *Presbyterian Pioneer Missionaries in Manitoba, Saskatchewan, Alberta and British Columbia.* Toronto, 1924.

——. *Presbyterian Pioneer Ministers.* Toronto: Murray, 1924.

McNab, John. *They Went Forth.* Toronto: McClelland & Stewart, 1933.

Middleton, Jesse Edgar, and W. Scott Downs, eds. *National Encyclopaedia of Canadian Biography.* 2 vols. Toronto, 1935-37.

Moir, John S., ed., *Called to Witness: Profiles of Canadian Presbyterians, a Supplement to Enduring Witness.* III. Hamilton: Committee on History, Presbyterian Church in Canada, 1991; IV, 1999.

——, and C.T. McIntire, ed. *Canadian Protestant and Catholic Missions, 1820s-1960s: historical essays in honour of John Webster Grant.* New York: Peter Lang, 1988.

Morgan, Henry J. *Sketches of Celebrated Canadians.* Quebec: Hunter, Rose, 1862.

Murray, J. Lowell. *Nation Builders.* Toronto: The Mission Boards of the United Church of Canada, 1925.

Patterson, George. *Biographical Notes of Presbyterian Ministers in the Lower Provinces.* N.P., n.d.

Rattray, William J. *The Scot in British North America.* 4 vols. Toronto, [1880-84].

Reid, W. Stanford, ed. *Called to Witness: Profiles of Canadian Presbyterians, a Supplement to Enduring Witness.* Vol. 1. Toronto: Presbyterian Publications, 1975. Vol. 2. [Toronto]: Committee on History, Presbyterian Church in Canada, 1980.

——, ed. *The Scottish Tradition in Canada.* Toronto: McClelland and Stewart, 1976.

Roberts, Charles G.D., and Arthur L. Tunnell, eds. *A Standard Dictionary of Canadian Biography: The Canadian Who Was Who.* 2 vols. Toronto, 1934.

Rose, George MacLean. *A Cyclopedia of Canadian Biography.* Toronto: Rose, 1886.

Roy, James A. *The Scot and Canada.* Toronto: McClelland and Stewart, 1947.

Scott, Hew. *Fasti Ecclesiae Scoticanae: the succession of ministers in the Church of Scotland from the Reformation.* 10 vols. Edinburgh: Oliver and Boyd, 1915-1981.

Scottish Tradition. Canadian Association for Scottish Studies. [Annual, irregular.]

Sellar, Robert. *A Scotsman in Upper Canada.* Toronto: Clark, Irwin, 1969.

Thomson, E.A. *Keepers of the Faith.* Toronto: Presbyterian Publications, 1939.

Wallace W. Stewart, ed. *The Macmillan Dictionary of Canadian Biography.* Toronto: Macmillan, 1963. Rev. ed. by William MacKay, 1980.

Who's Who and Why: A Biographical Dictionary of Men and Women of Canada and Newfoundland. Vancouver, 1914.

Yoo, Young Sik. *Earlier Canadian Missionaries in Korea: A Study in History 1888-1895.* Mississauga: Society for Korean and Related Studies, 1987.

7. Religious Practice and Pastoral Care

Bowman, F. *Communion Tokens of the Presbyterian Church in Canada.* Toronto: Canadian Numismatic Association, 1965.

Burns, Robert. *Substance of Speeches and Addresses at the Presbyterial Visitation of Knox Church.* Toronto: MacLear, 1856.

Campbell, Douglas F. "Ecumenists and Entrepreneurs: A Study of Coalition Leadership." *Revue d'études canadiennes/Journal of Canadian Studies,* 27, 3 (Automne/Fall 1992): 28-46.

Canadian Presbyterian Pulpit: Sermons. Toronto: James Campbell, 1863.

The Charlton Standard Catalogue of Canadian Communion Tokens. 1st ed. Toronto: The Charlton Press, 1992.

Cowan, C.L. ("Roman Collar"). *The Parson Hits Back.* Toronto: Thorn, 1937.

Craik, W.A. *Canadian Communion Tokens.* 1912.

Crysdale, Stewart. *The Changing Church in Canada.* Toronto: United Church Publishing House, 1965.

———, and Les Wheatcroft, eds. *Religion in Canadian Society.* Toronto: Macmillan of Canada, Maclean-Hunter, 1976.

Ferrier, Andrew. *Christ Wounded in the House of His Friends.* Brantford, UC: Herald, 1851.

fon Wearinga, Juw. "The First Protestant Ordination in Canada." United Church Archives, *The Bulletin,* No. 11 (1958): 19-32.

Fotheringham, T.F. *The John Knox Liturgy: with an introductory note by The Rev. Principal Allan Pollok of Halifax College, N.S.* Halifax, n.d.

Fraser, Brian J. "The 'Progress in Theology' Debate: Consensus and Debate in North Atlantic Presbyterianism." *Proceedings of the Canadian Society of Church History* 3-4 June 1987 (1988): 45-52.

———. "The Public Pieties of Canadian Presbyterians." In Robert E. Vandervennen, ed. *Church and Canadian Culture.* Lanham, MD: University Press of America, 1991. Pp. 87-104.

———. *Fire in the Sanctuary: Leadership in The Presbyterian Church in Canada.* Vancouver: St. Andrew's Hall, 1993.

Gauvreau, John Michael. "History and Faith: a study of Methodist and Presbyterian thought in Canada, 1820-1940." Ph.D. thesis, University of Toronto, 1985.

———. "War, Culture and the Problem of Religious Certainty: Methodist and Presbyterian Church Colleges, 1914-1930." *Journal of the Canadian Church Historical Society* 29, 1 (April 1987): 12-31.

———. *The Evangelical Century: College and Creed in English Canada from the Great Revival to the Great Depression.* Montreal: McGill-Queen's University Press, 1991.

George, James. *The Sabbath School of the fireside; and the Sabbath School of the Congregation, as it ought to be.* Kingston, UC, 1859.

Grant, George Monro. *Address on Temporalities.* N.P., 1882.

Gray, J.W.D. *A Brief View of the Scriptural Authority and Historical Evidence of Infant Baptism; and a Reply to Objections Urged in the*

Treatise of E.A. Crawley. Halifax: W. Cannibal, 1837. Pp. 305.

Gregg, William. *Book of Prayers for Family Worship.* Toronto: James Campbell, 1873.

Hay, J. Charles. *The Face of the Church in the 90's.* Toronto: Board of Congregational Life, Presbyterian Church in Canada, 1991. Pp. 25.

Jenkins, John. *Letter concerning the Christian Duty of Adequately providing for the support of Ministers.* Montreal, 1869.

Johnson, Robert. *Presbyterian Worship; its spirit, method, and history.* Toronto, 1901.

Johnston, John A. *Through the Years with the Ontario Presbyterian Young People's Society.* Toronto, 1952.

Laing, John. *Marriage with the sister of a Deceased Wife considered in connection with the Standards and Practice of the Canada Presbyterian Church.* Toronto: Adam Stevenson, 1868.

"Lay Presbyterian." *The So-called Heresy Case at Galt.* Toronto: Imrie and Graham, 1889.

"Layman." *A Letter of a self Reliant Layman.* Reprinted from *Colonial Presbyterian.* [St. John's?:] Barnes, 1861.

MacLennan, George A. *The Story of Old-Time Communion Service and Worship, and also the Metallic Communion Tokens of the Presbyterian Church in Canada, 1772.* 1924.

Macleod, Donald. *Presbyterian Worship: Its Meaning and Method.* Richmond, VA: John Knox Press, 1965.

Martinello, Sandra. "A Member in Good Standing: Communion Tokens of the Presbyterian Church in Nova Scotia." *Canadian Collector* 16 (May/June 1981): 47-8.

McLachlan, R.W. *Canadian Communion Tokens.* 1891.

Melton, J.W., Jr. "The Reshaping of Presbyterian Worship by Nineteenth Century America." Ph.D. thesis, Princeton University, 1966. *Dissertation Abstracts* 27 (1966-1967): 246-A.

Mol, Hans. *Faith and Fragility: Religion and Identity in Canada.* Burlington: Trinity, 1985.

Ormiston, William. *A Pastoral Letter addressed to Members of the Canada Presbyterian Church.* Hamilton, 1869.

Osborne, Alexander Campbell. "Pioneer sketches and family reminiscences." *Papers and Records of the Ontario Historical Society* 21 (1924): 213-26.

Polity of the Presbyterian Church of Canada in connection with the Church of Scotland. N.P.: Synod, c. 1868.

Presbyterian Church in Canada. *Ministry of the Presbyterian Church in Canada.* Toronto: Committee on Recruitment and Vocation, Presbyterian Church in Canada, in co-operation with P.S. Ross and Partners, 1969.

Presbyterian Church of Canada, in connection with the Church of Scotland. *Proceedings of the Presbytery of Toronto in the case of Messrs. Leach and Ritchie.* Toronto: "Colonist," 1843.

Rintoul, William. *A Pastoral Letter from the Synod of the Presbyterian Church in Canada in connexion with the Church of Scotland.* N.P., 1837.

Waldie, John R. "The Influence of the Kirk Session on the Administration of Justice and Regulation of the Social Life of the Community," M.A. thesis, Queen's University, Kingston, 1933.

Woodley, E.C. *The Bible in Canada.* Toronto: J.M. Dent, 1953.

8. Missions

Binnington, A.F. "The Glasgow Colonial Society and Its Work in the Development of the Presbyterian Church in British North America, 1825-1840." D.Th. thesis, Toronto Graduate School of Theological Studies, 1960.

Boyle, George. "The Foreign Mission Committee of the Presbyterian Church in Canada, 1854-1925." United Church Archives, *The Bulletin*, No. 8 (1955): 37-44.

Burns, Robert. *Report presented to the Colonial Committee of the Free Church of Scotland in Canada and Nova Scotia.* Paisley, Scotland: Colonial Committee, 1844.

——. *Reports of the Glasgow Society in connection with the Established Church of Scotland for promoting the religious interests of the Scottish settlers in British North America.* 1826.

Call and Response: A History of the Women's Missionary Society, W.D., 1864 1914 1964. [Toronto?:] History Book Committee, n.d. Pp. 110.

Canada's Share in World Tasks. Toronto: Canadian Council of the Missionary Education Movement, c. 1920.

City Missions, Board of. *City Missions of the Canada Presbyterian Church.* Montreal: J.C. Becket, 1865.

Croil, James. *The Missionary Problem—A History of Protestant Mission.* Toronto: William Briggs, 1883. Pp. 224.

——. *"The Noble Army of Martyrs," being a roll of Protestant Missionary Martyrs, 1661-1891.* Philadelphia: Presbyterian Board of Publication and Sabbath-School Work, 1894. Pp. 175.

Dunn, Zander. "The Canadian Presbyterian Church in Guyana." M.A. thesis, Queen's University, Kingston, 1972.

Gale, James S. *Korean Sketches.* 1898.

Goforth, Jonathan, and Rosalind Goforth. *Miracle Lives in China.* London, 1930.

Goforth, Jonathan, and Allan Rech. *Gospel Triumphs in Manchuria: The Story of Canadian Presbyterian Mission 1927-1935.* Toronto, 1935.

Gordon, C.W. "The Presbyterian Church and its Missions." In Shortt and Doughty, eds., *Canada and its Provinces* (1913-1917), XI: 1, 249-300.

Grant, John Webster. *Moon of Wintertime: Missionaries and the Indians of Canada in Encounter since 1534.* Toronto: University of Toronto Press, 1964.

——. "Presbyterian Home Missions and Canadian Nationhood." *Biblioteca della Ricerca, Cultura Straniera* 30, Estratto de "Canada ieri e oggi 2," 1988, 139-53.

——. "The Reaction of WASP Churches to Non-WASP Immigrants." Canadian Society of Church History, Papers, 1968, Part I, 1-15.

Grant, K.J. *My Missionary Memories.* Halifax, 1923.

Gunn, William T. *His Dominion.* Toronto: Canadian Council of Missionary Education Movement, 1918.

Holman, J.D., ed. *The History of Our Society.* Toronto: Women's Missionary Society (W.D.) of the Presbyterian Church in Canada, 1934.

"In the Heart of India." Toronto: Presbyterian Board of Foreign Missions, 1916.

Johnson, Edward Hewlett. "Rethinking Mission—1955." *Canadian Journal of Theology 1* (2), July 1955, 109-16.

Johnston, Geoffrey. *Unknown Country: A Centennial Account of Missions, the Presbyterian Church in Canada.* Toronto: Presbyterian Church in Canada, [1973?]. Pp. 80.

——. *Of God and Maxim Guns: Presbyterianism in Nigeria, 1846-1966.* Waterloo: Wilfrid Laurier University Press, 1988.

Kannawin, W.M. *Go, Teach.* Toronto: Board of Sabbath Schools and Young People's Societies, 1940.

Kennedy, Margaret F. *Flame of the Forest.* Toronto: Board of World Mission, 1980.

Lindsey, Robert G. "Evangelization of the French Canadians by the Presbyterian Church, 1863-1925." B.D. thesis, Emmanuel College, Toronto, 1956.

Lynch, Sr. Claire, O.S.B. "William Thurston Boutwell and the Chippewas." *Journal of Presbyterian History* 58, 3 (Fall 1980): 238-254.

Macdonald, Caroline. *A Gentleman in Prison.* New York: Doran, 1922.

MacDonald, Alexander S. "Overseas Missions of the Presbyterian Church in Canada, 1875-1950." B.D. thesis, Presbyterian College, Montreal, 1955.

MacKay, George Leslie. *From Far Formosa: The island, its people and missions.* 1896.

MacLean, A.H. *The Galloping Gospel.* Boston: Beacon, 1966. [The author's experiences as a Presbyterian missionary in Western Canada.]

MacLeod, Duncan. *The Island Beautiful.* [Formosa:] N.P., n.d.

MacVicar, D.H. "Canadian Presbyterian Mission Fields." *Knox College Monthly,* 1891?, 311-27.

Martell, Anne Patricia. "The Canadian Presbyterian Mission to Trinidad's East Indian Population, 1868-1912." M.A. thesis, Dalhousie University, 1975. Canadian Theses on microfiche: 24942.

McKenzie, F.A. *The Tragedy of Korea.* N.P., n.d.

——. *In Other Tongues.* Toronto: Thorn, 1939.

McPherson, Margaret E. "Head, Heart and Purse: The Presbyterian Women's Missionary Society in Canada 1876-1925." In Dennis L. Butcher, ed. *Prairie Spirit: Perspectives on the Heritage of the United Church of Canada in the West.* Winnipeg: The University of Manitoba Press, 1985. Pp. 147-70.

McTavish, William Sharpe, ed. *Reapers in Many Fields: a survey of Canadian Presbyterian Missions.* Toronto: Westminster, 1904.

——. *Missionary Pathfinders.* Toronto: Musson, 1907.

Mills, Thora McIlroy. *The Contribution of the Presbyterian Church to the Yukon during the Gold Rush, 1897-1910.* Toronto: Committee on Archives of the United Church of Canada, 1977.

Moir, John S., and C.T. McIntire, ed. *Canadian Protestant and Catholic Missions, 1820s-1960s: historical essays in honour of John Webster Grant.* New York: Peter Lang, 1988.

Moir, John S., co-ed. *Selected Correspondence of the Glasgow Colonial Society 1835-1840.* Toronto: The Champlain Society, [1994].

Mount, Graeme Stewart. *Presbyterian Missions to Trinidad and Puerto Rico: The Formative Years, 1868-1914.* Hantsport: Lancelot, 1983.

—. "The Canadian Presbyterian Mission in Trinidad 1868-1912." *Revista Interamericana* (Puerto Rico) 7, 1 (1977): 30-45.

Olender, Vivian. "The Reaction of the Canadian Presbyterian Church Towards Ukrainian Immigrants (1900-1925): Rural Home Missions as Agencies of Assimilation." D.Th. thesis, University of St. Michael's College, Toronto, 1984.

Our Jubilee Story 1864-1924. Toronto: The Women's Missionary Society, Presbyterian Church in Canada, W.D., 1924.

Platt, H.L. *The Story of the Years: A History of the Woman's Missionary Society in Japan, from 1881 to 1906.* 2 vols. Toronto: The Woman's Missionary Society of the United Church of Canada, 1915; n.d. for Vol. 2.

Presbyterian Church in Canada, Woman's Missionary Society, Eastern Division. *The World for Christ: Woman's Missionary Society of the Presbyterian Church in Canada, Eastern Division, 1876-1976.* [1976?]. Pp. 78.

A Quarter Century in North Honan. Shanghai: Mission Press, c. 1910.

Report of the COMMITTEE OF THE GENERAL ASSEMBLY OF THE CHURCH OF SCOTLAND *for promoting the religious interests of* SCOTTISH PRESBYTERIANS IN THE COLONIES. *Given in by The Rev. Professor Stevenson, D.D., convener, May 1864.* Edinburgh: Thomas Paton, 1864. Pp. 25.

Robertson, H.A. *Eromanga: The Martyr Isle.* Toronto: Upper Canada Tract Society, 1902.

Sinclair, James M. "Mission: Klondike." *Presbyterian Record,* February 10-14; March 12-16; April 11-14; May 14-16; June 10-13, 1975.

Stephenson, William. *Report of the Committee of the General Assembly of the Church of Scotland for Promoting the Religious interests of Scottish Presbyterians in the Colonies.* Edinburgh: T. Paton, 1864-1866.

Stevenson, L. June. *Seed Time and Harvest.* Don Mills: Women's Missionary Society of the Presbyterian Church in Canada, 1987. Pp. 31.

Strang, Peter. *History of Missions in Southern Saskatchewan.* Regina, 1929.

Summons of the Spirit. Toronto: Board of Missionary Education, 1960.

Warden, Robert H. *The Statistics and General Working of Home Missions in Canadian Churches with special reference to the Chatham Presbytery of the Canada Presbyterian Church.* London: Free Press, 1873.

Women's Missionary Society. *The Planting of the Faith.* N.P., n.d.

———. (W.D.). *The Royal Road.* Toronto: Bryant Press, 1927.

———. *The Story of Our Missions.* Toronto: Women's Missionary Society of the Presbyterian Church in Canada, 1915.

Woods, Desta E. Brown. *Graham Stoddart, Minister: a story of the Gatineau.* Serialized in *The Presbyterian,* 1914-15.

Young, Sik Yoo. *Earlier Canadian Missionaries in Korea: a study in history 1888-1895.* Mississauga, Society for Korean and Related Studies, 1987.

9. The Arts

Alexander, Thomas. *Prayers for the Young.* Toronto: James Cleland, 1840. Pp. 33.

Anderson, George. *The Psalmist, being a choice selection of sacred music. Adapted to the use of churches and schools in British North America with initiatory lessons on the art of singing.* Edited and published by George Anderson, precentor, St. Andrew's Church. Montreal: J.C. Becket, 185?. Pp. 68.

Angus, Margaret. "The Old Stones of Queen's, 1842-1900." *Historic Kingston* 20 (1972): 5-13.

Bingham, Neil R. *A Study of the Church Buildings in Manitoba of the Congregational, Methodist, Presbyterian and United Churches of Canada.* Winnipeg: Government of Manitoba, Historical Resources Branch, [1989].

Book of Praise, rev. 1972, authorized by the General Assembly of the Presbyterian Church in Canada. Don Mills: Presbyterian Church in Canada, 1972.

Book of Praise, authorized by the General Assembly of the Presbyterian Church in Canada. Toronto: Humphrey Milford (Oxford University Press), 1918.

Celebrate. Waterloo: Waterloo Music Co., 1983.

"Christ in architecture—a review article." *Journal of Presbyterian History* 45 (1967): 49-56. [A discussion of modern church-architecture as it confronts several Protestant groups, occasioned by D.J. Bruggink and C.H. Droppers, *Christ and Architecture: building Presbyterian/ Reformed churches.*]

Choix de Cantiques à l'usage de l'Église presbytérienne française du Canada. Quebec: William Neilson, 1844.

Estey, Zebulon. *New Brunswick Church Harmony: A Collection from Approved English and American Authors.* Saint John: Blakslee & Estey, 1835.

Ferguson, George. *Signs and Symbols in Christian Art.* London: Oxford University Press, 1961.

Fraser, John. *Address on Instrumental Music as delivered at the Synod of the Canada Presbyterian Church, June 12, 1868.* Kincardine, [1868?].

Harvey, D.C. "The intellectual awakening of Nova Scotia." *Dalhousie Review,* 13 (1933): 1-22.

Hymnal of the Presbyterian Church in Canada, for use in Sabbath Schools, with accompanying tunes. Prepared by a committee of the General Assembly. Toronto: Assembly's Hymnal Committee, 1884.

Hymnal of the Presbyterian Church in Canada: prepared by a committee of the General Assembly. Approved and commended by the General Assembly. Toronto: C. Blackett Robinson; Montreal: W. Drysdale, 1881.

Hymns for the use of Sabbath Schools in Connection with the Canada Presbyterian Church. Toronto: James Campbell, 1862.

Johnston, John Alexander. "The Organ Question." *Presbyterian History* 2 (March 1960): 1-2.

———. "The Presbyterian Press." *Presbyterian History* 3:2 (June 1959): 1-2.

Knyha Khvaly [Ukrainian Book of Praise]. Toronto: Home Missions Boards of the Presbyterian and Methodist Churches, 1922.

Mahon, A. Wylie. *Canadian Hymns and Hymn Writers.* Saint John, NB.: Globe, 1908.

McDonald, Donald. *Laiodhean spioradail.* Charlottetown, 1835.

———. *Hymns for Practice, not to be used in the Solemn Worship of the Sanctuary. . . . For the Church of Scotland in connection with the Presbytery of Prince Edward Island.* Charlottetown: Excelsior, 1870.

McNaughton, Duncan. *The Wife of Fairbank, or Kirks and Ministers.* Toronto, 1893. [Fiction.]

Memorial to the Presbytery of Toronto in connection with the Church of Scotland on the Organ Question. Toronto: Lovell and Gibson, 1859.

"Minister of the Canada Presbyterian Church." *A Catechism on the Organ, or The Organ Question Discussed by way of Question and Answer.* Toronto: Lovell and Gibson, 1867.

Old Choir Selection. New Glasgow: Synod of the Maritime Provinces of the Presbyterian Church in Canada, 1942.

Organ Question: Line upon Line or Instrumental Music in Presbyterian Churches. Montreal: Murray, 1868.

Praise Ways. Don Mills: Presbyterian Church in Canada, 1975.

Presbyterian Book of Praise. Approved and commended by the General Assembly of the Presbyterian Church in Canada. [N.P.:] Oxford University Press, 1897.

Presbyterian Church of Canada in Connection with the Church of Scotland. *Hymns for the Worship of God, selected and arranged for the use of congregations connected with the Church of Scotland.* Montreal: Lovell, 1863.

——. *The Presbyterian Psalmody, being a selection of tunes for the use of Presbyterian churches, families, and schools throughout Canada.* Montreal: John C. Becket, 1851.

Rennie, Frederick. "Spiritual Worship on a Carnal Instrument." M.A. in Theology thesis, Knox College, Toronto Graduate School of Theological Studies, Toronto, 1969. [Organ controversy in the Presbyterian Church.]

Sharman, V. "Thomas McCulloch's Stepsure: the relentless Presbyterian." *Dalhousie Review* 52 (1972-73): 618-25.

Smith, Neil Gregor. "Communion Tokens." *Presbyterian History* 9:2 (October 1965): 1-3.

Smith, Mary A., ed. (The St. Mary's Presbyterian Church Ladies.) *The St. Mary's Quilt.* St. Mary's, Ontario: St. Mary's Presbyterian Church, 1990. Pp. 46.

Songs of Faith; prepared for the Guyana Presbyterian Church. Don Mills, ON: Presbyterian Church in Canada, Board of World Mission, 1985.

Songs of Praise for Sabbath Schools and Families. Montreal: Lovell, 1861.

St. John's Church Sunday School hymn book; compiled for the use, chiefly, of the Sunday School of St. John's Church (Church of Scotland), Cornwall, Ontario. By the Superintendent. Montreal: John Lovell, 1870.

The Choir: A Collection of Sacred Vocal Music for the Use of the Congregations and Families of the Presbyterian Church of the Lower Provinces, B.N.A. Halifax: A. & W. MacKinlay, 1885.

The Harmonicon: a collection of sacred music, consisting of psalm and hymn tunes, anthems, &c., selected from the best authors; with a copious introduction to vocal music. 2nd ed., improved and enlr. Pictou: James Dawson, 1841.

Woodruff, A. *The Memorial Hymn Book.* Shanghai: Presbyterian Mission Press, 1890.

10. Education

Betts, E. Arthur. *Pine Hill Divinity Hall, 1820-1970: a History.* Truro, NS: Executive Print for the Board of Governors, Pine Hill Divinity Hall, Halifax, 1970. Pp. 62, illus.

Bush, Peter G. "John Edgar McFadyen and the Ewart Missionary Training Home." *Presbyterian History* 37, 1 (May 1993): 1-5.

———. "The Presbyterian Church in Canada and Native Residential Schools, 1925-1969." *Presbyterian History* 37, 2 (October 1993): 1-7.

Calvin, D.D. *Queen's University at Kingston.* Kingston: Trustees of the University, 1941.

[Campbell, Peter Colin.] "A Master of Arts." *Thoughts on the University Question, respectfully submitted to the members of Both Houses of the Legislature of Canada.* Kingston, UC, 1845. Pp. 36.

Defence of the Plan of University Reform Proposed by the Senate of the University of Toronto. Being a Statement Drawn up at the Request of the Board of Trustees of Queen's College. Kingston, UC, 1863. Pp. 32.

Falconer, Sir Robert. "Scottish Influence in the Higher Education in Canada." *Proceedings and Transactions of the Royal Society of Canada,* 3rd series, 22, Section 2, 7-20.

Fraser, Brian J. *Church, College, and Clergy: a History of Theological Education at Knox College, Toronto, 1844-1994.* Montreal and Kingston: McGill-Queen's University Press, 1995.

Glazier, Kenneth MacLean. "The Place of Religion in the History of the Non-Catholic Universities of Canada." Ph.D. thesis, Yale University, 1944.

Grant, Rudolph W. "Politics, Religion and Education: The Canadian Presbyterian Church and the Struggle over Schools in Guyana." *Journal of Caribbean History* 27, 2 (1993): 176-96.

Greer, A. "The Sunday Schools of Upper Canada." *Ontario History* 67, 3 (1975): 169-84.

Gregg, William. "The History of Knox College." *Knox College Monthly*, November 1888, 9(1), 1-15.

Harvey, D.C. "Dr. Thomas McCulloch and liberal education." *Dalhousie Review* 24 (1943-1944), 352-62.

Hodgins, J. George, ed. *Documentary History of Education in Upper Canada*. 28 vols. Toronto: King's Printer, 1894-1910.

Hughes, Nora Louise. "A History of the Development of Ministerial Education in Canada from its inception until 1925 in those churches which were tributary to the United Church of Canada in Ontario, Quebec, and the Maritime Provinces of Canada." Ph.D. thesis, University of Chicago, 1945.

Johnston, John A. "Factors in the Formation of The Presbyterian Church in Canada 1875." Ph.D. thesis, McGill University, 1955.

———. "A Presbyterian University System for Canada." *Presbyterian History* 5, 2 (May 1961): 2-3.

———. "The Presbyterian College, Montreal, 1865-1915." M.A. thesis, McGill University, 1953.

———. *Through the Years with the Ontario Presbyterian Young Peoples Society.* [N.P.: n.p.,] 1953. Pp. 26.

———. *Presbyterian Youth Activities and Organization in Central Canada.* MS, 1953. Pp. 125.

Krepps, Rex. "The Indian Residential School, File Hills, Sask." *Presbyterian History* 17, 2 (December 1973): 1-2.

Macdonnell, D.J. "The Bible in Schools." *Canadian Educational Monthly* 1888, p. 53.

MacKenzie, R. Sheldon. *Gathered by the River: The Story of the West River Seminary and Theological Hall, 1848-1858*. [N.P.:] Hignell, 1998.

Manual for Presbyterian Young Peoples Societies. Board of Sabbath Schools and Young Peoples Societies. N.P., n.d.

Markell, H. Keith. *History of The Presbyterian College, Montreal 1865-1986.* Montreal: The Presbyterian College, 1987.

Marr, Lucille. "Sunday School Teaching: A Women's Enterprise. A Case Study, from the Canadian Methodist, Presbyterian and United Church Tradition, 1919-1939." *Histoire sociale / Social History* 52 (November 1993): 329-44.

McDougall, Elizabeth A., ed. "Towards the Establishment of a Church of Scotland University in the Canadas: selected letters from the manuscript correspondence of the Glasgow Colonial Society." United Church Archives, *The Bulletin*, No. 21, 1969-1970, 3-27.

McLaren, William. *Knox College, Past and Present.* Toronto, 1894.

Neatby, Hilda. "Queen's College and the Scottish Fact." *Queen's Quarterly* 80 (1973): 1-11.

——. Frederick W. Gibson and Roger Graham, eds. *Queen's University: Vol. 1, 1841-1917: And Not to Yield.* Montreal: McGill-Queen's University Press, 1979.

Owen, Michael. "Keeping Canada God's Country: Presbyterian School-Homes for Ruthenian Children." In Dennis L. Butcher, ed. *Prairie Spirit: Perspectives on the Heritage of the United Church of Canada in the West.* Winnipeg: The University of Manitoba Press, 1985. Pp. 184-201.

Queen's University; a centenary volume, 1841-1941. Toronto: Ryerson, 1941.

Rawlyk, George A., and K. Quinn. *The Redeemed of the Lord Say So: A History of Queen's Theological College, 1912-1972.* Kingston: Queen's Theological College, 1980.

Ross, W. MacKenzie. "Morrin College." *Presbyterian History* 8, 1 (May 1964): 3-4.

Snodgrass, William. *Report of the General Committee on the endowment of Queen's College.* Toronto, 1871.

Somerville, John. *Historical Sketch of Knox College, 1844-1912.* N.P., 1912.

Queen's College Trustees. *Circular to the Subscribers to Queen's College,* August 9, 1845.

University Question, Chalmers vs Burns. 1847.

Vaudry, Richard W. "Theology and Education in Early Victorian Canada: Knox College, Toronto, 1844-1861." *Studies in Religion/Sciences Religieuses* 16, 4 (Fall 1987): 431-47.

Wallace, Robert. "Reminiscences of Student Life in Canada fifty Years ago, and the origins of two Presbyterian Colleges." *Knox College Monthly,* August 1892.

Watson, John. "Thirty Years of Queen's University." *Queen's Quarterly* 10 (2), October 1902, 188-96.

Wigney, Trevor. "Manifest Righteousness: The Presbyterian Church, Education and Nation Building in Canada, 1875-1914." In A. Chaiton, and N. McDonald, eds. *Canadian Schools and Canadian Identity.* Toronto: Gage, 1977.

Wisse, Frederick. *Free of Charge: Preaching the Gospel to Students of Theology.* Montreal: Presbyterian College, 1988. Pp. 84.

11. Migration and Settlement

Bradawl, Caroline B. "From Catholics to Presbyterians: French-Canadian Immigrants in Central Illinois." *American Presbyterians* 63 (Fall 1985): 285-98.

Bridgeman, Harry John. "Three Scots Presbyterians in Upper Canada: A Study in Emigration, Nationalism and Religion." Ph.D. thesis, Queen's University, Kingston, 1978. *Dissertation Abstracts.* (March 1979).

Idyll of the shipbuilders: being a brief account of the life and migrations of the families from the Highlands of Scotland that finally settled at Waipu, North Auckland. Auckland, NZ: Clark & Matheson, [192?].

MacDonald, Gordon. *The Highlanders of Waipu, or, Echoes of 1745: a Scottish Odyssey.* Dunedin, NZ: Coulls Somerville Wilkie, 1928.

MacDonald, Marvin. "The Reaction of Methodist and Presbyterian Churches in Fort William and Port Arthur toward Immigrants from Continental Europe, 1903-1914." M.A. thesis, Lakehead University, 1977.

Martynowych, Orest T. "Canadianizing the Foreigner: Presbyterian Missionaries and Ukrainian Immigrants." In Jaroslav Rozumnyj, ed. *New Soil—Old Roots: The Ukrainian Experience in Canada.* Winnipeg: Ukrainian Academy of Arts and Sciences in Canada, 1983. Pp. 33-57.

Owen, Michael. "The Presbyterian Church Views The Foreigner in the City." 1981. Ms.

Putnam, Ada McLeod. *The Selkirk Settlers.* Toronto: Presbyterian Publications, 1939.

Smith, W.G. *Building the Nation: a study of some problems concerning the churches' relation to the immigrants.* Toronto, 1922.

12. Politics, Labour and Social Thought

Addresses arranged by the Committee on Evangelism and Social Action of the Synod of Toronto and Kingston in the Presbyterian Church in Canada. Galt, 1956.

An Abstract of the Minutes of the SYNOD OF THE PRESBYTERIAN CHURCH IN CANADA, *(in connection with the Church of Scotland,) Session II, held at Toronto 31 August-6th September, 1837.* Toronto: William J. Coates, 1837. Pp. 23.

Barkwell, Gordon. "The Clergy Reserves in Upper Canada: a study in the separation of Church and State 1791-1854." Ph.D. thesis, University of Chicago, 1953.

Boudreau, Michael. "The Emergence of the Social Gospel in Nova Scotia: The Presbyterian, Methodist and Baptist Churches and the Working Class, 1880-1914." M.A. thesis, Queen's University, Kingston, 1991.

Christie, E.A. "The Presbyterian Church in Canada and its Official Attitude toward Public Affairs and Social Problems, 1875-1925." M.A. thesis, University of Toronto, 1955.

Christie, Nancy, and Michael Gauvreau. *A Full-Orbed Christianity: the Protestant Churches and Social Welfare in Canada, 1900-1940.* Montreal: McGill-Queen's University Press, 1996.

Clendennan, D.W. "Some Presbyterian U.E. Loyalists." Ontario Historical Society *Papers and Records* 3 (1901): 117-22.

Cross, Harold. *One Hundred Years of Service with Youth.* Montreal, 1951.

Crysdale, Stewart. *The Industrial Struggle and Protestant Ethics in Canada.* Toronto: Ryerson, 1961.

Elgee, William H. *The Social Teachings of the Canadian Churches. Protestant. The Early Period, before 1850.* Toronto: Ryerson, 1964.

Emery, George N. "The Lord's Day Act of 1906 and the Sabbath Observance Question." In J.M. Bumstead, ed. *Documentary Problems in Canadian History.* Toronto, 1969. Vol. 2, pp. 23-51.

Fraser, Brian J. *The Social Uplifters: Presbyterian Progressives and the Social Gospel in Canada, 1875-1915.* Waterloo: Wilfrid Laurier University Press, 1988.

——. "Theology and the Social Gospel among Canadian Presbyterians: A Case Study." *Studies in Religion/Sciences religieuses* 8, 1 (Winter, 1979): 35-46.

Historical Report of the Administration of the Temporalities' Fund of the Presbyterian Church of Canada in Connection with the Church of Scotland 1856-1900. Montreal: Board of the Temporalities' Fund, 1900. Pp. 15.

Kiesekamp, Burkhard. "Community and Faith: The Intellectual and Ideological Bases of the Church Union Movement in Victorian Canada." Ph.D. thesis, University of Toronto, 1974.

Kilpatrick, Thomas B. *New Testament Evangelism.* Appendices by J.G. Shearer. Toronto: Westminster, 1911.

Laverdure, J.F. Paul. "Canada on Sunday: The Decline of the Sabbath, 1900-1950." Ph.D. thesis, University of Toronto, 1990.

MacDougall, John. *Rural Life in Canada.* [Toronto?:] Presbyterian Board of Social Service, 1913. Reprint, Toronto: University of Toronto Press, 1973.

Manson, I.M. "Serving God and Country. Evangelical Piety and the Presbyterian Church in Manitoba, 1880-1900." M.A. thesis, University of Manitoba, 1986.

Markell, Keith. "Canadian Protestantism against the background of urbanization and industrialization in the period from 1885 to 1914." Ph.D. thesis, University of Chicago, 1971.

McIntosh, W.R. *Social Service: A Book for Young Canadians.* Toronto: Presbyterian Publications, 1911.

—, ed. *Canadian Problems.* Toronto: Presbyterian Publications, 1910.

Miller, J.R. *Equal Rights: The Jesuits' Estates Act Controversy.* Montreal: McGill Queen's University Press, 1979.

Moir, John S. ed. *Church and State in Canada, 1627-1867: Basic Documents.* Toronto: McClelland & Stewart, 1967.

—. *Church and State in Canada West: three studies in the relation of denominationalism and nationalism, 1841-1867.* Toronto: University of Toronto Press, 1959.

—. "The Roots of Disestablishment in Upper Canada." *Ontario History* 60 (3), (September 1968): 247-58.

—. "The Settlement of the Clergy Reserves, 1840-1855." *Canadian Historical Review* 27, 1 (1956): 46-62.

Morris, William. *Reply of WM. MORRIS, MEMBER OF THE LEGISLATIVE COUNCIL, to SIX LETTERS addressed to him by JOHN STRACHAN, D.D. Archdeacon of York.* Toronto: Scotsman Office, 1838. Pp. 54.

———. *The Correspondence of the Hon. William Morris with the Colonial Office as the Delegate from the PRESBYTERIAN BODY IN CANADA.* 1838. Pp. 28.

Murison, Barbara C. "The Disruption and the Colonies of Scottish Settlement." In S.J. Brown, and M. Fry, eds. *Scotland in the Age of Disruption.* Edinburgh: Edinburgh University Press, 1993. Pp. 135-150.

Owen, Michael. "Keeping Canada God's Country: Presbyterian Perspectives on Selected Social Issues, 1900-1915." Ph.D. thesis (education), University of Toronto, 1984.

Parker, Ethel. "The Origins and the Early History of the Presbyterian Settlement Houses." In Richard Allen, ed. *The Social Gospel in Canada.* Ottawa: National Museums of Canada, 1975. Pp. 86-121.

Peddie, Gordon A. *"The King of Kings": the Basis of Union of the Presbyterian Church in Canada and its Relationship to the Present Need of the Church for a Confession of Faith in Jesus Christ as Lord of Church and State together with the Petition of a Memorial of the Presbytery of Paris to the General Assembly, 1942.* Toronto: Age Publications, 1942.

Reid, W. Stanford. *The Church of Scotland in Lower Canada, Its Struggle for Establishment.* Toronto, 1936.

———. "The Struggle of the Church of Scotland for Equal Rights and Privileges with the Church of England in Canada." M.A. thesis, McGill University, 1936.

Rennie, Ian. "The Free Church and the Relations of Church and State in Canada, 1844-54." M.A. thesis, University of Toronto, 1954.

Rienks, Gabe. "Social Concerns within the Presbyterian Church in Canada, 1875-1925." M.Th. thesis, Knox College, Toronto, 1966.

Ross, Murray. *The Y.M.C.A. in Canada.* Toronto: Ryerson, 1951.

Smart, James D. *Evangelism and Social Education in the Local Church.* Toronto: Synod of Toronto and Kingston, 1963.

Smith, W.H. *The Church and Men.* Toronto: Presbyterian Publications, 1914.

Storey, Norah. "The Church and State 'Party' in Nova Scotia, 1749-1840." *Collections of the Nova Scotia Historical Society* 27 (1947): 33-57.

Strachan, John. *Letters to the HONORABLE WILLIAM MORRIS, being STRICTURES on the correspondence of that gentleman with the Colonial Office, AS A DELEGATE from the PRESBYTERIAN BODY in Canada.* Cobourg, UC: R.D. Chatterton, 1838. Pp. 57.

Watts, J.R. *Fifty Years of Rural Canada.* [N.P.:] Board of Home Missions, United Church of Canada, 1933.

Wood, E.H. "Ralph Connor and the Canadian West." Ph.D. thesis, University of Saskatchewan, 1975.

13. Church and Society

Brown, Jennifer S.H. "Diverging Identities: The Presbyterian Metis of St. Gabriel Street, Montréal." In Jacqueline Peterson, and Jennifer S.H. Brown, eds. *The New Peoples: Being and Becoming Métis in North America.* Winnipeg: University of Manitoba Press, 1985. Pp. 195-206.

Harris, William. *Statement and Correspondence of the Pictou Presbytery respecting the Antigonish Riot.* Pictou, 1874.

Jones, A., and Rutman, L. *In the Children's Aid: J.J. Kelso and Child Welfare in Ontario.* Toronto: University of Toronto Press, 1981.

Kiesekamp, Burkhard. "Response to disruption: Presbyterianism in Eastern Ontario, 1844." The Canadian Society of Church History, *Papers 1967,* 31-51, notes, 1-4.

Moir, John S. "The Smouldering Bush—The Presbyterian Church in Canada Faces its Second Century." *Chelsea Journal* 2, 2 (1976): 97-9.

Statement and correspondence of the Pictou Presbytery, Presbyterian Church of the Lower Provinces, respecting the Antigonish Riot. Pictou: W. Harris, 1874. Pp.76.

14. Women and Religion

Anderson, Grace N. *God Calls, Man Chooses: a study of women in ministry in Anglican, Baptist, Presbyterian and United Churches.* Burlington: Trinity, 1990.

Brouwer, Ruth Compton. "Canadian Women and the Foreign Missionary Movement: A Case Study of Presbyterian Women's Involvement at the Home Base and in Central India, 1876-1914." Ph.D. thesis, York University, 1987.

———. *New Women for God: Canadian Presbyterian women and India missions, 1876-1914.* Social History of Canada, 44. Toronto: University of Toronto Press, 1990.

———. "Wooing 'the Heathen' and the Raj: Aspects of Women's Work in the Canadian Presbyterian Mission in Central India, 1877-1914." *Proceedings of the Canadian Society of Church History,* 3-4 June 1987 (1988): 17-32.

Buchanan, Ruth. *My Mother.* Toronto: Women's Missionary Society of the Presbyterian Church in Canada, 1938.

Campbell, Jean. *A Lively Story: Historical Sketches of the Women's Missionary Society (Western Division) of the Presbyterian Church in Canada 1864-1989.* Toronto: WMS (W.D.), [1990?].

Church, W.R. *History of Moncton Presbyterial of the Women's Missionary Society of the United Church of Canada, 1884-1961.* [Moncton, 1961?].

Committee on the Order of Deaconesses. *A History of the Deaconess in the Presbyterian Church in Canada.* [Toronto:] Women's Missionary Society, 1975.

Hall, Nancy. "The Professionalism of Women Workers in the Methodist, Presbyterian and United Churches of Canada." In Mary Kinnear, ed. *First Days, Fighting Days: Women in Manitoba History.* Regina: Canadian Plains Research Centre, University of Regina, 1987. Pp. 120-33.

Hamilton Presbyterial, Women's Missionary Society (W.D.) *In His Service, One Hundred Years, 1886-1986.* Hamilton: Wharton Graphics, 1986.

Historical sketches of churches and W.M.S. auxiliaries in the Saint John Presbytery of the Presbyterian Church in Canada. Moncton, NB: Saint John Presbytery of the Women's Missionary Society, 1968.

Holman, J.D. *The History of our Society.* Toronto: Women's Missionary Society (W.D.), 1934.

Moir, J.S., ed. *Gifts and Graces: Profiles of Canadian Presbyterian Women.* I. Hamilton: Committee on History, Presbyterian Church in Canada, 1999; II. 2002.

Penfield, Janet Harbison. "Women in the Presbyterian Church—an historical overview." *Journal of Presbyterian History* 55, 2 (1977): 107-124.

Reith, Louise A., ed. *Call and Response.* Toronto: Women's Missionary Society, 1964.

Women in the Church, Committee on the Place of. *Putting Woman in her Place.* [Toronto, 1963?]

The Women of the Kirk. Charlottetown, 1977.

Women's Missionary Society, W.D. *The Royal Road.* 1927.

———. *Our India Story.* Toronto: Thorne, n.d.

Whale, Mary E. *On Wings of Faith.* Sarnia: Haines Frontier, 1984. Pp. 62.

———. *Women who Witnessed, Go and Tell.* Oshawa: Tern Graphics, 1989.

15. Ecumenism and Inter-church Relations

Allan, Hugh. *Address to the members of the Presbyterian Church of Canada in connection with the Church of Scotland, on the subject of the proposed grant from the clergy reserves fund, in aid of the Theological Faculty at Queen's College, Kingston.* Montreal, June 1, 1852.

"Anglo-Canadian." *Ten Letters on the Church and Church Establishments, in Answer to certain Letters of the Rev. Egerton Ryerson.* Toronto, 1830.

Barkwell, Gordon. "The Clergy Reserves in Upper Canada: A Study in the Separation of Church and State, 1791-1854." Ph.D. thesis, Divinity School, University of Chicago, 1953.

Basis of Union of the United Church of Canada as prepared by the Joint Committee on Church Union and approved by the Presbyterian Church of Canada, the General Conference of the Methodist Church, the Congregational Union of Canada; also a brief historical statement. Toronto: Joint Committee on Church Union, January 1924.

Bayne, John. *Reasons of Dissent by the Rev. Bayne and others anent Decision of Synod on the basis of Union with the United Presbyterian Church, June 1859.*

——. *Was the recent disruption of the Synod of Canada, in connection with the Church of Scotland, called for? An address to the Presbyterians of Canada who still support the Synod in connection with the Church of Scotland.* Galt, UC: James Ainslie, 1846. Pp. 83.

Beattie, Robert Hartley. "Church Union in Canada, 1925." *Presbyterian History* 24, 2 (October 1980): 1-6.

Bennet, James. *The Kirk on Union of Presbyterians in New Brunswick criticised in a series of Letters.* Saint John: Barnes, 1861.

Campbell, Robert. *The Relations of the Christian Churches; to One Another, and Problems Growing out of Them, Especially in Canada.* Toronto: William Briggs, 1913.

——. *On the Union of Presbyterians in Canada.* Montreal: Grafton, 1871.

Brymner, Douglas. *Faults and Failures of the Late Presbyterian Union in Canada.* London: Free Press, 1879.

Burnet, Robert. *Presbyterian Trade-Union or The Plot to Rob the Kirk of Scotland in Canada.* Hamilton: Duncan Stewart, 1875.

——, et al. *On the Union Question.* 1874.

Burns, R.F. *Address in the Presbyterian Union, delivered in Halifax, July 13, 1875.*

Burns, Robert. *Letter addressed to the Ministers and Elders of the Synod of Canada on the Present duty of the Presbyterian Church.* Montreal: J.C. Becket, 1844.

——. *Report presented to the Colonial Committee of the Free Church of Scotland on Canada and Nova Scotia.* Paisley, Scotland, 1844.

Cameron, John P. "The Story of Church Union of 1925 in the Presbytery of Pictou of the Presbyterian Church in Canada." B.D. thesis, Presbyterian College, Montreal, 1969.

Campbell, Douglas F. "Ecumenists and Entrepreneurs: A Study of Coalition Leadership." *Journal of Canadian Studies/Revue d'études canadiennes* 27, 3 (automne 1992 Fall): 28-46.

Campbell, Robert. *The Pretensions Exposed of Messrs. Lang, Burnet & Co.* Montreal: W. Drysdale, 1878.

Carmichael, James. *Organic Union of Canadian Churches: with a comparison of Authorized Standards.* 1887.

Chown, Samuel Dwight. *The Story of Church Union in Canada.* Toronto: Ryerson, 1930.

Clark, Thomas. *Letter of Sympathy to the Moderator and other Members of the Presbyterian Church in Canada in connexion with the Established Church of Scotland.* September 20, 1844.

Clifford, N. Keith. "Charles Clayton Morrison and the United Church of Canada." *Canadian Journal of Theology* 15 (1969): 86-92.

——. "The Impact of the Presbyterian Controversy over Church Union on the Methodist Church in Canada." Canadian Methodist Historical Society, *Papers*, 2 (1982): pp. 21.

——. *The Resistance to Church Union in Canada, 1904-1939.* Vancouver: University of British Columbia Press, 1985.

Cunningham, Rev. Dr. *Letter to Rev. Henry Esson.* Montreal: J.C. Becket, 1844.

Draft of an Answer to the Dissent and Protest of certain Ministers and elders who have seceded from the Synod of Canada in connexion with the Church of Scotland, by a committee appointed by the Synod . . . . Kingston, UC, 1844. Pp. 30.

Esson, Henry. *An Appeal to the Ministers and Members of the Presbyterian Church on the question of adherence to the Church of Scotland as by Law Established.* Montreal, 1844.

——. *A Plain and Popular Exposition of the Principles of Voluntarism.* Galt, UC: P. Jeffray & Son, 1851.

Ferrier, Andrew. *Christ Wounded in the House of His Friends: A Brief Review of Some Proceedings in Different Courts of the Presbyterian Church of Canada.* Hamilton, UC, 1850.

Grant, George Munro. "Organic Union of Churches: how far should it go?" *Canadian Methodist Magazine* 20, 1884.

Grant, John Webster. *The Canadian Experience of Church Union.* Ecumenical Studies in History, No. 8. London, England: Lutterworth, 1967.

Hamilton, James. *The Harp on the Willows: The Trials and triumphs of the Free Church of Scotland.* No. 1. Montreal, 1844. Pp. 31.

Historical Sketch of Steps taken to bring about a Union of the Presbyterian Church of Canada with the Canada Presbyterian Church in 1866 and 1870. Montreal: John Becket, n.d.

Jenkins, John. *A Protestant's Appeal to the Douay Bible, and Other Roman Catholic Standards, in support of The Doctrines of the Reformation.* 2nd ed. Montreal, 1853.

Johnston, John A. "Presbyterian Union 1875." *Presbyterian History* 1, 2 (June 1957): 3-4.

——. "Presbyterian Disruption in British North America." B.D. thesis, Presbyterian College, Montreal, 1953.

——. "Factors in the Formation of the Presbyterian Church in Canada 1875." D.Th. thesis, McGill University, 1955.

Kiesekamp, Burkhard. "Presbyterian and Methodist Divines: Their Case for a National Church in Canada, 1874-1900." *Studies in Religion/Sciences religieuses*, 2, 4 (1973): 289-302.

——. "Community and Faith: the intellectual and ideological bases of the church union in Victorian Canada." Ph.D. thesis, University of Toronto, 1975.

King, Andrew. *Narrative of Events issuing in the Institution of the Free Church of Scotland in separation from the State.* Halifax: James Barnes, 1861.

Lang, Gavin. *The Union Question.* Montreal, 1874.

——. To the Rev. *Presbytery of Montreal in connection with the Presbyterian Church in Canada.* Montreal, 1876.

——. *Supplementary Statement to the First Article in March 1875 number of "The Presbyterian."* Montreal, 1875.

——. *Letter to the Synod of the Church of Scotland in Canada, when a delegate to the Scottish Assembly, Edinburgh, May 26, 1875.*

—- et al. *Memoranda relating to the Present position of the Question of Union between the Presbyterian Church of Canada in connection with the Church of Scotland and other Presbyterian Churches for the information of members of the different Legislatures of the Dominion.* N.P., n.d.

Mason, Gershom W. *The Legislative Struggle for Church Union.* Toronto: Ryerson, 1956.

McCulloch, Thomas. *Popery again Condemned by Scripture and the Fathers.* Edinburgh: A. Neill, 1810.

——. *Popery Condemned by Scripture and the Fathers.* Edinburgh: J. Pillans, 1808.

[McGill, Robert.] *Brief Notes on the Relation of the Synod of Canada to the Church of Scotland.* Niagara, UC, [1844].

McLean, T.A. et al. *Protest against the so-called Basis of Union.* N.P., n.d.

McLelland, Joseph C. *Towards a Radical Church.* Toronto: Ryerson, 1967.

McNeill, John T., and James Hastings Nichols. *Ecumenical Testimony: the concern for Christian unity within the Reformed and Presbyterian Churches.* Philadelphia: The Westminster Press, 1974.

"Member of Synod." *Rev. Gavin Lang and Union.* 1875.

Middlemiss, James. *Letters on the Union with the Church of Scotland and on Church Independence.* Toronto: James Bain, 1874.

Moffat, John. *Remember Zion or the Captivity and Persecution of the Scotch Church in Canada.* Toronto: Hunter Rose, 1877.

Moore, Donald Stewart. "Disruption in the Canadian Presbyterian Church." M.A. thesis, Pine Hill Divinity Hall, Halifax, 1972.

———. "Presbyterian Non-concurrence and the United Church of Canada." United Church of Canada Archives, *The Bulletin* 24 (1975): 28-39.

Morrow, Ernest Lloyd. *Church Union in Canada; its history, motives, doctrine and government.* Toronto: Thomas Allen, 1923.

Morton, Arthur S. *The Way to Union. Being a study of the principles of the foundation and of the historical development of the Christian Church as bearing on the proposed union of the Presbyterian, Methodist and Congregational Churches in Canada.* Toronto, 1912.

Petition, presented to the Legislative Assembly of the Province of Ontario, containing a summary of the legal aspects of the case of members and adherents of the Presbyterian Church of Canada in connection with the Church of Scotland. Ottawa, 1874.

Presbyterian Union and the College Question. William Baillie, 1871.

Presbyterian Union Bill Discussions, February, 1875, as reported in the Montreal *Herald* and *Daily Commercial Gazette,* February 15, 16, 1875.

Present Position of the Union Question. Reprint for *Presbyterian,* March 1872.

The Present Duty to preserve the Presbyterian Church. A brief Reply to the nine Advocates of the Desertion of our Church for a New Denomination by Dr. McLeod, Barrie, July, 1915. [Barrie?,] 1915.

Protest of Certain Ministers and Elders belonging to the Synod of Canada in connection with the Church of Scotland, July, 1844.

R., A.I.D. *Why We are out of the Union.* Seaforth, n.d.

Reid, Allan S. "The Pilgrim Boat or Scuttling the Ship." *Presbyterian History* 4, 2 (March 1960): 4.

Remarks upon the Late Disruption and Present Position of the Synod of Canada. Toronto: Banner, 1844.

Remarks on Dr. Burns' visit to Nova Scotia, and his proceedings on behalf of the Free Church; by a member of the Established Church of Scotland. Pictou, 1844. Pp. 15.

Rennie, Ian. "The Free Church and the Relations of Church and State in Canada 1844-1854." M.A. thesis, History, University of Toronto, 1954.

Report on the Part of the Convener of the Synod's Committee to Negotiate on the Subject of Reunion with the Seceding Brethren (Presbyterian Church) 1845. Pp. 8.

Report of the Union Committee of the Presbyterian churches in the Provinces of British North America on the subject of Union, 1870-1875.

Report of the discussion of the late disruption in the Presbyterian Church which took place in St. Andrew's Church, Galt, on Tuesday, May 27, 1845, between the Rev. Principal Liddell, D.D., of Queen's College, Kingston, and the Rev. John Bayne, minister of the Presbyterian Church of Canada, Galt: taken in shorthand, and revised by the speakers. Galt, UC: Dumfries Courier, 1845. Pp. 60.

Riddell, Walter Alexander. *The Rise of Ecclesiastical Control in Quebec.* New York: Columbia University, 1916.

Ross, John, et al. *Dissent from joining the Union of 1875, contained in "Why We are out of Union."* 1875.

Ross, John Arthur. "A Study of Presbyterian Dissenters in the Canadian Church Union of 1925." Ph.D. thesis, McMaster University, 1973.

———. "Regionalism, Nationalism and Social Gospel Support in the Ecumenical Movement of Canadian Presbyterianism." Ph.D. thesis, McMaster University, 1974.

Scott, Ephraim. *"Church Union" and the Presbyterian Church in Canada.* Montreal, 1928.

Scrimger, John. *Jesuit morals; a paper . . . and correspondence between Prof. Scrimger and Rev. Father Jones, S.J.* Montreal, 1890.

Silcox, Claris Edwin. *Church Union in Canada: its causes and consequences.* New York: Institute of Social and Religious Research, 1933.

Smith, Neil Gregor. "By Schism Rent Asunder: a study of the Disruption of the Presbyterian Church in Canada in 1844." *Canadian Journal of Theology* 1, 3 (1955): 175-83.

Statement of the Presbyterian Church Association to all Presbyterians who desire to continue the Presbyterian Church throughout Canada. Toronto: Presbyterian Church Association, August 1924.

Union of Presbyterian churches in the Dominion of Canada: A Statement of the steps which have been taken towards its consummation for the information of the Venerable, the General Assembly of the Church of Scotland, submitted by the members of the Deputation from the Synod of the Presbyterian Church of Canada in connection with the Church of Scotland, appointed to appear before the Assembly, at Edinburgh, on the 20th May, 1875. Montreal: Lovell, 1875.

Union of the Presbyterian Churches in Canada, Circular regarding the contemplated union. 1874.

United Presbyterian Church. *An Account of the Proceedings of the Committees of Union appointed by the Synod of the Presbyterian Church of Canada and the Synod of the Missionary Church in Canada.* London, UC: Wm. Sutherland, 1849.

Welsh, David. *Letter of Reply from the Convener of the Colonial Committee of the Free Church of Scotland to the Moderator of the Synod of Canada.* Montreal: Beckett, 1844.

16. Religion, Ethics and Health

Bell, Ernest A. *War on the White Slave Traffic.* Reprint, Toronto: Coles Publishing, 1980.

Royal Commission on the Liquor Traffic. *The Facts of the Case: . . . . Compiled by FS Spence [for] The Dominion Alliance for the Total Suppression of the Liquor Traffic.* Toronto: Newton and Thriller, 1896. Reprint, Toronto: Coles Publishing, 1973.

Shearer, John George. *Our Laws affecting Morals and their Enforcement.* Toronto: Presbyterian Church in Canada, Board of Social Service and Evangelism, n.d.

—— and T.A. Moore. *Canada's War on the White Slave Traffic.* Toronto: Presbyterian Church in Canada, n.d.

17. Theological Thought

An Historical Digest of the Work in Articles of Faith. Don Mills: Presbyterian Publications, 1967.

Barr, A.T. *New Lights From Old Lamps.* Toronto: Thorn, 1937.

——. *Our Presbyterian Church.* Toronto: Westminster, n.d. Pp. 12.

——. *Torchbearers of Recovery.* Toronto: Thorn, 1938.

Boudreau, M.E.R. *What We Believe As Presbyterians.* Durham: Chronicle Printing, 1936.

Brown, W.G. *Sermons In Answer to Questions.* Saskatoon: Saskatoon Printers, 1938.

Bryden, Walter W. *Why I Am A Presbyterian!* Toronto: Presbyterian Publications, 1934.

——. *The Christian's Knowledge Of God.* London, England: Jas. Clarke, 1960.

———. "Continental Movements and The Theological Thought of Tomorrow." *United Church Observer,* 15 June 1941, 11, 28.

———. "Shall We Adopt the Statement of Faith?" *Presbyterian Record,* October 1946, 269-70.

———. *Separated Unto The Gospel.* Toronto: Burns and MacEachern, 1956.

———. *The Significance of The Westminster Confession of Faith.* Toronto: University of Toronto Press, 1943.

Campbell, John. "The Perfect Book and the Perfect Father." *Queen's University Sunday Afternoon Addresses.* Kingston, Ontario, 1893-1894.

———. *The Great Election.* Montreal: Lovell, 1894. Pp. 28.

Canada Presbyterian Church Pulpit, First Series. Toronto: James Campbell, 1871. Second Series. Toronto: James Campbell, 1873.

Caven, William. *A Vindication of Doctrinal Standards with Special Reference to the Standards of the Presbyterian Church.* Toronto: James Campbell, 1875.

Chambers, Calvin H. *In Spirit and in Truth: Charismatic Worship and the Reformed Tradition.* Ardmore, PA: Dorrance, 1980.

Cochrane, William. *Christian Responsibility in the Matter of Popular Amusements.* Stratford, Ontario: Beacon, 1874.

———. *The Church and the Commonwealth: Discussions and Orations on the Question of the Day. Practical, Biographical, Educational and Doctrinal.* Brantford, Ontario: Bradley Garretson, 1887.

———. *The Heavenly Vision and Other Sermons.* Toronto: Adam, Stevenson, 1874.

———. *The Negative Theology and the Larger Hope.* Brantford, Ontario: J.R. Salmond, 1892.

———. *Warning and Welcome: Sermons Preached in Zion Presbyterian Church in Brantford During 1876.* Toronto: Adam, Stephenson, 1877.

Cowan, C.L. ("Roman Collar"). *This Warfare.* Toronto: Thorn, 1941.

Dickie, R.W. *Presbyterianism: Its Origins and Principles.* Montreal: Presbyterian Association, 1925.

DiGangi, Mariano. *Twelve Prophetic Voices. Major Messages from the Minor Prophets.* Wheaton, Illinois: Victor, 1985.

Dunn, Peter A. *Presbyterianism in the Twentieth Century.* Toronto: Presbyterian Publications, n.d.

Falconer, J.W. *Religion and the War.* Toronto: Presbyterian Church Commission on the War and Spiritual Life of the Church, 1917.

The Face of the Church. Being a volume of sermons to contemporary Presbyterians. Presbyterian Church in Canada: Centennial Committee, 1967.

Farris, Allan Leonard. *Reformed and Reforming.* Toronto: Presbyterian Publications, 1960.

———. *An Historian looks at the Book of Revelation: an Address given to the annual international Meeting of the Clergy of Niagara Falls, New York and Niagara Falls, Ontario, held in the Canadian City, 1956.* Niagara Falls: Kiwanis Club, Niagara Falls, printed for private distribution only, 1956. Pp. 4.

Fraser, T. *The Religion of the Soldier.* Toronto: Presbyterian Church Commission on the War and Spiritual Life of the Church, 1917.

Fraser, Brian J. "The 'Progress in Theology' Debate; Consensus and Debate in North Atlantic Presbyterianism." *Proceedings of The Canadian Society of Church History* 3-4 June 1987 (1988): 45-52.

General Assembly of the United Presbyterian Church in the United States of America. *Book of Confessions.* 2nd ed. New York: General Assembly UPC, 1970.

Grant, George Monro. "How to Read the Bible." *Queen's University Sunday Afternoon Addresses.* Kingston, 1891.

———. "The Old Testament and the New Criticism." *Queen's University Sunday Afternoon Addresses.* Kingston, 1892.

———. *The Religions of the World in Relation to Christianity.* New York: Fleming H. Revell, 1894.

Hayes, Stephen A. *Being a Presbyterian in Canada Today.* Don Mills: Presbyterian Publications, 1978. Pp. 39.

Henderson, Dorothy. *Glorifying and Enjoying God—the People, Practice and Promise of the Presbyterian Church in Canada.* Life and Mission Agency, Presbyterian Church in Canada, c. 1995.

Kannawin, W. M. *Our Church.* Toronto: Presbyterian Publications, 1935.

Kilpatrick, Thomas Buchanan. *The War and The Christian Church.* Toronto: Presbyterian Church Commission on the War and Spiritual Life of the Church, 1917.

Klempa, William, ed. *What it means to confess the Christian Faith Today.* Toronto: Committee on Church Doctrine, The Presbyterian Church in Canada, 1972. Pp. iv, 35.

Knox, John. *The Church and Its Creed; the address delivered before the annual assembly of the Prince Edward Island Association, Monday, the 20th July, 1857.* Charlottetown: Haszard, 1857. Pp. 92.

Lang, Gavin. *Address to the Synod of the Church of Scotland in Canada, February 15, 1882.*

LeBlanc, Philip, and Arnold Edinborough, eds. *One Church, Two Nations?* Don Mills: Longmans, 1968.

Liddell, Thomas, et al. *Address to the office bearers and members of the Presbyterian Church of Canada on the subject of the commemoration of the Westminster Assembly.* Kingston, UC: Chronicle and Gazette, 1843.

MacBeth, R.G. *The Burning Bush and Canada.* [Toronto]: Westminster, c. 1912.

Macdonnell, Daniel J. *Death Abolished: Sermon Preached at St. Andrew's Church, March 1889.* Toronto, 1889.

MacEachern, N.A. *The Challenge*. Toronto: Presbyterian Publications, 1930.

——, Neil G. Smith and David W. Hay. *The Faith We have Received: a brief Exposition of the Apostles' Creed*. Toronto: Presbyterian Publications, 1946.

McDowall, Robert. *Discourses on the Sovereign and Universal Agency of God in Nature and Grace*. Albany, New York, 1806.

McLaren, William. *The Unity of the Human Race*. Belleville, UC: E. Miles, Chronicle, 1860.

McLean, J.L.W. *The Church Presbyterian*. Toronto: Presbyterian Publications, 1960.

McLelland, Joseph C. *Why Our Pond is Lukewarm, or Forty Years in the Wilderness*. Toronto: Synod of Toronto and Kingston, 1965. Unpaged.

——. *The Other Six Days*. Toronto: Burns and MacEachern, 1959.

McNab, John, ed. *What Do Presbyterians Believe?* Toronto: *Presbyterian Record*, 1957.

—— and F. Scott Mackenzie. *Our Heritage and Our Faith*. Toronto: 75th Anniversary Committee, 1950.

Miller, A. Neil and Arthur Cochrane. *The Word says No! The Word of God and the Foundation Fund Campaign in the Presbyterian Church in Canada*. Port Credit: Port Credit Publishing, n.d.

Morley, F.S. *Why a Presbyterian Church?* Calgary: Albertan Printers, 1955.

Parker, S.G. *The Guest Chamber*. Toronto: Thorn, 1938.

——. *Jesus Asks A Question*. Toronto: Thorn, 1937.

——. *Yet Not Consumed*. Toronto: Thorn, 1946.

Presbyterian Church Association. *Statement of the Presbyterian Church*. 1924.

Proceedings of the Presbytery of Toronto in the case of Messrs. Leach, and Ritchie. Toronto: British Colonist, 1843.

Reed-Maroney, Nina. "Christian Darwinism in the Knox College Monthly, 1883-1896." *Journal of Canadian Church Historical Society* 31, 1 (April 1989): 15-32.

Reflections from the Pulpit of MacNab Street Church, 1854-1969, containing a sermon preached by each of the six ministers of MacNab Street Church. Hamilton, 1969. Pp. 22.

Robertson, Ian Ross. "The Bible Question in Prince Edward Island from 1856 to 1860." *Acadiensis* 5, 2 (Spring 1976): 3-25.

Sandeen, Ernest R. "The Princeton Theology: One Source of Biblical Literalism in American Protestantism." *Church History* (September 1962): 307-21.

Shaw, J.M. *The War and Divine Providence.* Toronto: Presbyterian Church Commission on the War and Spiritual Life of the Church, 1917.

Sins relating to the Gospel Ordinances, being reasons for a National Fast, appointed by the commission of the General Assembly in 1650. Kingston, UC: Chronicle and Gazette, 1844.

Smart, James D. *What A Man Can Believe.* Philadelphia: Westminster, 1943.

Smith, Neil Gregor. *Facing A Second Century: The Challenge of Canada's Second Century for the Presbyterian Church.* N.P., 1967.

Thomson, E.A. *Keepers of the Faith.* Toronto: Thorn, 1937.

Wasson, Joseph. *The Light of Love.* Toronto: Presbyterian Publications, 1938.

also available from Laverdure & Associates:

CHRISTIANITY *in* CANADA
HISTORICAL ESSAYS *by John S. Moir*

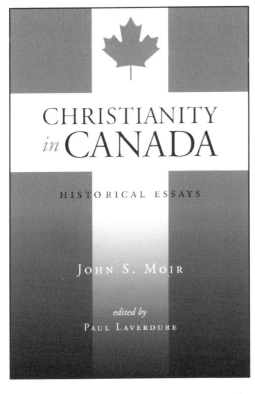

This volume includes:

- Religious Determinants in Canadian History.
- The Sectarian Tradition in Canada.
- The Canadianization of Protestant Churches.
- Towards the Americanization of Religion in Canada.
- Loyalism and the Canadian Churches.
- The Canadian Baptist and the Social Gospel.
- Origins of the Separate School Question.
- A Study of Canadian Religious Historiography, and several other essays.

An appreciation by Mark McGowan (St. Michael's College, University of Toronto) gives an excellent overview of the major themes.

Send your order with purchase order number or cheque for $19.00 for each copy (includes all taxes, shipping and handling) to:

LAVERDURE & ASSOCIATES
Box 246, Gravelbourg, SK, Canada, S0H 1X0
FAX: 1-306-648-3614   E-MAIL: drpaul@sk.sympatico.ca

While supplies last. Price subject to change without notice.